Corruption in Latin America is a most needed book to understand deeply the complexity of corruption practices from their social and cultural roots. From this angle the fight against its pervasive and destructive effects in all societies might emerge.
 Gabriela Coronado Susan, University of Western Sydney, Australia

This book offers an interesting and novel approach on corruption in Latin America; exploring corruption as a socially-embedded game. This generates new insights into the sociological, cultural and organizational aspects of the phenomenon. It also includes a rich analysis of anticorruption efforts in the region, and of the reasons behind persistent meagre results. The book truly is a valuable resource for students, as well as for practitioners and policymakers that are interested in understanding corruption and imaging new solutions to old problems.
 Fernando Nieto Morales, El Colegio de México, Mexico

This is a 'must' for those interested in understanding corruption in Latin America. It adopts a realistic approach not only to comprehend, but also to tackle this problem our citizens face on a daily basis.
 Cristian Pliscoff, Universidad de Chile, Chile

CORRUPTION IN LATIN AMERICA

In *Corruption in Latin America*, the reader is presented with an alternative starting point for understanding corruption in this key region. The author asserts that corruption is a stable and rational social and organizational mechanism. Seen through this lens, we can begin to understand why it persists, and how to implement strategies to control corruption effectively.

Beginning with an in-depth, nuanced examination of the concept of corruption, the author establishes the theoretical basis for viewing corruption as a social construct. An analysis of the experiences of four countries in the region—Argentina, Brazil, Guatemala, and Mexico—provides the reader with concrete data from which they can understand how and why these behaviors are reproduced, validated, and tolerated in everyday settings between governments and citizens, governments and firms, and firms and clients. Once we see corruption as the socially sanctioned norm for getting business done, we can begin to produce and propose effective solutions to reduce corruption in Latin America by designing and implementing instruments that transform this dynamic.

This rigorous and original approach will challenge the reader's assumptions about corruption, and will appeal to students of corporate governance, international business, public management, and business ethics.

David Arellano-Gault is Professor in the Public Administration Division at the Center for Research and Teaching in Economics (CIDE), Mexico. He has been coeditor and Senior Editor of *Organization Studies*.

CORRUPTION IN LATIN AMERICA

David Arellano-Gault

NEW YORK AND LONDON

First published 2020
by Routledge
52 Vanderbilt Avenue, New York, NY 10017

and by Routledge
2 Park Square, Milton Park, Abingdon, Oxon OX14 4RN

Routledge is an imprint of the Taylor & Francis Group, an informa business

© 2020 Taylor & Francis

The right of David Arellano-Gault to be identified as author of this work has been asserted by him in accordance with sections 77 and 78 of the Copyright, Designs and Patents Act 1988.

All rights reserved. No part of this book may be reprinted or reproduced or utilised in any form or by any electronic, mechanical, or other means, now known or hereafter invented, including photocopying and recording, or in any information storage or retrieval system, without permission in writing from the publishers.

Trademark notice: Product or corporate names may be trademarks or registered trademarks, and are used only for identification and explanation without intent to infringe.

Library of Congress Cataloging-in-Publication Data
Names: Arellano Gault, David, author.
Title: Corruption in Latin America / David Arellano-Gault.
Description: New York, NY : Routledge, 2020. | Includes bibliographical references and index.
Identifiers: LCCN 2019033676 (print) | LCCN 2019033677 (ebook) | ISBN 9781138583702 (hardback) | ISBN 9781138583719 (paperback) | ISBN 9780429506543 (ebook)
Subjects: LCSH: Political corruption–Latin America. | Corruption–Latin America. | Fraud–Latin America.
Classification: LCC JL959.5.C6 A74 2020 (print) | LCC JL959.5.C6 (ebook) | DDC 364.1/323098–dc23
LC record available at https://lccn.loc.gov/2019033676
LC ebook record available at https://lccn.loc.gov/2019033677

ISBN: 978-1-138-58370-2 (hbk)
ISBN: 978-1-138-58371-9 (pbk)
ISBN: 978-0-429-50654-3 (ebk)

Typeset in Bembo
by Taylor & Francis Books

 Printed in the United Kingdom
by Henry Ling Limited

CONTENTS

List of illustrations	*x*
Acknowledgments	*xii*
List of Abbreviations	*xiv*
Introduction	1

SECTION I
Corruption as a Dense Social Relationship 15

1 Corruption: The Battle for Its Definition	17

Corruption: A Political Concept 17
Corruption: A Diverse, Heterogeneous Phenomenon 25
The Debate and the Fight to Define Corruption 35
Summary and Next Steps 44

2 Corruption as a Cultural and Social Process	53

Corruption as a Social Relationship 53
Social Relations, Reciprocities, and Exchanges 59
The Logic of Favors and Exchanges in Various Countries 65
Studying the Mechanisms for the Exchange of Favors: The Palanca
as a Double-Edged Sword 83
Palancas: The Social Density of Relationships between
Acquaintances 92

viii Contents

*The Logic of Favors and Exchanges and Their Relationship
with Corruption 96*

SECTION II
Latin American Anticorruption Strategies   107

Introduction to Section II 107
Anticorruption Agencies 110
Main ACA Models 113

3   The Anticorruption Agency of Argentina   121

Limits of Anticorruption Agencies in Latin America 121
The Conceptual Logic of ACAs 125
Anticorruption Agencies: Conditions and Context 128
The Argentinean Anticorruption Office as a "Strategy" 130
Lessons from the OOA 136

4   The Mexican National Anticorruption System: White Elephant
    or World-Class Innovation?   142

Introduction 142
The Logic of the SNA 151
The Anticorruption Reform Proposals (2012–2016) 151
Anticorruption Reform 154
Implementation and Stagnation (2016–2018) 156
*The Substantive Challenges of the SNA in a Country such
as Mexico 160*
*Final Reflections on the Mexican Case: Political Corruption as the
Mother of Administrative Corruption 163*

5   Brazil: The Success and Crisis of a Decentralized Mechanism for
    Controlling Corruption   170

Introduction 170
The Brazilian Institutional Anticorruption Framework 172
Operation Lava Jato (Car Wash) 183
Final Reflection on the Brazilian Case 189

6   The International Commission against Impunity in Guatemala   192

Introduction 192
Background 194

Normativity 195
Organization 196
Institutions Involved 197
La Línea Case 199
More Investigation by the CICIG 203
Final Considerations 206

Index *210*

ILLUSTRATIONS

Schemes

I.II.1	Factors that determine the independence of an anticorruption agency	112
I.II.2	ACA mandates	113
I.II.3	Composition of the ICAC	115
4.1	*Palancas* as a social mechanism	144
4.2	Sequence of the use of *palancas* in Mexico	146
4.3	*Palancas* as quasi-mafias	148
4.4	Mexico National Anticorruption System, 2016	152
4.5	Mexico SNA features	162
5.1	Brazil. Year of presentation of proposals on corruption in process in both legislative houses 1992–2016	185

Tables

1.1	Definitions of corruption	27
1.2	Corruption acts and uses	45
I.II.1	Types of Anticorruption agency models	111
I.II.2	Laws that grant functions to the ICAC	114
I.II.3	Procedure for the investigation and prosecution of corruption offenses by the ICAC	114
I.II.4	Examples of the failure of anticorruption initiatives	119
3.1	Design and principal functions of the OAA	131
4.1	Mexico: The anticorruption reform proposals, 2012–2016	155

| 4.2 | Mexico Anticorruption Reform. Secondary laws: 2015 | 157 |
| 4.3 | Basic pillars of the SNA | 158 |

Boxes

| 1.1 | Traffic police and bribery | 46 |
| 1.2 | The President and the contractor | 47 |

ACKNOWLEDGMENTS

Writing a book is always an adventure, a journey where you get to know new people, learn to interact with your family and friends in a whole new way, and are forced to face yourself, your ideas, and your thoughts, often in a tough and not always pleasant way.

It is, nevertheless, an adventure: you depart from port one day and you intuit that your world will be different when you come back. Hopefully, the important persons in your life will be there when you return; perhaps, if you are lucky enough, they will be ready to keep walking together with you in search of the next adventure.

Laura, Ana, and Ricardo, my family and close allies. They have been with me in all sorts of adventures: living in a foreign country while I was studying my Ph.D. or adapting their routines to the academic sort of neurotic and disordered way of life, full of books, papers, deadlines, field trips and, of course, eventual writer's block. Nevertheless, I'd like to think, we have been a happy family, full of love and abounding in fun.

The group of my whole-life friends: Raul, Lourdes, Guillermo, Hilda, Alberto, and Maribel. All important journeys require accomplices, people who understand you, sometimes even better than you understand yourself. Maribel just left us unexpectedly and with her we lost an important part of our existence and happiness. Memories prevail, though, and I cherish all and each one of them.

I consider myself a fortunate person. I have had several mentors and professors that have supported me through different stages of my professional career. And I have been lucky enough for some of them to have also become my friends. Among others, I particularly would like to thank my professors and mentors: Enrique Cabrero, Jorge Arias, Juan Recabarren, Mike Cortes, Linda and Peter de Leon, and Sam Overman.

I would like to thank my friends and colleagues here at CIDE, this publicly funded research center in Mexico, where you can freely debate, discuss, and have a lot of fun looking for fresh organizational and public policy ideas and solutions to this troubled but overall wonderful region of the world, Latin America.

I am very grateful to the Routledge team for believing in this project. I found in them not only professionalism but also kindness and patience for this non-native English speaker academic.

My final thanks go to Jair Trejo and Cristian Murguia, former students of mine and currently good colleagues who helped me during several critical moments in this research, finding information and lending me their helping hands to tackle important details to write this book.

David Arellano-Gault
CIDE, Santa Fe, Mexico City
May 2019

LIST OF ABBREVIATIONS

ACA	Anticorruption Agencies
ACFE	Association of Fraud Examiners
APN	National Public Administration Agencies in Argentina
ASF	Superior Audit Office of the Federation
BCE	Before Christ Era
BPI	Bribe Payers Index
CEP	The Public Ethics Commission
CGU	The Office of the Comptroller General of the Union
CICC	Inter-American Convention Against Corruption
Ciciacs	Commission for the Investigation of Illegal Bodies and Clandestine Security Apparatuses
CICIG	International Commission against Impunity in Guatemala
CJF	The Council of the Federal Judiciary
COAF	Financial Activities Control Council
CPC	Citizen Participation Committee
CPI	Corruption Perceptions Index
CPIB	Corrupt Practices Investigation Bureau of Singapore
CPRFB	Political Constitution of Brazilian Federal Republic
CSB	Civil Service Office of Hong Kong
ENCCLA	The National Strategy to Combat Corruption and Money Laundering
ENCIG	National Survey of Government Quality and Impact 2013
FCPA	Foreign Corrupt Practices Act of 1977
FGR	General Prosecutor's Office
FIOA	Institutional Strengthening of the Anticorruption Office
GCB	Global Corruption Barometer
IAACA	International Association of Anticorruption Authorities

ICAC	Hong Kong's Independent Commission against Corruption
IGSS	Guatemalan Social Security Institute
IMF	International Monetary Fund
INAC	National Anticorruption and Control Institute
INAI	National Institute of Transparency, Access to Information and Data Protection
INEGI	Institute of Statistics, Geography, and Information Technology
MP	The Public Prosecutor's Office
NAD	National Anticorruption Directorate of Rumania
NGO	Non-Governmental Organization
NRSNF	Steering Committee of the National Supervision System
OAA	Argentinean Anticorruption Office
OECD	Organization for Economic Cooperation and Development
OSC	Open Society Foundation
PAN	National Action Party
PETROBRAS	Petróleo Brasileiro S.A.
PF	The Federal Police
PNC	National Civil Police of Guatemala
RIC	Registry of Cadastral Information
RPEI	Illicit Political-Economic Networks
SAT	Tax Administration Superintendency
SEC	Securities and Exchange Commission of the United States
SFP	Secretariat of Public Administration
SLAC	Local Anticorruption Systems
SNA	National Anticorruption System
TCE	Transaction Cost Economics
TCU	The Court of Accounts of the Union
TFJA	Federal Court of Administrative Justice
TI	Transparency International
UEFAC	Special Prosecutor's Office for CICIG
UN	United Nations
UNDP	United Nations Development Program
USAID	United States Agency for International Development
USSR	Union of Soviet Socialist Republics
WB	World Bank

INTRODUCTION

This book addresses a phenomenon that has recently attracted a great deal of international attention, even though it is a phenomenon that has been present in society since its inception. Corruption is an age-old problem, yet one that continues to fascinate because of the enormous difficulty of controlling, let alone eliminating, it. Part of the reason why it is so difficult to understand and control has to do with the fact that, in practice, corruption is a heterogeneous set of social practices which, at some point, require someone to define them credibly and legitimately as unethical and even illegal. Since corruption is wrapped up in a normative logic, it requires a kind of shared social agreement to draw the line between the collective and the individual, the public and the private. At some time in the past, in a certain society, a certain practice was allowed, whereas at another point in history or in another society, it was declared unethical. And in the case of corruption, this always has to do with how private, individual logic illegitimately affects or abuses a collective or public agreement. Establishing what is illegitimate and what constitutes abusing what is collective or public (both categories are also very difficult to clearly establish in all circumstances) is precisely what requires a broad, legitimate social agreement.

Corruption is not only a set of practices regarded as unethical, which change from society to society and from one historical moment to the next. It is also a set of extremely heterogeneous social practices, ranging from bribing a public official at a window, through to fraud by an important businessman, to the misappropriation of funds in a cooperative, fraud in government contracting with a non-governmental organization, and conflicts of interest in a decision by a transnational firm or a decision by the president of a country. All these practices are usually lumped together in a single category: corruption. But they are quite clearly different situations, where quite distinct social relations come into play between various individual and collective agents. In other words, they represent acts and

2 Introduction

relationships that are socially, legally, economically, and organizationally different. Corruption is an umbrella concept that tries, with limited success, to group dozens of different social practices under a simple title: corruption.

This umbrella concept tends to be used in everyday language to refer to a multitude of illegal, or at least undesirable, behaviors that can be observed in virtually any type of organization: government agencies, private companies, judicial and legislative organizations, NGOs, and international organizations. And they are present in every country, to at least some degree. The key issue for this book is to understand that the corruption category encompasses a myriad of heterogeneous behaviors: from bribing a government employee at a window, through conflicts of interest in government contracting, to millionaire frauds in large companies, to an employee's pilfering, while for some, inefficiency, or shoddy work, can also be a form of corruption. One concept, dozens of highly different behaviors, linked only by an extremely abstract normative idea: the abuse of a position of responsibility (collective) to obtain a personal, individual benefit, for oneself or others (the last of which, incidentally, further complicates the issue).

Corruption, then, is a concept that is difficult to summarize, since it is extremely malleable. It has become a commonly used generalization but one that, actually, attempts to define many things at the same time. This means that it is virtually possible to speak of corruption in accordance with the preferences or values of the person observing or defining it. It is also, obviously, a morally loaded concept. The person who corrupts bears an obvious burden of guilt and probably of malfeasance assigned by others, either by society or the law. But the person who allows himself to be corrupted, or ignores it, although often to a lesser extent, is nevertheless subject to a certain amount of disapproval, suspicion, and probably social or group contempt, depending on the circumstances.

Corruption is an improper act by one or more people who have acted "wrongly" according to a particular legal or moral parameter. This begs the question of why they do it. Did they make bad decisions? On their own, caused by their own failings and ethical limitations? Were they socially and organizationally forced to do so? Answering these questions accurately in any case and circumstances is extremely complicated. One possible explanation could be that, in actual fact, people rarely decide or act in isolation. An act of corruption is usually a social act: there are other actors present in the act, sometimes as accomplices, sometimes as victims, sometimes as deceived parties, sometimes as unwanted observers who are potentially there and can become accusers or witnesses. One way of seeing this presence of others is easily understood when it is perceived that a corrupt act usually develops in two critical stages: the first is the performance of the questionable act in itself (such as fraud or embezzlement). But a second act may then be needed: hiding or concealing the wrongful act to avoid punishment or the disapproval of others (Dubbink, 2015, p. 9). Concealment, in itself, is an operation that is often complicated because it usually requires a complex operation, whether the cover-up has been planned at length with willful intent, or is carried out more subtly through justifications, excuses, and rationalizations that may be shared to a certain extent by other members of the group or the organization. Accordingly, concealment can involve a blend of different degrees of combination between an obvious crime carried out with malice aforethought and at the other extreme, an act which, in the eyes of those who commit it and probably of a particular group close to the act, is to a certain extent justifiable, rationalized in such a way that it is not only seen as a normal act but as one that is morally harmless. Typical examples include people who say that they did not hurt anyone, that they only did what is always done in the organization or in the group (the act is defended as a normal act). Other more classic arguments include the person who claims they followed orders and that they were only a cog in a larger, well-oiled machine.

All of this suggests that studying corruption poses an enormous analytical and methodological challenge. It is an extremely interesting challenge for at least three critical reasons. First, it is an act that can be performed out of the sight of others. Second, some actors may be intent on concealing, justifying, or rationalizing it, in a systematic and even organized manner, as mentioned earlier. But there is a third reason that is often overlooked and which contributes to the problem of studying corruption: the fact that it is morally loaded means that people, groups, and organizations who raise their voices and can become agents who position themselves as anticorruption experts tend to appear, encouraging the organizational, social, and even international agenda to address the "problem" of corruption. Let us examine each of these reasons.

The first reason is typical: investigating acts of corruption generally involves a legal and persecutory view of illegitimate acts. A person who knows or suspects this type of act is being committed usually carries it out in such a way that it is less likely to be observed or identified as an improper act by concealing and rationalizing it. Concealment, then, is usually an integral element of the phenomenon of corruption. However, this does not only happen in acts of corruption clearly classifiable as illegal acts. It also occurs in those that are usually justified in certain societies: for example, giving gifts to government bureaucrats to facilitate the granting of services, licenses, or contracts. Or encouraging social relationships and even friendship between businesspeople and public servants through parties or lunch or dinner invitations (which eventually lead to advantages or preferences for certain people). This, as a second reason, also makes the empirical study of corruption a challenge because, rather than being a discrete, self-explanatory act, it tends to involve a series of previous acts, agreements, and relationships that enable the execution of the corrupt act itself. In other words, an investigation to determine whether a particular act is corrupt not only has to explore the cover-up, but also requires investigating the past to understand the history of the relations between different people that led to the consummation of the act and its implications. Take, for example, the case of a civil servant or a manager of a private company who facilitated a particular case of fraud. Fraud can be the result of a long chain of interactions that developed over time between the fraudster and the person affected by the fraud, involving many people from different areas of the organization and even from other organizations. It is a process of gestation,

4 Introduction

induction, planning, and concealment, in which many people intervened, consciously or unconsciously, with or without malice, but which led to the final effect of a probable fraud. Mutual gifts, parties or meetings, and family ties can be part of a long chain of interactions, none of which are perhaps illegal, yet which, when combined, explain the process of fraud and its cover-up. The fact that it is a hidden, dense, and often concealed act are classic elements for explaining the difficulty of studying corruption; since it involves a set of acts that some people can classify as illegal and immoral, the emotional burden that generally accompanies the phenomenon is high. It is therefore a phenomenon that is usually loaded with guilt. In other words, people experience guilt when they are accused and punished for being corrupt and therefore immoral in a certain sense. Legal punishment may or may not occur, be necessary, or be minimum or maximum. But a person accused of corruption can be socially marked. The element of shame and social branding, the emotional burden this phenomenon can entail for those involved (the malicious and Machiavellian, but also secondary players, observers, who were only suspected) is a substantive element for understanding the plot and social drama of corruption.

Finally, the third reason that socially brands the dense phenomenon of corruption is an actor who is usually forgotten: those who manage to assign themselves the role and the social, sometimes legal and therefore, in this case, moral power to label others as corrupt. We are speaking of course of judges, police officers, and investigators who, as part of their work, must prevent, investigate, and punish. But this includes other groups which, particularly in recent times, have emerged in the anticorruption arena. Non-governmental organizations, which are sometimes international, journalists, academics, and participants in social networks have set themselves up as being crucial to addressing the problem and usually assign themselves a certain moral and technical quality for reducing corruption and labeling others as corrupt.

In effect, a person accused of corruption is not only saddled with the legal definition of a crime, but also with the moral judgment of being negligent and having failed to control themselves and make the right decision not to act to the detriment of certain predetermined values. And someone must assign those values and then defend them, by setting themselves up as the guardians of those values by establishing rules and norms and assigning blame, but above all making moral judgments of others. Thus, corruption, as with a a few acts of dubious legitimacy, requires a dynamic, intricate social process that defines and socially constructs it in order for it to be identifiable, but also to define the way it is addressed. This is because, as the very concept of corruption implies, in its most profound moral sense, certain people are acting to destroy and allow the social system, relationships, institutions, and the social order itself, to rot. And they do so as a result of a moral flaw, a negligence that must be socially condemned. Accordingly, because of this heavy emotional toll, it is usually necessary to have actors, groups, and institutions who establish moral "normality". And it is difficult for these actors not to set themselves up as the guardians or agents on a not only legal but also moral pedestal, who therefore have the possibility of establishing the parameters according to which others will be judged and classified. Studying a morally charged social phenomenon is difficult because it is not only intended to conceal, but to justify: the people involved may actually be in a confused area where formal and informal rules are not in line with each other. But the emotional burden also leads to greater complexity because it is a subject that swiftly becomes polarized: Who are those untainted actors who set themselves up as judges and establish the definitions and labels to impose on others? At the end of the day, those who set themselves up as judges and demarcators can also be considered to be ethically bounded, like anyone else (Chugh, Bazerman & Banaji, 2005, p. 75). Are these actors—who regard themselves as having the morals and legitimacy to brand and reveal the corrupt—themselves exempt from social forces, the specific dynamics that occur in a society so that certain people can engage in practices which in certain circumstances can be regarded as corrupt? In any case, one thing is clear: since corruption is supported by a series of social practices, it involves virtually the whole of society: those who define them, those who persecute them, those who commit them, and those who investigate and punish them, both legally and morally.

If there were social clarity about what a world with a total absence of corruption would be like, the issue might be easier to solve. The problem is that such a world does not exist. The phenomenon of corruption has been identified since ancient times. It is an apparently perennial one (Bardhan, 1997; Noonan, 1984) due to its obviously normative content: it encompasses everything that implies abuse or deception as regards what a community or group expects to be everyone's behavior in order to maintain and achieve the common objectives of that community or group.

Since it is a social act of interrelationship between people and groups, organizations and institutions, which is also morally charged, it is conceivable that a process of definition and construction, which is also social, is required. Corruption is not a "natural" phenomenon, so to speak, one that exists outside the social sphere that defines it: it is a normative construction that seeks to guide and affect the most common practices of people through the exchange of money, power, influence, and objectives. On a day-to-day basis, in all kinds of transactions between people, societies can be said to constantly negotiate the boundaries between what is and is not an improper act: what is globally unethical and unethical from the day-to-day perspective of specific people in specific acts. Moreover, many practices that were common and legitimate in the past may now be defined as unethical: exchanging gifts or having a social or political presence thanks to certain family ties or friendships has existed in every society. But today, in certain countries, several of these exchanges have been regulated, in certain circumstances. And it should be added that in any contemporary society, friendships or families are still important sources for obtaining social presence and influence. When is it considered that these relationships have legitimate or illegitimate effects? This is still a matter of debate in many societies. In practice, attempts

6 Introduction

have been made to obtain mechanisms that will make it possible to delimit that border in certain circumstances: nepotism is almost universally frowned upon, if one is talking about government issues and in very specific circumstances. In any case, rules and forms of measurement are required: What degree of kinship involves nepotism? Does nepotism always potentially lead to influence peddling? And, even more so in practice, it may be not so obvious that an act of nepotism is de facto affecting the honest performance of a person (if anything, the damage may lie, in this respect, in the suspicion of a specific code of impartiality, which, in any case, would have to be proved). That is why attempts to regulate family and social relationships in certain circumstances usually continue to experience difficulties in being effective or making people understand them in practical situations. The "social density" of corruption does not end here. It is also necessary to construct enforcement mechanisms, and people who have or are assigned the duty to be on a kind of pedestal of morality to establish punishments and enforce sanctions on others.

For all these reasons, corruption is an emotionally charged social concept that needs to be socially negotiated. It must be negotiated because it is essential to take action: rules must be made, institutions built, resources assigned, and functions and those responsible defined. And it will be these socially constructed elements that can aspire to have some legitimacy to then establish the politically and socially legitimate border between an unethical and an ethical act. The definition of this socially legitimized border is extremely important, yet far from perfect. This is logical: every day, in any society, millions of exchanges, transactions, and interactions take place between people with a wide array of links. Assuming the existence of precise, clear borders between the ethical and the unethical, the individual and the collective, the public and the private, in all circumstances and contingencies, would stretch the limits of credibility. This imperfection is obviously greater in some societies than others. Generally, when discussing a phenomenon such as corruption, this border ends up being imprecise, at least in a fair number of situations. This is why so many people accused of corruption tend to deny they were engaging in an illegal or unethical act: An act of corruption is usually the culmination of a series of different kinds of interactions, often legitimate, carried out over time, in which many people may have participated, and where the ability to conceal, deceive, and hide can produce a plot that is extremely difficult to unravel. How can one clearly establish faults and judgments? The border between unethical and ethical acts is extremely important: not only are regulatory burdens are established, as noted above, but also and very importantly, moral burdens that create important emotions in the people involved.

The need for certain people and organizations to attempt to set themselves up as those who define this border, and establish the legal and emotional charges for those who fail, is a critical element to consider among the difficulties and challenges of studying corruption. In the end, these people and organizations cannot easily detach themselves from the social dynamics and emotions an issue such as corruption produces. They are ultimately people and organizations in social contexts, with political intentions and interests, like anyone else. Obtaining the social title of an anticorruption person or organization, who is not corrupt, is untainted, and has no conflict of interests, implies a social process in itself: it implies setting oneself up, creating a discourse and an image, building a reputation, and obtaining the social power to define borders, concepts, even punishments and social and moral charges (Eisenstadt & Roniger, 1984, p. 25). None of this is automatic, nor is it harmless, socially speaking. Who establishes the parameters for certain acts to be socially regarded as illegitimate or even contemptible? Under what circumstances and with what qualifications or operators can someone be burdened with the moral weight of being corrupt? What political processes were set in motion to establish those groups and people who become anticorruption strategists, or judges and moral bastions of a society? The fight against corruption is waged through the lenses, definitions, strategies, prejudices, values, ideas, and sense of morality of certain actors and organizations. Even words matter: "fight", "war", "battle against corruption" show how emotionally charged addressing the phenomenon has become. And it is necessary to attempt to make explicit these burdens and the political and social nature of the people and institutions that build and defend them and seek to impose them on societies. If corruption is a dense social phenomenon, anticorruption, as a stance, strategy, and public policy, can also be socially and politically constructed as a form of domination capable of imposing burdens and judgments on others.

On the basis of these considerations, this book seeks to better understand both the logic of corruption and the limits and possibilities of the instruments within our reach. And it does so by taking as a case study one of the regions which, by common agreement, is apparently regarded as having the most corruption in the world: Latin America (Faughnan & Seligson, 2015, p. 212). Latin America, with the possible exceptions of Chile, Costa Rica, and Uruguay, is seen as a region with extremely corrupt governments. Or rather, governments and societies. Indeed, corruption has accompanied the region since colonial times. Those times of imperial governments imposed norms and principles from Europe at a distance, which tended to be adapted and transformed by local powers almost immediately. There is a famous phrase dating from the colonies at that time: "Obey but do not comply". The colonial administration was plagued with exceptions, rules that were obeyed on paper and in form but were modified and adapted to the circumstances, people and their social position, and the intervention of influencers or influential actors who intervened in administrative procedures or processes in favor of certain people.

In the contemporary era, corruption and fraud scandals in the Latin American region continue and appear to be worsening. This not only includes cases of illicit enrichment of rulers and businesspeople in constant collusion, but now those of truly regional impact as in the case of the Brazilian company Odebrecht, which has had an impact on a significant number of countries in the region, from Brazil itself to Mexico, Colombia, and Peru, among others. It is a case that not only involves national governments, but also local ones. And all kinds of businesspeople,

8 Introduction

including, of course, those from countries that are tax havens. It is a Latin American case of transnational corruption.

For this reason, for some decades now, Latin America has proved to be a major focus for what has been called "the anticorruption industry". In other words, the group of people, groups, and organizations that have emerged as a fundamental conglomerate to determine what corruption is and to define ways, rules, and mechanisms for reducing it. On the basis of a metaphor with a heavy moral burden, "the cancer of corruption", a group of international organizations, both governmental and non-governmental, have set the tone for a battle, a war that countries identified as highly corrupt urgently require because of the danger that corruption will get out of control and put an end to the viability of the countries themselves. Central Europe, Africa, certain regions of Asia and Latin America, are often the venues of choice for the experiments of these organizations.

In this book, we discuss how the logic of the anticorruption instruments that have permeated Latin America, especially those from the so-called "anticorruption industry", is facing greater resistance than expected. One of the reasons is that in many countries there are obviously very powerful, resistant spaces for organized corruption. In Latin America, political corruption based on clientelism and patronage have been the fundamental bases of regimes. The reason for the perseverance of these political dynamics, as a second reason related to the previous one, is that they are intimately related to a series of centuries-old, deeply rooted social practices that determine and define the relationship people have with each other, but above all, with different types of authorities. Indeed, in Latin America, as noted earlier, since colonial times, the link between people and authorities is not that of the classic vision of the Weberian rational-legal bureaucracy, so to speak. In the rational bureaucratic ideal, authority has legitimacy because it is an impersonal and impartial power. The opposite is true in Latin America. Authority in Latin America is often seen as the privilege of a particular group, which uses this authority precisely to sustain and legitimize itself—a privileged group separate from the common people (Arellano-Gault & Del Castillo, 2004; Dealy, 1977). The authorities therefore have their own political and social logic: one of dominance and reproduction of the social dynamics of relationship and exchange that make sense precisely as a means of maintaining power. In other words, power is maintained by these groups thanks to their ability to reproduce social exchange practices that preserve them as privileged groups, and the only ones with the necessary means to solve people's problems. In this scenario, interpersonal relationships are fundamental: acquaintances, networks of acquaintances, can provide advantages, influence the processes of the authorities, and speed up results, services, and treatment. And it is this rich, dense social dynamic that constructs a particular way of interaction that is widespread in these countries, where interests, institutions, formal and informal norms, and even laws and political practices intersect, lending broad stability to the constant logic of corruption that exists in this part of the world. Politics and power, and the reproduction of their dynamic economic and social rules, are inseparable aspects for understanding the stable paths of corruption (Johnston, 2005).

This is why this official definition of corruption as a cancer or an anomaly is so odd, since in many social and political settings, corruption is an integral part of the political order, however paradoxical this may sound. Or rather, the numerous practices involving the exchange of favors and influences, construct the path of a stable grid or social fabric that paradoxically appears to be supported in many ways by various acts that are unethical or overtly corrupt. The networks of exchanging favors, the dynamics of the networks of acquaintances constitute the everyday social fabric of these realities. And corruption, therefore, is part of this social breeding ground, making the definition of unethical and ethical acts unclear and opaque, broadening the gap between formal and informal, legal and real social norms, the latter being where people give meaning to their action because they are the ones that "really" work. However strange this may sound, they make corrupt or unethical practices part of a dynamic which, at certain times, and for certain people in certain specific circumstances, can be regarded as functional practices. They are undoubtedly dysfunctional in the social aggregate, producing bureaucratic pathologies and other formalistic conventions of social action, but are functional in the practice of many people on a day-to-day basis and in many circumstances (Debiel & Gawrich, 2013).

Discussing and understanding these social practices, these interpersonal and intergroup dynamics, can prove to be an extremely productive strategy—not only to understand the underlying reasons for the limited success that the "anticorruption industry" type strategies have had. It will be useful, precisely, to increase the understanding of other types of additional options that could be attempted to reduce or control corruption in countries such as those in Latin America. Corruption is a socially negotiated concept. In other words, it requires a broad debate and communication in society to define as legitimately as possible the border between appropriate and inappropriate acts. But if the world of formal and informal rules is so disparate, and the practices, organizations, and institutions of these societies reproduce the abyss between what formal rules establish and what happens in everyday practice, generic anticorruption strategies, with a classic vision of a disease, a war of good against bad, paladins against miscreants, are unlikely to succeed. In a society that begins with the principle that the authorities say one thing formally and do another in reality, a group or organization setting itself up as a champion of morality and the war against corruption can only be suspect. In several societies, there have been several studies on how formal rules and norms coexist perfectly with informal ones that operate on a day-to-day basis. The former constitutes the formal framework while the latter is the space where there is flexibility and specific practical solutions. This strange interaction can be functional, precisely if it gives people a hope of solving their problems with distant and opaque authorities, who are Kafkaesque in the strict sense of the word (Hodson, Martin, Lopez, & Roscigno, 2012). But they are functionally Kafkaesque, in that these same authorities benefit from informal exchanges outside the formal rules, yet within a dynamic that has become socially normal (Torsello, 2015, p. 166). People in these societies have learned to live in two parallel worlds: what formal rules say and what informal

10 Introduction

practices, which are effective in day-to-day reality, say. Given these circumstances, it is hardly surprising that social practices based on acquaintances, influences, and the exchange of favors continue to be more effective and credible, however many new laws and regulations are issued.

What is being described speaks of societies that have undoubtedly built a solid shell of cynicism—but a type of cynicism that works: For example, the essence of this cynicism is that there is a kind of popular wisdom in various experiences (such as those in Argentina and Mexico we shall study in Chapters 3 and 4) which says that the anticorruption authorities themselves probably used their influences and acquaintances to secure these positions. In other words, these anticorruption authorities find it difficult to avoid the very social logic of exchanges between acquaintances. This implies the existence of a very stable vicious circle, a social trap that seems to explain what societies in Latin America are experiencing: de jure societies with impersonal, impartial formal rules and institutions that coexist and acquire logic in the real dynamics of everyday life, based on networks of acquaintances, exchanges of favors and, therefore, not supported de facto by impersonal or impartial rules. Hence the importance of understanding their practices, contradictions, and the ways these very practices paradoxically reproduce what they seek to address: the particularism of the authorities, the deep social and political interaction that supports systemic, even organized, corruption in these countries.

Despite this, regional efforts to control or reduce corruption have been quick to materialize. And in various countries, with many of these social practices involving the exchange of favors, influence peddling, and systemic corruption, some innovations are being implemented, with very different patterns and instruments. They all hope to find the mechanisms that will enable Latin American societies to negotiate and define the concept of corruption in order to make it socially undesirable, to control it at least as a phenomenon to curb its expansion in the government, firms, and the non-governmental organization sector. In this book, I have chosen to discuss four of these national efforts, all different and all to a certain extent desperate acts by societies beginning to realize that it is necessary to control and reduce corruption if they wish to remain viable as nations. They are more or less desperate efforts to, above all, negotiate and socially construct a clearer border between ethical and unethical acts. They include Argentina and its anticorruption agency, created in 1999 and attacked and boycotted since its inception by the very powers it is supposed to monitor and control. Another example is Brazil with its long, solid history of a civil service born in 1930, which has been able to build a network of institutions whose only mission is to attack corruption, but thanks to the fact that each one does what it is supposed to do, has managed to detect, investigate, and punish extremely serious cases that have shaken Brazilian society. This success has, nevertheless, some people have begun to suggest, paradoxically jeopardized the political system, since it is based on influential practices, the exchange of favors, and the normalization of corruption. We also describe the case of Guatemala and the spectacular innovation of a hybrid organism—both international and national—which in a focused manner has managed to create an

Introduction **11**

extremely solid technical capacity for investigating acts of corruption. This experience has also included the need to strengthen institutions in the judiciary branch as a key element for advancing the gradual reduction of the organized acts of corruption linking the highest levels of government with business. It is an experience which at the time of writing, is under strong attack by the Guatemalan executive itself, which wishes to terminate the agreement with the UN in order for this hybrid organization known as the CICIG (International Commission against Impunity in Guatemala) to leave the country. This comes precisely at a time when the CICIG is investigating the president for the misuse of funds in his political campaign. Lastly, there is the Mexican case, with the construction of a National Anticorruption System. This elephantine structure involves the federation, the states, and the municipalities, in a dream of institutional coordination of national scope, composed of many parts, which, if they manage to coordinate, could at last reduce and affect the core of the organized, systemic corruption historically experienced by this country. If successful, this innovation will undoubtedly serve as an international reference. If not, it will also serve as an international benchmark for a costly and ambitious strategy that must be avoided because of its arrogance.

In any case, it seems important to study the experience of Latin America. This is because it is a region that is making innovative efforts to control a type of corruption that seems to be spinning out of control in a society based on the common, widespread, learned, and extremely solid use it makes of networks of acquaintances and the exchange of favors. These practices work for people, on a day-to-day basis, in micro interactions. At the same time, however, they create a social trap full of paradoxes: practices that reproduce the very inequalities and inequities it seeks to address.

This book consists of six chapters, divided into two parts. The first part presents the basic elements guiding this study: the battle for the definition of corruption and the intricate network of practices underpinning corruption in various countries, including those in Latin America. Thus, Chapter 1 discusses the difficulties caused by an umbrella concept such as corruption. It is actually a label that seeks to encompass a multiplicity of very different practices and acts; the degree of variation in the concepts of corruption is already a well-known obstacle in the debate to address the phenomenon. Therefore, it is argued, there is a real battle for definition. A battle that is not innocuous: as noted before, corruption is defined and addressed through a social and political process. It is necessary to create organizations, rules, and institutions that impose penalties and affect people, groups, and organizations. Those who manage to impose and convince others about a definition of corruption therefore set themselves up as the judges and those responsible for ensuring enforcement. For many people, nowadays, there is a real "anticorruption industry" that has sought to become hegemonic. And one that obviously has its own interests. On the basis of a definition-metaphor of corruption as a cancer, global anticorruption prescriptions have been created that include ideas and formulas involving economic liberalization, the withdrawal of the government from various activities, and new formulas of contracts to further privatize public

12 Introduction

services. It is not the purpose of this chapter to discuss the political and economic consequences these ideas have had. It simply seeks to explain in some detail the argumentative logic of this hegemonic vision of corruption, with its virtues and limitations. This will allow us to observe more clearly the need to take an additional step that is pushing to continue studying corruption more as a socially integrated phenomenon and less as an exogenous factor, a pathology that comes from outside social dynamics and is resolved through generic formulas involving liberalization and an open economy.

In Chapter 2, precisely one of the most neglected options for understanding corruption is taken up as a powerful perspective to be studied: corruption as a social process. A social process in which corruption forms part of a series of practices that are extremely widespread and necessary in any society: the exchange of favors. The exchange of favors happens all the time, in the family sphere and in the ambit of close friends and acquaintances. It forms part of an indispensable glue which, on the basis of reciprocity, creates stable, constant bonds between people. It is a universal phenomenon. But in certain societies, this dynamic of exchanging favors crosses boundaries and becomes indispensable for people to succeed in achieving their own objectives. We speak of societies where the exchange of favors determines the effects and logics of a wide array of relations: between people and government, between firms, between people and all kinds of authorities.

In many Latin American countries, the dream of contemporary societies of patterns of exchanges under universal patterns of rules and merits coexists with another social logic: one of favors and networks of acquaintances that are critical for things to work. Thus, those who have contacts and acquaintances can solve their problems, with all kinds of authorities, whether government or private, through these contacts. Two issues are discussed in this second chapter. First, the enormous strength of the social glue these practices of exchanging favors create. They become indispensable for maintaining exchanges and relations between people. Second, the enormous diversity and richness of these practices—of their informal rules, logic, communication, rules of etiquette, and even ethics. Several of these practices are reviewed, such as *guanxi* in China, *blat* in Russia, and *protekzia* in Israel. But particular emphasis is placed on two solid, widespread practices in two Latin American countries: *jeitinho* in Brazil and *palancas* in Mexico. Linking these practices to corruption allows us to provide a different, more open and dynamic perspective, which allows us to have a better understanding of the challenges and limitations of anticorruption efforts. Indeed, in these societies, formal anticorruption instruments must be effective in transforming a profound social reality, full of old practices, which creates a stability that must be transformed. It probably needs to be transformed from within.

The second part of the book begins with these elements. This section is dedicated to observing the opportunities and challenges some Latin American countries face in controlling the phenomenon of corruption. It examines four countries that have addressed corruption through major risky efforts, as described above. Chapter 3 explores the case of the Anticorruption Agency of Argentina and its desperate effort to survive in the face of boycotts and threats from the very political system it is designed to control. Chapter 4 is dedicated to Mexico and the extremely risky innovation of a National Anticorruption System—a system whose ambitiousness and cost could, oddly enough, be part of the reasons for its possible failure. Chapter 5 examines the case of Brazil and its decentralized, professional effort to eliminate corruption, whose success is, for some, part of the cause of the political crisis this great country is experiencing today. Lastly, Chapter 6 deals with the international innovation of CICIG in Guatemala, a hybrid, international, and national organization that has enjoyed great success through a solid research technique and a complex political operation enabling it to operate. Yet paradoxically, because of its success, it is about to be canceled by the government itself.

The studies in the second section of the book are an excellent step forward to seeing the complex political and social processes that exchange practices have created in action. Its most worrying feature is its stability: the practice of exchanging favors has created a social network of micro-actions so widespread and powerful that the extremely powerful and ambitious efforts made in Latin America have achieved limited and even paradoxical results. However, this book shows that the road is still open, and hopes are high. It will probably be necessary to use the over-simplification of the anticorruption industry formulas to push toward formalization and greater transparency in relations between society and the authorities. But it will also be essential to understand that emphasis will have to be placed on social and political practices and customs in order to reveal the perverse, powerful logic of the exchange of favors. It is a logic that has its own rules, which may be paradoxical but no less functional as a result. And this should be used to re-assess efforts such as those discussed in this book, in order to ensure that they have the expected effect of building more equitable societies in Latin America, based less on the privileged structures of a few.

Bibliography

Arellano-Gault, D., & Del Castillo, A. (2004). Maturation of public administration in a multicultural environment: Lessons from the Anglo-Saxon, Latin and Scandinavian political traditions. *International Journal of Public Administration*, 27(7), 519–528.

Bardhan, P. (1997). Corruption and development: A review of issues. *Journal of Economic Literature*, 35, 1320–1346.

Chugh, D., Bazerman, M., & Banaji, M. (2005). Bounded ethicality as a psychological barrier to recognize conflict of interests. In D. Moore, D. Cain, G. Loewenstein, & M. Bazerman (Eds.), *Conflict of interest* (pp. 74–95). Cambridge, England: Cambrdige University Press.

Dealy, G. C. (1977). *The public man: An interpretation of Latin American and other Catholic countries*. Amherst, MA: The University of Massachusetts Press.

Debiel, T., & Gawrich, A. (Eds.). (2013). *(Dys)Functionalities of corruption: Comparative perspectives and methodological pluralism*. Heidelberg, Germany: Springer.

Dubbink, W. (2015). Organizational integrity and human maliciousness. In P. Hardi, P. Heywood, & D. Torsello (Eds.), *Debates of corruption and integrity* (pp. 7–37). Basingstoke, England: Palgrave Macmillan.

Eisenstadt, S. N., & Roniger, L. (1984). *Patrons, clients and friends*. Cambridge, England: Cambridge University Press.

Faughnan, B., & Seligson, M. (2015). Corruption in Latin America. In P. Heywood (Ed.), *Routledge handbook of political corruption* (pp. 212–224). Abingdon, England: Routledge.

Hodson, R., Martin, A., Lopez, S., & Roscigno, V. (2012). Rules don't apply: Kafka's insights on bureaucracy. *Organization, 20*(2), 256–278.

Johnston, M. (2005). *Syndromes of corruption.* Cambridge, England: Cambridge University Press.

Noonan, J. (1984). *Bribes: The intellectual history of a moral idea.* Berkeley, CA: University of California Press.

Torsello, D. (2015). Corruption as a social exchange: The view from anthropology. In P. Hardi, P. Heywood, & D. Torsello (Eds.), *Debates of corruption and integrity* (pp. 159–183). Basingstoke, England: Palgrave Macmillan.

SECTION I

Corruption as a Dense Social Relationship

1

CORRUPTION

The Battle for Its Definition

Corruption: A Political Concept

It is no exaggeration to say that there is a global battle to reduce corruption. It is battle which, for various reasons, has mainly been concentrated in developing countries in order to encourage them to design and implement policies and strategies to control and even eliminate corruption. Several of these campaigns have been created by international organizations and supported with funds from developed countries, establishing a clear, dominant pattern showing that the problem is predominantly located in developing countries. International concern over the issue has become a kind of necessity and sometimes obsession, even becoming a clause in international trade treaties and a condition for sending aid to countries in crisis. Perhaps that is why it is increasingly common for various people to advocate studying this phenomenon; in other words, to analyze the reasons why so many organizations and countries have placed so much emphasis on the battle against corruption in developing countries. The question is, for example, what economic and political interests do these organizations and their assistance pursue? Is this battle a disinterested effort by all those involved? Is the central objective of this battle really to reduce corruption effectively and thereby achieve the common good?

Beyond the clearly normative arguments usually established by the defenders and believers in the war against the cancer of corruption, for various analysts of the subject it is also possible to argue that this international battle is a well-orchestrated campaign, with a discourse that tries to dominate the debate, and even an ideology. An ideology that is the front of diverse economic and political interests that have been able to dominate in the field of the creation of instruments, rules, and anticorruption policies induced (and sometimes imposed) in developing countries. What interests lie behind and according to what logic are anticorruption policies and

18 Corruption as a Dense Social Relationship

instruments promoted? This chapter presents the background of this political battle, which, in many ways, is based on the debate over the definition of corruption.

Indeed, everything would seem to suggest that there is a political and economic struggle to take the lead in the way corruption is defined, as a point of departure to hegemonize an entire structure of organizations, people, and ideas seeking to lead in the international sphere in this matter. An international anticorruption regime, so to speak, which becomes the main gateway to defining the concepts, tools, and prescriptions and rules for the distribution of resources to be used by all those wishing to address corruption. This regime has therefore obviously become the acceptable parameter, the indispensable door to legitimizing or certifying the anticorruption efforts of any country or government. A country or government that needs to obtain international support, strengthen its trade, certify its government or corporate contracting practices, in one way or another, needs to rely on the advice of that group of organizations that have become expert spaces with legitimized experts to give advice and design anticorruption instruments. That is why they have been called "the anticorruption industry", since they comprise a myriad of organizations and people that exist, negotiate, and work full time in the development of this field of knowledge that has proved so fruitful in recent years. Nowadays, the anticorruption industry is undoubtedly strong and powerful, as is the growing criticism it is facing, not only because of its questionable results in various experiences, but also because of its unwillingness to discuss the interests of the industry itself (Vogl, 2016). The point, in any case, is that, as a discourse and an international device, the metaphor and conceptualization of corruption as a battle, a cancer that must be eliminated, is based on a series of interests and political positions that must be discussed and debated.

Achieving a dominant definition of what corruption is and ways to reduce it, whether it is a hegemonic definition or accepted mostly in the international arena, is extremely important. The reason for this is extremely simple: a person who presents a particular perspective in a polysemic phenomenon such as this, with many angles, is capable of skewing international discussion to promote a specific political and economic view. Let us examine this in more detail.

Making a particular definition of the phenomenon dominant gives one the upper hand in setting the rules and conditions to direct, propose, and impose, if necessary, the keys and "right" ways to build anticorruption policies, institutions, norms, and programs (De Graaf, Wagenaar, & Hoenderboom, 2010, p. 100). Having this leadership makes it possible to establish the political line of what is corrupt versus what is "honest, clean, and correct". And of course, what is honest and clean cannot be wrong. In other words, a "moral" battle is won by framing the defenders of these policies as champions of the right policies. For many, for example, it is increasingly evident that the dominant anticorruption solutions have been coupled with issues such as the imposition of a vision of the reduction of government intervention, defending pro-market and pro-deregulation restructuring (Kajsiu, 2014), couched in a moralistic discourse. This is anticorruption discourse at the end of the day, but with aims that go beyond the phenomenon itself:

anticorruption policies as a small part of a general framework of ideas and instruments aimed at the construction of a certain international economic order.

In fact, just as the issue of corruption has been important for several decades, the crusade against corruption has not only been an academic idea or a fashion merely to be debated in the classroom (Argyriades, 2001). The way corruption has generally been defined as a "disease" or a "cancer" is no coincidence. And this way of constructing the phenomenon of corruption is key to directing the battery of reforms to change the economic and governmental practices of various countries.

Anticorruption policies as part of a more general scheme of economic liberalization and the reduction of state intervention would appear to be the dominant international strategy. The die has been cast since the 1996 World Bank director defined corruption as a cancer. An international body with the importance and weight of the World Bank therefore set the tone of the debate and predefined the framework on which legitimate solutions could be built, both technically and politically. Thus, the dominant discourse was outlined: a functional market economy, a government that does not intervene excessively, a strategy of constant deregulation are the prerequisites of a "corruption-free society". In other words, corruption is a phenomenon characteristic of societies with governments that intervene too much and therefore with imperfect market economies with weak institutions. From this frame, any anticorruption strategy would make sense insofar as it points to the gestation of these societies in a particular international order (neoliberal, some would say).

Corruption seen as an illness seems an obvious and even harmless formula at bottom, but the consequences of the metaphor have been many and obvious. If the cancer of corruption needs to be removed, this implies that it must be done without thinking twice about it: it is a fight by the good guys against the bad guys; there are no intermediate spaces. The next step is therefore to make it clear that instruments and experts are required to deal with the disease. This is how what Sampson (2010) called the anticorruption industry was born. A growing group of organizations and individuals emerged that would make their *modus vivendi* acting as experts in a range of activities and knowledge in the war on corruption. These ranged from how to identify and measure it "correctly", to how to promote the creation of public policies in various nations to "extirpate" cancer. A professional intervention industry grew up that diagnoses, implements, and acts under a very specific paradigm of corruption as a social disease.

Words matter; they have a key rhetorical weight: if it is a cancer, then it is a destructive disease. It is a disease created by strange, exogenous, and identifiable agents that must be vaccinated against and destroyed. Moreover, in this particular paradigm, by removing the cancer, a healthy organism is created, which becomes nothing less than the goal. One of the oddest aspects of this paradigm is the problems it has in operationally defining the goal: Where is there an example of a world free of corruption, that is totally "healthy"? It is odd that precisely this metaphor has been chosen, which was probably inspired by the war against cancer, launched in the USA in the early 1970s. The similarities with this case are quite interesting. For the case of

20 Corruption as a Dense Social Relationship

the "war on cancer", Mukherjee (2011) has argued that this military metaphor of a battle against cancer trivialized the problem of a disease that is created not by external agents that can be eliminated but by the very dynamics of the cells and, therefore, means that there is no single solution or treatment. Cancer does not have a single cause; it is produced by mutations of the cells themselves and therefore requires a myriad of solutions, many of which are designed to strengthen the defenses of the biological system itself. The resemblance to corruption is very interesting: What happens if corruption is not a social disease, which is treated as if it were caused by externalities? In other words, what happens if corruption is built from within, on the basis of relationships between people, their networks and links of exchange and communication, in a logic of social interrelation? The metaphor of corruption as cancer undoubtedly has very different types of implications, because its discourse and instruments point to a particular way of understanding and addressing the phenomenon.

If corruption is a cancer, according to this rhetoric, there must be "doctors" who know how to diagnose and eradicate the disease. It requires professional experts proficient in the art of curing social diseases such as this. It cannot therefore be left to laymen. It requires experts ready to act in a battlefield: one would expect a war with casualties and fatalities, good against evil, heroes against villains. It should be added, of course, that in this dominant definition, the greatest burden of responsibility and problems has fallen on developing countries, with the assumption that developed countries do not experience or experience very little corruption. It may be obvious that the forms and scope of corruption may be different in the latter, and that corruption in various forms is a reality in countries such as the USA, Germany, and the UK (Asencio, 2018; Hine & Peele, 2012; Schluter, 2017; Tanzler, Maras, & Giannakopoulos, 2012), but the practical effect is well known: the recipes of the anticorruption industry are mainly designed for developing countries.

This has been in many ways the prevailing rhetoric of recent years regarding the issue of corruption. One can easily imagine, then, that the issue is not merely an academic one or that it was placed on the international agenda by chance. The international anticorruption regime has been built by identifiable individuals and organizations, which has paved the way for intervening in the phenomenon. This route almost always goes through policies and action programs that are suggested or encouraged in certain governments as standards that must be met in order to be accredited in the international community. Corruption has become a solid issue on the international political agenda, with many people working to define the instruments to diagnose and attack the problem in the battlefield, which is mainly countries in the developing world. The military language used may not be a coincidence in this respect: battle, war, fight against corruption, against the corrupt and their institutions that do not allow democracy and the market to flourish. The force behind the argument is still Manichean, in many ways: It is a battle, a war that makes sense because it serves to win a morally correct world to the cry of, "A world without corruption or death". And those who doubt the importance of the war against corruption undoubtedly do so because they have interests in maintaining those perverse political and economic dynamics. It is therefore not easy to question the dominant paradigm that has been created at the risk of being placed "on the wrong side of history". That is how Manichean this discourse can be.

Observing the phenomenon of corruption over and above the bias that the anticorruption industry has created and hegemonized can be a fundamental academic effort, but also a political one. Some argue that this bias is not free of plausibly identifiable powerful, economic, and political interests (Brown & Cloke, 2001, p. 118; Wedel, 2009). Beyond this discussion of the interests behind the anticorruption industry is the need to continue the quest to better understand the phenomenon of corruption. The simplistic metaphor of war may be limiting the identification of other aspects of the phenomenon that may be essential to understanding its logic and nature. The bias or veil the anticorruption industry has placed over the phenomenon has significant disadvantages. To begin with, it conceals the interests created by the participants themselves in the anticorruption industry: The metaphor of the fight between good and bad is a very appropriate way to subtly divide the group into two parts, ensuring that the side of the good guys is unlikely to be wrong. In this respect, it is evident to many that the anticorruption industry is part of the chain of organizations and groups that defend deregulation in commercial and financial exchanges, the highest possible freedom for foreign investment and the flow of capital as part of the global economic model (Kajsiu, 2014). If fighting corruption is good, then the recipe must be good: liberalization and deregulation, with no room for debate or dissent.

The militaristic metaphor of the fight against corruption therefore simplistically divides the issue into two groups (bad versus good), creating an undoubtedly limited environment to maintain a more inclusive discussion among many groups, people, and organizations which can be part of the solution. If corruption is such a widespread social phenomenon (and not only in developing countries, incidentally), then the social density that makes corruption possible must be much greater than the simplistic idea of two opposing groups. Losing sight of the way corruption is embedded in the social and political processes of a society is a part of this social history of corruption that ends up hidden or concealed, and is probably essential to understand in order to address it (Marquette & Peiffer, 2015).

Another possible disadvantage of this rhetorical vision of the battle of good versus bad or of corruption as a disease is that it prevents one from understanding that corruption is actually a politically created concept, and therefore ambiguous and imprecise. Corruption is an umbrella concept, one that brings together a wide array of acts in very different circumstances and spaces: it exists in the public sector, but also in the private and social (or non-profit) sectors. The interaction between governments, politicians, citizens, and civil society organizations are all spaces where a normative concept of corruption is identifiable. It is not merely a matter of government or political actors: corruption is a social relationship that is expressed and depends on the exchange between citizens, politicians, governments, organizations, and companies.

22 Corruption as a Dense Social Relationship

Additionally, there is a solid body of evidence showing that the definition of corruption as the act of individual people making calculations of the disadvantages and advantages of acting corruptly has failed to explain why some people engage in these acts and others do not. It has also failed to explain the permanence of corruption in many societies (Depuy & Neset, 2018, p.2). Corruption involves many acts that generally involve different forms of reciprocity and interrelation, which can be seen and justified by different people in different ways according to the specific circumstances of the region or country. The deep and dense social dynamic that surrounds corrupt acts makes the concept constantly debatable and negotiable, both culturally and politically. As a concept, corruption encompasses acts, customs, practices, and social relationships that may be supporting entire political systems and intricate cultural interpretations (Baez-Camargo & Passas, 2017). These can, incidentally, evolve over time, meaning that an act that was acceptable in the past may be inappropriate in the present.

Corruption, then, as an umbrella concept involving an array of acts that are part of a network of interrelations among many people, is therefore one where not only individual but also groups and even organizations are involved (whether partially or fully, Burke, Tomlinson, & Cooper, 2011; Fleming & Zyglidopoulos, 2009; Zyglidopoulos, Dieleman, & Hirsch, 2019; Zyglidopoulos, Hirsch, de Holan, & Phillips, 2019). Corruption is a phenomenon which, in certain concrete and specific circumstances, may or may not have broad social agreement that is an unethical act. To make these acts effectively be socially regarded as unethical generally requires the social capacity to reconstruct the social history of the relations and reciprocities that led to the fact that in a certain situation, corruption ended up dominating or determining what eventually happened. In other words, corruption can usually be told as a story, as a saga where certain people did or stopped doing various things while interacting with each other. And in that story, there are many acts, some unethical and others not necessarily so. The point is that the saga will have to end up defining the narrative: for one reason or another, this history of relations between people and organizations ended up being corrupt. A corrupt act is a social act with a past that links other acts and practices. And it probably also has a future. In order for this unethical act to remain as a possibility in time and to avoid being identified and punished, the relationship and practice must be stable, justified, often even rationalized (that is, the agents involved create a story or justification in their actions to make them appear less incorrect, at least in their mind). The formula of good guys against bad guys evaporates when faced with an empirical reality based on a rich series of acts and practices, not all unethical or completely ethical, with a multitude of intermediate grays rather than black and white tones.

Bribery, conflict of interest, fraud, influence peddling, and coercion are just some of the acts that can be regarded as being linked to corruption. But basically, each of the concepts referred to above are of a very different social and political or economic nature. Some refer to monetary exchanges, but not always (influences can be exchanged); some of them materialize in basically forced acts (as in a bribe

Corruption: The Battle for Its Definition **23**

with threats), but in others there may be a relatively agreed on exchange (as in a bribe that benefits both parties). In certain acts of corruption, the parties involved benefit from each other and the victim is actually identified in a very abstract way: society or citizens or the shareholders of an organization.

In others, such as fraud, there is no strict exchange, although there is cheating and opacity when acting, which implies that some participants have a fairly good grasp of the rules and organizational relationships that must be understood in order to engage in fraud. Fraud requires knowing the organizational paths, relationships and rules of hierarchy and oversight, the organizational culture of interactions and obedience to rules, so that the deception is successful. Continuing with fraud, for many it is evident that this is another umbrella concept that can itself be divided into dozens of forms of fraud, each with its own logic and specificity (ACFE, 2016, p. 11).

Let's talk, for example, about conflicts of interest. These conflicts can be real, identifiable, and punishable, almost immediately. But it is not always that simple. In the case of a conflict of interest, it is almost never that simple. Generally, a conflict of interest may also be potential or apparent: the mind of a civil servant or the manager of a firm may be in the process of being adversely affected by a private or particular interest. The point is that the conflict of interest can negatively affect the judgment of a person in a position where he/she should protect the interests of others. It is, in other words, a failure of the self-discipline a person must have so that in his/her position of decision in the organization, he/she puts the interest of the organization, the client, the citizen, above his/her personal interest. A conflict of interest can be extremely subtle and even difficult to identify for the very person who is supposed to maintain that self-discipline to avoid engaging in that conflict. In the case of a potential or apparent conflict of interest, the conflict itself has not happened, but has only been observed by someone outside the organization (a journalist, for example, who draws other people's attention to the potentially negative effects if the conflict of interest materializes). In other words, even though the de facto conflict of interest has not happened, the fact that it has been identified as possible or likely has already harmed the organization or the government. In other words, it may be that in fact there was no conflict of interest. But the possibility that it may have happened, that the people involved did not take precautions to prevent their judgment from being adversely affected against the interest of the group or the general interest, is already harmful. One example serves to clarify the situation: the case of the president of a country whose wife accepts a loan for a contractor to build her house. The president's wife is a well-known artiste, is paid for her work, and is the person who secured the loan. But the contractor turns out to have obtained contracts from the government led by the president in question, through a tender. The president does not formally participate in hiring decisions, which are decided by competition or tender. But the case made headlines. Could it be that the president's judgment was affected by the existence of his wife's loan and that this in some way affected the awarding of contracts to the contractor in question? It is difficult to know. But the possibility that it may have happened is an apparent conflict of interest. Perhaps it had no effect, but no-one knows for sure.

24 Corruption as a Dense Social Relationship

Could it have been avoided? The answer is yes, steps could have been taken to prevent this from happening: self-discipline and foreseeing that this type of contract and agreement, although perhaps not strictly illegal, is unethical. Was there corruption? No single answer appears to have achieved total consensus. Conflict of interest is one of the clearest examples of the difficulty of classifying in black or white a practice that can be regarded as corruption at some point.

In short, each of these concepts that are usually identified under the very generic umbrella of corruption actually identify very different acts and relationships with each other, involving extremely varied and heterogeneous social and organizational relationships, with very different effects and quite disparate levels of severity (whether organizational or social). The fact that corruption is in fact an umbrella concept for so many dissimilar and heterogeneous acts is an enormous practical, intellectual, and political problem.

It is therefore worth encouraging readers to explore the diversity and social richness of the phenomenon of corruption. Indeed, corruption is an umbrella concept encompassing many different types of actions and acts. Many are illegal, but not all, depending on the country and even the region. Many of these acts which can be considered illegitimate (and even illegal) require people to build relationships and links, exchanges that involve building (paradoxical as this may sound) certain bonds of trust and reciprocity. And many of those relationships and bonds are dense, socially rich, builders of ties that can be seen as legitimate by many people, for various reasons, in a particular society.

Corruption actually comprises many types of practices and acts, which imply various forms of action and relationship between people. In a normative way, under certain circumstances, those acts or practices are converted or described or qualified by some as improper and even illegal, with different justifications ranging from the fact that they are inequitable (corruption creates unjustifiable inequalities of power), to moral judgments (acts of corruption are bad). Since we are talking about acts that involve relationships between people, corruption rarely implies a relationship at a discrete point in time: a corrupt act usually requires a series or chain of events that unfold over time, with a past as a reference and possibly with a future as a possibility. The chain of acts that can lead to an effect or an ending that can be classified as corrupt can therefore be seen as corruption, although there are some acts in the chain that are not illegal and sometimes not even socially illegitimate. As an example, imagine an average public servant in a contracting area that follows all the established normative steps for a large contract with a supplier. However, he/she notes that several of the specifications in that contract are too specific. He/she requests information and finds that there are no complaints from competitors, nor is any particular rule being violated. Quite simply, it is clear, for an expert on the subject of hiring, that the conditions seem too specific. Proving that there is collusion between some of the contractors and a section of the government which is hiring would involve a lengthy, complex technical process, and the public servant responsible for observing the rules and regulations does not find a quick and inexpensive way to show that there is something strange going on. In

Corruption: The Battle for Its Definition   **25**

this example, if corruption is involved, it places this public servant in the chain of events that led to it. But he/she is not a conscious or formal participant. The example also shows that corruption can involve a chain of acts, organizations, and people at different times, which means that identifying corruption in such a situation is neither evident nor exempt from heavy research costs. Such investigation obviously involves risks: there may not be legal and reasonable evidence of corruption, either because there was none or because it was very well concealed. And it is important to understand that an anticorruption investigation can be expensive, since it requires technical capacity, and specialized computer and human resources.

From now onwards, the concept of corruption will continue to be used in the book. This simplified concept is used for the sake of convenience, but readers will understand that what is actually being talked about are the different forms and acts that can take the form of an act of corruption. The central point of the argument is that it is a rich, diverse, intense, and motley social phenomenon, full of exchanges, reciprocities, cultural imaginaries, justifications, concealment, and rationalizations. This is a good time to be very clear: it is also a phenomenon of interests, of political and economic ambitions, which often involve and feed veritable political and economic mafias that use illegality and even violence and extortion as a way of life. Indeed, saying that corruption is a dense, rich, intense, and diverse social phenomenon does not mean that it is not part of the social fabric of illegality and potentially of crime, in ways that form the basis of the creation of mafias, which, through corruption, reproduce a social scheme that is very likely to be unequal, inequitable, partial, and unfair (Philp, 1997). The social richness of the phenomenon does not make it less worrisome or reduce the need to address it and there is a growing literature on international crime and the corruption structures it builds (Berdal & Serrano, 2002; Boll-Stiftung & Schonenberg, 2013; Rotberg, 2009; Williams & Savona, 1996). Accordingly, without trying to reduce the importance of the efforts designed to reduce crime and the social impacts it has, it is necessary to construct a more realistic vision, socially speaking, separating it from the discursive Manichaeism that produces the idea of a war or a battle against corruption, which is the standard discourse, among others, of the anticorruption industry. In other words, the point is to create the capacity for the analysis, research, and understanding of the rich social dynamic (which is intimate, sometimes illegal and even violent, but always socially diverse) behind this phenomenon.

Corruption: A Diverse, Heterogeneous Phenomenon

Corruption has a long history of existence. Some claim that the first references to this concept date from the Hammurabi Code (1750 BCE). Noonan (1984) finds references to bribery in the Roman Empire itself (27 BCE). And since these remote times, corruption has actually described various phenomena with different names and meanings. In general, the most recurrent synonym has been bribery in transactions with public servants. While bribery is the first thing that comes to mind for many people when talking about corruption, it is also often equated with various

26 Corruption as a Dense Social Relationship

forms of fraud. And various forms of deception and concealment of information to obtain illicit profits in all kinds of firms or organizations also appear as corruption (Comer & Stephens, 2013; Iyer & Samociuk, 2006). What often happens is that corruption, however it is defined, appears to depend on a normative justification, on an attempt to behave correctly. It is a phenomenon that is an infringment of a particular duty or obligation that a person, a fiduciary, so to speak, has committed against a collective (a group, shareholders, citizens). This group, which can be very abstract and general, has been deceived and negatively affected by one or more people who have abused the trust placed in them, violating the written or moral rules that can be explicit or even implicit.

It is a concept that tries to explain several de facto different and heterogeneous phenomena and is based on a normative construction that requires the establishment of a dividing line between what is ethical and what is unethical regarding a collective. Corruption is a poorly constructed concept, a concept that fails to provide clarity in practice. It is only by understanding these two problems to be addressed with the concept of corruption that a solution can be found: we are dealing with an umbrella concept, which is also a normative concept. The vagueness of this type of concept of corruption can be useful for certain purposes, but also becomes an obstacle in many situations. Let us examine this in more detail.

Let us begin with the classifications (Holmes, 2015), definitions, or what Nichols and Robertson have called: the galaxy of definitions of corruption (Nichols & Robertson, 2017, p.2). The following table contains some of the best known and most important definitions of corruption, from different disciplines and visions (see Table 1.1).

As one can see from this brief, incomplete list, definitions tend to emphasize various circumstances of heterogeneous phenomena: different acts in different contexts emphasizing either their legal, moral edge, or sometimes social or cultural aspects. Thus, at various times it has been thought that a legal definition would solve the problem. Although clear, intentionally illegal acts exist within corruption (such as fraud, once fraud has been proven by someone), there are others where what exists is a continuum between being an illegal act or an acceptable social practice (such as the influence of cronyism or kinship in a government operation or a company). Bribery, for example, may range from an obviously illegal act of giving money to obtain benefits in a government contract, to a present a citizen gives a public servant as reciprocity for good service or out of gratitude. The latter case can be so ambiguous that the gift can be regarded in a logic not of payment for present favors but of keeping the relationship and the link alive so that there is a probability of future favors. Depending on the social context, these gifts can be legitimate, even legal (or at least not entirely illegal). They can even be regarded by some as an act of good manners. But for others, even though these gifts or favors are not illegal, they are clearly regarded as immoral. The hope of resolving the problem of corruption exclusively through legal means evaporates in the face of this rich social and moral logic that corruption tends to involve.

TABLE 1.1 Definitions of corruption

Definition	Author
Corruption: It consists of the abuse of power for one's own benefit. It can be classified as large-scale, minor, or political corruption, depending on the amount of funds lost and the sector in which it occurs.	Transparency International (2009)
Large-scale corruption: Large-scale corruption consists of acts committed at the highest levels of government that involve the distortion of policies or central functions of the State, which allow leaders to benefit at the expense of the common good.	Transparency International (2009)
Minor acts of corruption: Minor acts of corruption consist of the everyday abuse of power by low- and middle-ranking public officials when interacting with ordinary citizens, who often try to access basic goods and services in areas such as hospitals, schools, police departments, and other agencies.	Transparency International (2009)
Public corruption: Manipulation of policies, institutions, and rules of procedure in the allocation of resources and financing by those responsible for political decisions, who abuse their position to preserve their power, status, and assets.	Transparency International (2009)
Corruption is "The abuse of public function for private benefit".	World Bank (1997, p. 8)
Corruption, like *corruptus*, the Latin word from which it derives, is a morally loaded term, evoking flaws of right conduct or integrity.	Wedel (2012)
Corruption has its roots in the meaning of a thing that changes from its naturally healthy condition, into something unhealthy, impure, degraded, infected, stained, adulterated, depraved, perverted, etc.	Philp (1997, p. 445),
"A transaction between actors in the public and private sectors, through which public goods become illegitimately private profits."	Heidenheimer, Johnston, and LeVine (1990, p. 6)
Aroca (undated, paragraph 9) suggests there may be three types of corruption: white, black, and gray: "White corruption is used to refer to practices that are not recognized as corrupt either by public opinion or minorities. In other words, corruption is so completely integrated into a culture that the problem is not even perceived... Black corruption has the same consensus, but in the opposite direction: everyone, minorities and citizens, agrees about stigmatizing certain practices. Disagreement arises in the gray option: what some define as corruption others do not consider as such. It is in this mismatch that there is a risk that a scandal will emerge, in the clash between the perceptions of some and the practices of others".	Aroca (undated, paragraph 9)
von Alemann (2004) categorizes five groups of understanding: as social decay, a logic of exchange, deviant behavior, perception, and as a policy in opacity or shadow. As one can see, these five are logics of observation and definition that make the concept of corruption an extremely amorphous one. It is a concept that apparently tries to reduce a series of different phenomena into a single category, so to speak.	von Alemann (2004)
Corruption is a socially negotiated concept, dependent on public perception and acceptance. There are enormous variations in whether certain actions are perceived as corrupt, and even if a certain behavior is close to being illegal it may nevertheless be accepted.	Moeen (2010, paragraph 12–13)

Definition	Author
"Corruption is essentially equated with bribery". Rose-Ackerman adds that subsequently, within the framework of the agent-principal model, the most susceptible part of the concept in economic analyses are monetary payments to agents. These payments are intended to "encourage agents to ignore the interests of their principals and to favor... the bribers instead".	Rose-Ackerman (2006, p. xiv)
According to Wedel (2012), the typical focuses of research on corruption to which economists have devoted themselves point out that these are activities (generally illegal)—especially bribery, bribes, extortion, "fast money" (unofficial payment to move a subject through bureaucracy), collusion, and fraud—and sectors, usually government purchases or service provision, tax collection, customs agencies, and surveillance.	Wedel (2012)
In the same vein, other economists point out that corruption is a "disease" or "disease [with] many... strains and mutations".	Klitgaard (1988, pp. 7, 21)
"Pathologies in the agent/principal relationship lie at the heart of the corrupt transaction."	Rose-Ackerman (2006, p. xvii)
"[B]ehavior that deviates from the formal duties of a public role due to pecuniary gains or private compensation (personal, close family, private clique), violating the rules against the exercise of certain types of private influence."	Nye (1967, p. 419)
"[T]he behavior of public officials that deviates from accepted norms to serve private ends."	Huntington (2006/1968, p. 59)
For Bauhr (2017), there are two types of corruption: corruption for need or for greed. The former is the one citizens require to access "fair" treatment or access from the authorities. The latter is the one that gives people an illicit advantage. Citizens, claims Bauhr, tend to mobilize to reduce the first type of corruption but not the second.	Bauhr (2017)
"[C]orruption is a violation of norms and standards of conduct."	Gupta (1995, p. 388)
According to Torsello and Venard (2016), researchers of organization use many definitions of corruption that can be divided into three types. "In the first tradition, corruption is synonymous with any misconduct in organizations... In the second tradition, academics use a limited definition common among researchers of organization: the misuse of public power for private benefit [similar to that accepted by Transparency International and the World Bank]... The third type of perspective is broader in scope: 'the misuse of an organizational position or authority for personal gain or organizational gain (or subunit), where misuse in turn refers to the deviation from accepted social norms'".	Torsello & Vernard (2016, p. 35–36)
Corruption in a broader sense, encompassing a series of illicit practices, "technically distinct from corruption, all of which however, none the less have in common with corruption their association with state, parastatal or bureaucratic functions, and also contradict the official ethics of 'public property' or 'public service', and likewise offer the possibility of illegal enrichment, and the use and abuse to this end of positions of authority".	Olivier de Sardan (1999, p. 26–27)

Definition	Author
A concept of corruption that captures key elements of an intermediation transaction, such as the organizational resources exchanged, the forms of exchange, and the structure of relations. In this respect, corruption is a transaction involving "informal exchanges of formally assigned resources. That is, resources that belong properly to a formal but not exclusively public organization".	Jancsics (2014, p. 3)

Source: Compiled by the author.

As can be seen in the case of gifts that can become bribes, the moral issue implicit in many definitions is key and problematic in any attempt to encompass an amorphous phenomenon such as corruption within a single concept. The same act can be considered by some as clearly immoral and by others to be in a gray or ambiguous, context-dependent zone. In other words, in abstract terms, without considering the specific social context of an act, it is possible that a bribe is always a bribe and therefore illegal and immoral. But what characteristics are required for a particular act to be clearly identifiable as a bribe? If the intention is what counts, giving an item to a public servant or to a person who grants a service may be unrelated, at least directly, to the granting of a favor or a resource. In certain circumstances, a person gives a present to another person, not to receive something immediately in return, but either to repay a past favor or to keep the relationship alive to resolve a possible future problem. If the basis of the moral judgment of this type of act is that it undoubtedly sought to receive something in return immediately or promptly, then there is a problem. Because rather than obtaining an immoral benefit, the primary purpose of giving the item may have to do with maintaining and cementing a stable and also reciprocal social relationship, (that is, the other party, who receives the gift or bribe, may be interested in maintaining the relationship in the long term). Obviously, at bottom, it has to do with the likelihood of obtaining a benefit. But it may be that this benefit is never needed in practice: the relationship becomes stable, but it may not be de facto necessary to exchange something in particular (the relationship exists, but the exchange is not repeated). So, what is there to punish, morally speaking, let alone legally? The aim of maintaining a social relationship foreseeing a possible future where one will in fact require the support of the other person for something immoral? The aim of building a social relationship or network of people with diverse affinities? These ambiguities that may arise in the moral but also the legal field usually involve the classic dilemmas that prevent one from being able to speak of a general theory of corruption or at least of a complete concept of it. The moral judgments that usually accompany the definitions of the concept tend to keep implicit the enormous ambiguities created in the concrete relations of exchange and bonding between people.

In the field of morality, one would expect or require something that is highly debatable: for the concept to have a precise capacity—in black and white without nuances—to elucidate what is an immoral or moral act, beyond the consequences

30 Corruption as a Dense Social Relationship

and the specific circumstances that occur between people in everyday, practical social relations. Trying to achieve some degree of clarity in this discussion is undoubtedly necessary, although it is usually an endeavor that is difficult to achieve, at least fully and unambiguously. Corruption is a mental and social construct, a collective desire to identify a clear line between unethical and ethical acts according to a shared, legitimated collective code. But the first dilemma is that in practice, the relationships and bonds between people in everyday life explode into a quantity, variety, and richness of exchanges and justifications, conceptual constructions and arguments, and interpretations that go beyond the dream of a concept and a unified theory of corruption.

In other words, corruption is one of the multiple forms of exchange and reciprocity that occur in social interactions. The key issue is that, for some (which in extreme cases can be for the vast majority or even for everyone), these forms of exchange and reciprocity, or at least some of these exchanges and reciprocities, for different reasons and in certain circumstances, can be regarded as immoral or illegal, or both. In other words, it is necessary for some agents, persons, or organizations to successfully and legitimately establish the border between an unethical or ethical act, for a collective. Moreover, it does not suffice to establish the precise line between what is ethical and what is not, since different acts may have very different levels of seriousness. Thus, some acts which, for some people are really serious and deplorable, for others may be unethical, but not serious or only deserve a proportional punishment. These "levels" of seriousness require an additional process of agreement and debate, which makes the umbrella concept of corruption even more ambiguous and problematic. This is because levels of severity can actually be discussed and analyzed in specific cases and require at least a basic study of relationships, quantities, and circumstances.

In the abstract, we could consider an overall, broad definition of corruption (Guerrero & Talledos, 2018). But in fact, it is in day-to-day practices that it is possible to determine a particular significance of the type of offense, its seriousness, impact, and the circumstances for all agents and in all circumstances. Corruption, in practice, speaks of an act that needs to be evaluated contextually, based on the circumstances and practicalities in which the acts took place. Therefore, it seems increasingly impractical and perhaps even futile to insist on an umbrella concept that frames all practices, in every society, in such a way that this definition or border will make sense (the same sense) for all people in all circumstances. It is probably this impossibility which makes it so difficult to find a single definition, a single concept of corruption that makes general sense. Corruption is based on an extremely abstract normative idea that seeks to capture a very large number of exchange practices that take place in multiple, disparate social contexts.

Corruption is therefore a simplified concept that attempts to encompass many social relationships that occur in practice on a day-to-day basis. The social logic of these practices is the key to this discussion. People relate to each other, and solve their interaction problems through bonds and pacts that link them in networks of interdependence and reciprocity. These ties are created and transformed into action

Corruption: The Battle for Its Definition   31

on a day-to-day basis. And they become stable insofar as they work; that is, to the extent that reciprocity is reproducible in a relatively accurate manner. There will always be uncertainty in the relationships between people: it will always be possible for communication to fail, or intentions to be misunderstood, or for the deceptions and fundamental secrets in these relationships to be used with intent (as Goffman, 1981 has shown). Accordingly, this increases the likelihood of these reciprocities occurring through several instruments at various levels of formality: legally, morally, and socially. And among all these levels, the question is that the everyday nature of interactions is decisive. Social relations exist in action, which is where they are materialized and reproduced, on a day-to-day basis. Everyday actions can be interpreted, or some people and groups can try to pigeonhole and make certain codes of conduct and communication about everyday forms of behavior obligatory. But their degree of success in encompassing or materializing these relationships will always be limited. People may decide during a particular action, on a day-to-day basis, to do something different. And they may be punished for departing from the norm imposed by others. But the actor can decide, for example, to rationalize certain practices and assume that they do not fall within the framework others have decided is illegitimate. Several people may decide to conceal those changes or seek to create another interpretation regarding these "deviations", refusing to acknowledge that they are in fact deviations. Lastly, circumstances have a critical importance: people can agree in the abstract that a practice is illegitimate, but in certain circumstances, the social trap in which they find themselves is so great, that they may be unable to see another alternative and consider that an illegitimate act was performed but that there were no reasonable possibilities to avoid that practice. In the process, they make the act less illegitimate. This is the case of many bribes or embezzlement in certain societies: there is simply no way to escape from using resources in that way given that there are actually no other reasonable options or resistance is difficult, ineffective, frowned on, or even dangerous.

In short, two things are being said. The first is that every society constructs and seeks to impose codes and definitions that bind all people to certain types of behavior and reciprocity. And second, every society is materialized in real interactions, on a day-to-day basis. How this interplay between what sociologists have called social structure and micro action occurs is key in many ways: how everyday actions, real interactions adapt or are forced to adapt to a series of rules imposed in abstract terms, normatively in both the legal and often in a more moral sense (in other words, regarding what is defined as good or bad).

It is very clear that any definition is in this respect a social product and seeks to establish these general rules, in a particular way. It inevitably establishes decontextualized definitions, yet which aspire to guide (or impose) the behavior of a large number of people. The key is to insist that normative definitions such as those involving corruption are a social and political product; in other words, a proposal by certain actors who seek to establish this definition as socially valid and to a certain extent compulsory (like Foucault [2010] who has studied issues such as illnesses, punishments, ideas about sexuality, and many other social constructions).

32 Corruption as a Dense Social Relationship

There is no such thing as a neutral or unbiased definition: any definition of what is normal, legitimate, or legal is related to the groups, people, and organizations that drive them, who try to make them general and impose them on others (for very different reasons and interests). Why are there people and groups who seek to define what is good, normal, and appropriate? What do they seek; what benefits do they obtain? What costs do they impose on others with these definitions? Who are they to seek to impose those codes on others? And even more importantly: are these codes about what is normal or appropriate useful; do they make sense and are they useful in practice, on a day-to-day basis? To what extent are they followed and obeyed by people and how much are they blatantly or secretly violated and with what consequences? Who and how will the enforcement of the rules created and imposed by these groups be carried out and what is the likelihood of their success?

The social factor in the definitions of corruption therefore matters. Some argue that instead, we should understand that corruption is a socially negotiated concept (Bratsis, 2003; Chibnall & Saunders, 1977, p. 139). In other words, what is inappropriate or not, normal or not, corrupt or not (and the ambiguities between these extremes of what is and what is not and the severity of the punishment that must be meted out) implies understanding how many practices have been socially constituted. And understanding why these practices (even if they are seen as illegitimate by many) have crystallized and stabilized. And if these practices are to be changed, it is important to discuss why, with what intent, with what costs and benefits (and for which groups) it is beneficial to impose these definitions and perhaps ensure that they are adopted by society.

What types of acts are undesirable (from the point of view of certain people and organizations), how much damage do they cause, and why is it necessary to change them? If corruption, in general, is undesirable or harmful, there is a need to socially negotiate to build an accepted perspective that defines the following: Who it is beneficial for? What creates the contradiction that it is socially harmful but beneficial to some or even to many in a society? What levels of seriousness do various unethical acts have, and therefore what kind of punishment (legal and moral) do they warrant? In other words, if giving a present to a public servant, or using funds clientelistically to win elections is common practice, acceptable on a day-to-day basis (perhaps not in the rules or in the abstract, but useful for materializing the interaction), what does it mean to make it undesirable, socially speaking? What negative implications does it have for everyone or many people in society? What costs will have to be paid to make it undesirable? Who will pay those costs? Who will benefit from that measure? What mechanisms will be sought to enforce compliance? What costs will it have for those who create those agencies of control that will be able to force others to comply with it?

Corruption is a socially negotiated concept because it is an expression of many social acts and practices that take place in specific contexts, on a day-to-day basis. Corruption forms part of the intricate web of acts and practices of interaction and reciprocity. And it is part of those acts which, socially, some or many are demanding be controlled, monitored, punished, or at least socially or morally frowned on. In all these issues, it seems that the moral debate regarding a phenomenon such as corruption matters. Accordingly, one cannot conceal the fact that the debate on corruption is in itself a social process full of interests at stake: the interests of people and groups who wish to impose controls and surveillance on others, with the respective social costs that some will have to pay or support. Defining corruption is an act of power with major consequences for the order and legitimacy of a political system and even for what some call an international order.

Accordingly, the battle for the definition of corruption will inevitably be a political battle. The fact that this is a political struggle for hegemony in the definition of corruption has been revealed, particularly in anthropological literature. Parties and political groups in various countries (both developed and developing) have found clientelism to be an important vein of political benefit. And again, these clientelistic logics generate concrete, day-to-day practices, expectations, and forms of interaction and reciprocity between citizens, parties, and government which are socially embedded and stabilized. Some anthropologists even suspect that, in many ways, the essence of many political systems in practice is linked to corruption (Blundo & Olivier de Sardan, 2001; Gupta, 1995; Nuijten, 2004). It is not an accident or pathology, it is not an exogenous "virus" that attacks a "healthy" political system, but an essential part of its modus operandi. Corruption therefore plays a paradoxical role in this regard: it is a word that defines immoral or illegal acts, yet at the same time, it defines social and practical acts which even politically or economically appear as substantive, crucial to the stability and modus operandi of groups, parties, and governments. The paradox of corruption is probably a substantive element of understanding and accepting so that different definitions make sense and can be discussed and debated.

If we combine these legal, moral, and social elements, then what we have is a major challenge. We can call it the paradox of corruption. Corruption is composed of acts and social relations, many of them necessary and indispensable in any society: the exchange of gifts, contacts, or influences. But many of these acts may be related to undesirable effects or consequences, at least for many within that same society. Corruption is usually perennial, stable, and sustained over time, despite being a phenomenon that may question the very foundations of a democratic society and its institutions (Warren, 2015, p.53) This paradox probably summarizes many of the conceptual limitations on understanding and addressing the phenomenon.

When we talk about corruption then, we are really referring to many things that may be processes, acts, relationships, and interactions. Let us examine this in more detail:

- Whether it is governmental (such as illegal hiring), economic (fraud in private or governmental companies), or political (it sustains the relationship between parties and citizens such as clientelism).
- Whether it is organized (mafia) or takes place on a small scale and is systemic, practically a "corruption industry" (Berkovich, 2015).

34 Corruption as a Dense Social Relationship

- Whether it is one of the multiple private acts that can be corruption or related to corruption: bribery, coercion, influence peddling, conflict of interest, nepotism, fraud, improper use of organizational resources, patronage, among other possibilities. Each and every one of them has a different social, political, organizational, cultural, and legal nature.
- Whether corruption is a discrete act or is actually part of a chain of social relationships and ties, many of which may or may not be corrupt.
- Whether there is a dispute regarding what is or is not considered an unethical act. That dispute may be in the normative area or may be in the field of social practice. This implies that people can be against corruption in the abstract but classify or understand their own concrete practices as being outside this classification, therefore regarding them as ethical, necessary, or unavoidable practices.
- Whether it is a social trap: in other words, people may agree that certain practices are wrong, but be in a trap where everyone else does this and nobody is willing to change. Or this trap may even be due to the fact that the actors who act as authorities say one thing about the law and act in a different, particularist way (Mungiu-Pippidi, 2015), which leaves some leeway to avoid engaging in these acts. Emerging from the social trap can be very costly on a daily basis, so that people and groups are willing to interpret acts that may be unethical in various ways. This is what psychologists call reduction of cognitive dissonance, or the mental process whereby people avoid thinking that an act or situation is negative, deceiving themselves that it is not negative, or at least, less so.
- Whether corruption is simply or at bottom a calculation by individuals regarding the costs and benefits of following the rules or violating them.
- Whether corruption is part of a chain of acts, many of them not corrupt, which may be hidden or difficult to evaluate, yet which in the end generate chains of reciprocity and commitment (partly what some call the normalization of corruption [Ashforth & Anand, 2003], as part of a process of falling down a slippery slope [Kobis, van Prooijen, Righetti, & Van Lange, 2017, p. 297]).
- Whether there are serious or less serious acts of corruption, and the specific ways of identifying them to create instruments of punishment proportional to the specific degree of severity identified. Identifying this often requires expensive and lengthy investigation processes.

This selection of the multiple possibilities included in the concept of corruption implies that there is a major challenge to be solved in practice if one wishes to advance in the debate and achieve the more transparent construction of proposals and instruments to control or reduce it. When you have a social phenomenon that is so intricate and embedded in social practices, and many of these practices are politically and legally defined as illegal or unethical, their identification, understanding, and prophylaxis become much more complicated to undertake. Therefore, what we see today in this area of discussion is a major struggle between groups, organizations, and people, with different interests, who are seeking to achieve hegemony in the definition of this phenomenon. Defining corruption is not a harmless act. It is an act full of political, economic, and social intentions, which must be opened up and debated.

The Debate and the Fight to Define Corruption

The previous section discussed how corruption is an umbrella concept that seeks to encompass (very imperfectly) a multiplicity of scattered, heterogeneous acts of people, groups, and even organizations. And it was argued that it is a social phenomenon that requires negotiation; that is, a social and political debate that attempts to establish the minimum elements of what are understood as acceptable or unacceptable, unethical or ethical acts or relationships, and in that respect, at least some of them are legal or illegal. It is a political act because in the end it distributes burdens and punishments among the different social agents, thereby distributing benefits and legitimizing the judges and those in charge of enforcement.

At the end of the day, we should accept the fact that corruption is an intrinsically confusing concept. It is confusing not only because it is generally an act that is hidden and clandestine. The confusion is also due to the fact that it is a socially constructed concept that requires a normative definition, from the perspective of what should be, of the border between what is ethical and what is not. That border will always be porous and will also be in continuous social and cultural debate. The border is porous because the way one should behave regarding abstract and general situations is an entirely different situation from what happens when this situation "is transported" to everyday situations, where people have to interpret the specific situation they face and make decisions. For example, a rule may state that in a procedure, the authorities grant services in exchange for certain requirements. But it turns out that these requirements are designed precisely so that people cannot easily and reasonably perform the process. The rule assumes that the authorities are impartial, but in everyday life, in many circumstances and societies, they are not. So, it may seem logical that if the authority that should be impartial is not, the rule that it is not right to give bribes can also be relativized. A second example can be nepotism and cronyism. In social and group settings, supporting family and close friends can even be considered a duty. But this rule changes if you are a public servant in a position of power: in that case, the general rule of supporting friends and relatives is frowned upon. The social and legal norms or customs in a specific work environment (in this case, that of the public sector) clash and contradict each other. Which rule takes prevalence and is therefore obeyed? There is a third example that is even more ambiguous: a person apparently legitimately wins a bid for a government contract and it is discovered that a government official who did not evaluate or know of the contest will be the administrator of some of the goods or services produced by the winner of the contest. And years ago, that administrator received a loan from the person who won the bid. If this relationship is proven, in many contexts, it can raise suspicion. It does not matter that it can be proved that the public servant did not exert any influence over the contract: *The appearance* of conflict of interest is enough to taint the process as being possibly corrupt. Everyday life marks situations and makes them contextual. The context may be important enough to end up explaining how abstract rules created for decontextualized logics end up being obeyed or not, or partially enforced (sometimes legitimately, at least for a significant number of people in society). When you have a social reality as confusing as corruption, it is logical to expect that there will be heated discussion and debate about it. Who defines what is unethical or ethical? And above all, what interests do they have in defending and imposing a certain definition?

Many definitions, as can be seen in the previous section, emphasize the role of the public sector in the existence of corruption. Accordingly, these definitions tend to overlook the fact that this also occurs in the private and social sector (non-profit) and in international organizations (Aaronson & Abouharb, 2015). Whenever there is the idea that a person with a position in the government or in an organization could have obtained benefits not considered legitimate (in this case, by acting in pursuit of a particular interest rather than that of the formally established beneficiary), it is possible to speak of corruption.

Moreover, in many cases, corruption is a two-way street: there must be a corrupter and a corrupted party (perhaps except in the case of simple fraud, although it usually happens that the fraud involves many people inside and outside the organization at various levels of deception and participation). And under the very strict logic of what it should be, corruption usually has a third actor involved (one that is usually very abstract): the group or social interest that is considered to be affected or deceived by an illegal transaction or interaction. Of course, the collective actor affected by corruption may be very specific and identifiable, especially when there are consequences: theft of property, construction flaws or disasters due to poor-quality materials, for example. But in general, it can be assumed that corruption is an attack that not only has concrete victims or people who are deceived, but significantly impacts on a collective called organization, citizens, or even society in general. An example would be the case of a bribe where the bribe obtains a resource which in theory could have been intended for another person who follows the formal rules. Although the second actor mentioned is not necessarily identifiable in a concrete way, the point is that a group of abstract people forming the group affected by corruption has been harmed (Della Porta & Vannucci, 2012).

Defining corruption and attempting to make that definition common, dominant, and accepted involves constructing very abstract situations regarding what should be, what is right, and what is ethical in the interaction between people and within a concept of a duty or very vague collective benefit. Defining corruption therefore implies trying to legitimize a vision of winners, losers, interests, and profits or costs that must be allocated and distributed among people in an organization or in society in general. For this reason, it is worth keeping in mind that in the definition of corruption there are effects that involve burdens on people and organizations and, therefore, interests at stake. Not only the interests of those who win or benefit from corruption, but interests behind defining the problem in a certain way. Defining corruption biases or directs the type of instruments and practices, policies, and legal and administrative regimes that will be built, financed, and legitimized. And thereby it establishes the social, moral, and economic burdens that will have to be distributed among the various social agents.

If corruption is a social relationship, there are logics of reciprocity that can be forced, but can also be accepted or agreed at different levels and moments. Reciprocity tends to be socially stabilized, as a means of coping with uncertainty and reducing risks in transactions or exchanges between people and groups. This normalization of ties and exchanges is substantive of all social processes. And corruption is no exception, as borne out by the interesting definition we saw earlier of white, black, and gray corruption. Different societies in agreement with their governments establish what is clearly corrupt or at least unethical (black corruption). But gray corruption speaks of those critical spaces of negotiation where interests and forms of relationship that have crystallized over time prevent agreement. And white corruption is very interesting precisely because it refers to that space of social relationships that form an intricate network of ethical and unethical acts that are confused and integrated. Either they are cynically justified (a kind of avoidance of cognitive dissonance) or frankly there is a social explanation, at least at the micro level, that it is a legitimate practice.

So, defining corruption is a fundamental act. It is not that there is only one way to do this work, nor is it easy to think that there is consensus. It is clear then that the very act of defining corruption is a political act. And those who manage to agree or impose a particular definition bias and establish the social visions of what is normal and are therefore in a better position to determine who should pay the costs and change their practices and behaviors. And also to establish what mechanisms and organizations are created in order to perform the all-important role of enforcement. The practical impacts of a particular definition can be very high as shown by Anechiarico and Jacobs (1996), regarding an extreme moralistic vision that seeks absolute integrity as a discourse, for example in the case analyzed by the authors, the unintended consequences of imposing a vision of absolute integrity led to the imposition of organizational and legal practices that made several processes, procedures, and services highly inefficient. At the same time, they failed to eliminate improper acts or generate a logic of realizable and practical integrity in the government in question.

That is why, logically, discussion about the actual repercussions of the international effort to impose a war on corruption has not been long in coming. The anticorruption industry has flourished at least partly under the aegis of a series of international organizations with certain specific interests and particular political and economic agendas. This primarily refers to the crusade launched in 1996 by the World Bank and closely followed by Transparency International: two organizations that have had many people in common in their ranks and that have been fundamental for the establishment of an international anticorruption regime (i.e. a regime as a set of organizations, rules, and principles that are at least minimally coordinated to create an orderly network with a major influence on the issue).

38 Corruption as a Dense Social Relationship

There have been variations over time, but the definition of corruption they have promoted has involved a moral crusade against corruption seen as a particularly persistent disease that occurs basically in governments and their administrations (although lately there has begun to be talk about corruption from and in firms).

To recap. The World Bank defined corruption as, "The abuse of public function for private benefit". And the metaphor, as already mentioned, was the cancer of corruption. A definition that immediately biased the concept of corruption as being a matter that begins and is generated in the public sector. It tended to frame firms and employers as victims in the process (Heissner, 2015; Wu, 2016). Moreover, in principle, the Bank focused its strategies for addressing corruption on developing countries. It was quickly assumed that the cancer basically existed in those countries, placing the corruption existing in developed countries at a different level of priorities. The logic was partly related to the launching of a crusade of support and therefore of intervention in the policies of developing countries (with particular emphasis at certain times on countries that had been within the sphere of power of the USSR). The alliance between the World Bank and Transparency International was crucial to promoting the so-called international anticorruption regime. It is a regime that many have thought has actually worked well, not necessarily to reduce corruption, but to promote strategies of economic liberalization and maximum deregulation of business activity and capital flow (Williams & Beare, 2000, p. 140)

It is worth examining one of the most characteristic examples of the contribution of these international organizations to the debate on corruption: metrics. Substantially based on methods such as the perception of entrepreneurs or certain people in different countries, metrics such as Transparency International's Perception of Corruption Index seek to show how corruption is perceived in various countries around the world. However, these metrics have very quickly been interpreted as an objective proof of corruption and their ranking has even been used to show that countries "rise" or "fall" in the index, as if that represented effectively raised or lowered corruption levels. It does not matter if methodologically, this type of ranking has a rather limited meaning in terms of the communication of a perception, which is undoubtedly important, but ultimately just a perception. Countries and analysts have become involved in bizarre discussions about what to do to improve the position of a country in the index. They are bizarre discussions because in fact, since this type of metrics is not equivalent to a ranking that measures the "amount" of corruption, they are unable to produce clear and precise prescriptive policies for "reducing" corruption and therefore "improving" a country's ranking. So, looking for solutions and instruments that "directly" change the position of a country in a perception index can be misleading. Although these limits of the Transparency International index are more or less evident, this has done less to prevent the emergence of organizations with experts with their instruments poised to engage in the battle against corruption, than to provide a clear perspective regarding the political logic and the specific means that construct and reconstruct the actual dynamics of corruption The anticorruption industry has therefore been characterized far more by generic prescriptions and global solutions than by a concern to understand the concrete phenomenon it wishes to affect.

An example of this generic and global strategy for the creation and implementation of standardized instruments is explained by Sampson (2010): the issue of anticorruption campaigns. The campaigns have usually been a portfolio in which both legal reforms and processes of economic liberalization, deregulation, and the change to public policies of market competition and the dismantling of governmental social protection structures are also discussed. These campaigns are full of generic, supposedly universal prescriptions, clearly based on the free market ideology and the dismantling of classic government policies of the so-called welfare state. There has been a strategy based on "campaigns" which, in other words, is extremely useful in avoiding a detailed explanation of the specific situation of corrupt relations and instead moving immediately to the instruments, which are always generic, with their standardized recipes (Kennedy, 1999).

With variations and exceptions of course, the general evolution of the discourse (or rhetoric) of the international anticorruption regime has emphasized a vision of the fight against corrupt acts largely focused on the surveillance of actions that take place within the public sector: bureaucracy, public services, and government purchases or actions. And it has primarily focused on developing countries, where interventions and reforms are regularly justified by the presence of inefficient bureaucracies.

Let us briefly review this evolution and some of its most important instruments.

A Nascent Internationalization

The enactment in the United States of the Foreign Corrupt Practices Act of 1977 (FCPA) is one of the first normative acts to criminalize behavior related to bribery that takes place between international companies and public servants (Sampson, 2010). This law arose as a result of investigations led by the Securities and Exchange Commission of the United States (SEC) in which the Watergate scandal—under the presidency of Richard Nixon—was related to money laundering matters in foreign countries and funds to bribe foreign public officials. The FCPA had two main objectives: 1) make accounting arrangements so that any company that had publicly traded securities in the United States should maintain records of the company's transactions; and 2) make it illegal to bribe or attempt to bribe an official in foreign governments.

Years before, during the first half of the 1970s, the Economic and Social Council of the United Nations (UN) made several efforts to place the anticorruption issue on the international agenda, but it was not until 1975 that the General Assembly of that agency adopted a resolution focused on combating corruption and bribery in international trade transactions. Despite this, it was only after two decades that a phase of intensification of anticorruption discourse and actions carried out by international organizations followed.

40 Corruption as a Dense Social Relationship

Chronologically, these two events were followed by a period in which international organizations developed a "complacent silence" (Bukanosky, 2006). When the FCPA was issued, companies in the United States and the world were dissatisfied with this law because it seemed to affect the international competition of companies. It was perceived as a hindrance to the international trade transactions carried out by international companies at the time. However, virtually no actions have successfully combated acts of bribery. In other words, for decades, international organizations such as the UN, the World Bank, the International Monetary Fund (IMF), and the Organization for Economic Cooperation and Development (OECD) maintained an inactive agenda on the subject. This does not imply, of course, that the agenda on corruption in international business is not a very intense agenda of analysis and development, both in academia and in private organizations of forensic auditing or fraud control (among many examples, we can cite Eicher, 2009; Lord, 2014; Bank, 2006). But the idea that corruption is a general phenomenon linked to the existence of government regulations and interventions as the main cause soon skewed the type of strategies to be generated: being an advocate of the free market and deregulation became a requirement for being accepted in the anticorruption circle of experts. The social density of the phenomenon of corruption was placed on the back burner: with general deregulation and transparency strategies, corruption would fall in a "healthy" market (i.e., an unrestricted one with minimal regulations).

The Intensification of a Common Anticorruption Discourse

The second important moment takes up the actions on an international scale which originated nearly 20 years earlier. First, in 1993, a non-governmental organization (NGO) with a global presence called Transparency International (TI) was founded by a former World Bank official, Peter Eigen, and several of his colleagues, specialists in international development, business and finance, and diplomacy, whose main objective was to maintain a "global movement, with a vision: a corruption-free world" (Transparency International, 2015). In addition, in 1996, another event triggered several institutional actions by international organizations and is considered the starting point of this phase of intensification of anticorruption discourse. Candidate for World Bank director James Wolfensohn gave a speech in which he pointed out that corruption was a "cancer" that had to be eliminated. Accordingly, "the economic development agenda was linked to the effectiveness of the government, which gave rise to new loan conditions [of the World Bank]" (Sampson, 2010, p. 274). Thereafter, intensification took the following route.

In the same year, in 1996, the UN General Assembly adopted a new resolution that called for cooperation to combat bribery, which became an annual convention for members' continuous follow-up of the issue (Bukovansky, 2006). The following year, in 1997, the OECD held the first convention on combating the bribery of public servants abroad in international business transactions. In the late 1990s, the actions of the UN, the World Bank, and the IMF focused on promoting the institutional conditions governments had to meet to be at the forefront of the fight against corruption.

On the one hand, Sampson (2010) points out that in the evolution of the anticorruption industry the conclusion was that good governance conditions—openness, accountability, and transparency in relations between governments and the private sector—in the countries were a precondition for development. Along these same lines, Bukovansky (2006) points out that, in the resolutions adopted by the UN between 1998 and 2002, anticorruption discourses evolved in such a way that they skewed the discourse toward countries with development problems, especially their governments or their public servants.

The evolution of discourse took an important turn in the second half of the 1990s. First of all, the UN resolutions recognized that development objectives should have an ethical basis, on the part of both the government and firms in their international commercial relations (until this point in time there seemed to be equality of circumstance between both actors). Second, they proposed that existing international laws, and the new laws criminalizing the bribery of public servants, should be fully enforced. Third, the resolutions overwhelmingly acknowledged that corrupt practices undermined the integrity and credibility of bureaucracies, thus placing emphasis on the public sector. Lastly, these resolutions exhorted and asked the private sector to become an ally with the aim of protecting the universal principles and norms put forward by the UN.

For its part, after 1995, the International Monetary Fund (IMF) and the World Bank reinforced their discourse in the same way as the UN. The IMF pointed out that corruption happened to the detriment of investment and economic development, and that it was necessary for governments to adopt governance policies—actions to improve their laws and ensure their compliance, improve efficiency and accountability in the public sector, and to reduce corruption—with the aim of generating stability in their economies. In the same way, the World Bank, as of 1997, presented a series of reports that positioned it as an organization with the financial capacity to help governments that required its monetary support in the fight against corruption (Bukovansky, 2006). In other words, the World Bank presented corruption as a problem that should basically be solved by governments and also defined strategies, or strategy packages (Sampson, 2010), to achieve this. The package sought to: 1) increase the accountability of the public sector; 2) seek the participation of civil society (TI subsidiaries in the countries); 3) make the private sector competitive; 4) promote institutional restrictions on power; and, 5) improve public sector management (Bukovansky, 2006). And in a collateral but substantive way, it should introduce the concept and measures of corruption as important data to be considered by the aid agencies of various developed countries (such as Rocham, 2015).

A Definition That Is Also Biased

Attempts were made to conceptualize the phenomenon of corruption in order to try to understand and analyze it in order to seek alternative solutions for addressing it. In

42 Corruption as a Dense Social Relationship

this regard, various national and international organizations, non-governmental organizations, researchers, and the government apparatus itself opted for a definition of this phenomenon that would enable them to offer actions to address it.

The World Bank (1997) established the basis for corruption to be understood as "the unethical use of a public position for private benefit". However, the roots of this widely accepted definition go back to Nye (1967) and Huntington (1968), and for authors such as Heidenheimer, Johnston, and LeVine (1990) the definitions of these authors accentuate the phenomenon as "public office-centered" acts, although they could also be understood as centered on the behavior dictated by the norms.

Moreover, due to the transactional nature that emanated from the Foreign Practices Corruption Act (FPCA) in 1977, Rose-Ackerman (1978, p. 7) pointed out that "essentially, corruption [was] equated with bribery", especially of public officials in international trade transactions. All these distinctions meant that the analysis of the phenomenon, initially, focused on the economic costs and benefits corruption entailed, assumed as a transaction cost.

In this way, just as quickly as the discourse did, the operationalized concept was crucial in the governance diagnoses that followed international actions and strategies, since corruption appeared as a "state capture", understood as "illicit control" of public policy by private actors in the form, for example, of undue influence or the buying off of judges or politicians (Sampson, 2010, p. 275).

In 1999, the Office of Latin America and the Caribbean, of the United States Agency for International Development (USAID), took up the World Bank definition. However, it broadened the concept to identify acts that included unilateral abuses by government officials such as embezzlement and nepotism, as well as abuse involving both the public and the private sector such as bribery, extortion, influence peddling, and fraud. A year later, TI proposed that corruption was the improper use of power granted for private benefit, which involves conduct by officials in the public sector and business managers, expanding the spectrum of actors and finally introducing a critical actor: the private sector. But in fact, there are very few international actors who emphasized this actor in this anticorruption regime.

For example, the Inter-American Development Bank (IDB) continued with the tradition of emphasizing the problem in governments, seeing it as acts carried out by officials who use their position for their own purposes, or do so at the request of others, in order to obtain benefits for themselves or third parties. Like other organizations, the IDB sought to identify practices or activities to exemplify this type of behavior: request, offer or receive bribes, considerations or clandestine commissions, extortion, improper use of information or assets, or influence peddling. For its part, in 2003, the UN—together with the United Nations Development Program (UNDP)—established that corruption is the misuse of public powers, office, or authority for private gain through bribery, extortion, influence peddling, nepotism, fraud, extraction of money to expedite procedures, and the embezzlement of funds.

Thus, the transactional nature with which corruption began to be understood (initially solely as bribes, and subsequently, as types of corrupt acts) focused much of its attention on the public sector. Moreover, the way in which the international bases for understanding corruption were established identified the focus of the metastasis of "cancer" called corruption: the behavior of civil servants. In other words, weak governmental institutions maintain and sustain unequal political relations with businesses and citizens, maintaining a paradoxical political equilibrium that even allows corrupt rulers to appear as if they had important political support (Manzetti & Wilson, 2007). And the solution: to free market forces from governmental encumbrances, especially their regulation. This point is critical to understanding the effects of the international anticorruption regime.

The Instruments Used to Measure Corruption

The third way the phenomenon of corruption focused rapidly on the effectiveness of bureaucracies in developing countries has to do with the instruments used by the anticorruption industry to measure the phenomenon. Since its inception in 1993, the NGO Transparency International has set out to leave a legacy, a "brand" that distinguishes it. Their mission is, as they themselves define it, a world without corruption. Their activism has a presence over most of the world and its influence affects the decisions of the groups of the most developed economies (Transparency International, 2015). In its 2015 Impact Report, TI indicates that it has a presence in 175 countries and territories in the world (with subsidiaries or offices in each). It also points out that it has secured the payment of $1.6 billion USD in fines for international bribery actions derived from business transactions. Moreover, TI shows that its influence in modifying norms in countries is equally powerful. It points out that in 1993, only 11 countries had transparency or freedom of information laws and that by 2015 there were 104 countries with this type of law, as a result of its international activism. TI is the "biggest non-governmental player in the anti-corruption industry" (Sampson, 2010, p. 274).

TI has generalized among public opinion (journalists, researchers, NGOs, and political class) three indices measuring the perception of corruption that citizens and business people have in the countries and territories that participate in the calculation of their metrics. The Corruption Perceptions Index (CPI), the Bribe Payers Index (BPI), and the Global Corruption Barometer (GCB)—measured since 1995, 1999, and 2011, respectively—allow us to discuss and compare the degree of corruption perceived in the country on a scale involving *rankings* or positions, which intentionally seek to distinguish the most corrupt countries from those that are not.

Some might think that "solid" metrics and international standards of comparison may not bias the discussion about where the analysis of corruption in the world is moving. However, a detailed analysis of the type of questions whereby each index is measured and the construct with which the type of corruption is operationalized shows that there is a focus of attention on the behavior of public sector officials.

First, the CPI measures the perception of corruption specifically for the public sector; generally, it measures the bribery of officials in various public services. Second, the IFS analyzes the propensity with which firms in the world's 30 largest economies offer bribes abroad; that is, to what extent a country perceives that firms that sell in its

44 Corruption as a Dense Social Relationship

territory are willing to offer bribes to public servants. Lastly, the GCB is an index that measures five ways of perceiving corruption in different regions of the world. In particular, the GCB measures 1) the perception of the change in the level of corruption in the past 12 months; 2) the perception of how the government is managing the fight against corruption; 3) the level of corruption perceived in the police force; 4) bribery rates, measured as the percentage of people who said they paid at least one bribe for 12 possible basic public services; and, 5) the perception of how much they believe people can make a difference in the fight against corruption.

Although the measurements of this international NGO have extended the indicators to different topics, it is striking that measures concerning the activities of the public sector prevail in the phenomenon of corruption, much more so than for the private sector. Although the IFS tries to serve a counterpart to measure the bribery of companies in the most developed countries, the last measurement was made in 2011, whereas the other two information sources are constantly updated.

Corruption metrics are diverse, heterogeneous, and very useful in several ways, but we need to advance a more realistic logic that will make it possible, rather than measuring corruption, to measure more precisely what Sampford, Shacklock, Connors, and Galtung (2006, p. 268) defined as "violations of integrity": bribery, nepotism, fraud, conflict of interest, embezzlement, among others. This implies, for the logic of the anticorruption industry, a break: there is not one corruption but many, and they are diverse in social, political, legal and, of course, ethical terms.

Summary and Next Steps

Corruption is an umbrella concept, which tries to encompass, with very little success in actual fact, a myriad of interactions between people in very different organizational and political spaces. Bribery, fraud, patronage, nepotism, conflict of interest, and embezzlement are all acts many would include as part of the concept of corruption. But many would not agree with including all these acts and there would be others who would argue that more acts are missing (people have even gone to the extreme of describing inefficiency or incapacity in organizations as corruption). It is therefore a concept in dispute and one that is extremely difficult to consolidate.

In this chapter we have claimed that as an umbrella concept, its usefulness is important for drawing attention to the problem, for example; but in practical terms, for discussion and its prophylaxis, it is necessary to state that there is not one form of corruption, but many. There are many forms of corruption, which comprise many different types of acts or interactions of a legal, political, and socially heterogeneous nature (Malem Seña, 2002, p. 13). The rhetoric of corruption becomes an enormous limitation when one enters the specific social reality of the different actors or processes we are talking about. They can be so different that they need to be understood in their specificity given their heterogeneity. And they are so different, in all senses, that it is striking that they can be encompassed in a category without losing their richness and intrinsic logic. Table 1.2 presents a schematic idea of this heterogeneity

TABLE 1.2 Corruption acts and uses

	Bribe	Fraud	Patronage	Clientelism	Conflict of interest	Embezzle-ment
Interaction logic	Agree-ment	Scam	Agreement	Agreement	Scam/ Agreement	Scam
Harmed who?	The person bribed (althoug-h they may obtain some-thing) A third party such as society	The main one	A third party such as society A third party on the basis of merit	A third party such as society (even if part of that society benefits from the agreement)	A third party such as society	The main one and society
Gray areas	Con-sidered as a gift No immedi-ate reci-procity is sought	Difficulty detecting decep-tion, especially when it is orga-nized	Legitimacy of social relation-ships and those with acquain-tances Political loyalty as a pretext	Difference between clientelism and support for "con-stituencies"	Difficulty proving it. Complex-ity of apparent and potential conflict	Difficulty detecting deception, especially when it is organized
Forms of prevention/ punishment	Investi-gation or detection in fraganti delicto	It may require expen-sive mechan-isms such as foren-sic audi-tingand internal control	Requires political control and institutions (such as civil service)	Requires political control	Prevention can be more effective	Investiga-tion or detection in fraganti delicto

Source: Author elaboration.

46 Corruption as a Dense Social Relationship

of different acts usually included in the concept of corruption. Their many differences, their heterogeneous social and legal logic, and therefore, the difficulties and differences in the instruments available for addressing them, are quite obvious.

Understanding corruption, the different possible types of corruption, involves a major effort. Not only because it is usually an act that is hidden or that can be frowned upon by others in society. Or because it is frankly illegal. Apart from this social nature that makes corruption a generally clandestine act, in actual fact, many people participate in exchanges and reciprocities that border dangerously on a gray area in legal terms or at least in terms of social legitimacy. Indeed, many of the acts that can be classified by some as corrupt can be part of a broad process of social interaction and customary exchanges between groups and individuals. These exchanges may be building and reproducing dense and even normalized dynamics of reciprocity. Corruption is composed of many types of acts, many of which require dynamics of reciprocity and trust building. The bribe trusts that once the resources have been handed over, the expected benefit will be delivered. The person who bribes expects the other party to receive his/her benefit and keep the transaction secret. The language and communication of a bribe can even be constructed with euphemisms that hide or attempt to reduce the moral impact of bribery: it is not a bribe; it is a form of assistance, an exchange of common agreement and benefit (see the case of the classic bribe of traffic police in Mexico City, Box 1.1). The conflict of interest can be subsumed in phrases such as: "Of course I knew him, but I did not participate in the decision that benefited him" (see the case of the loan for the house of the Mexican president with a government contractor, Box 1.2).

BOX 1.1 TRAFFIC POLICE AND BRIBERY

In Mexico City, the corruption of traffic police is legendary. It is almost inevitable that when arrested for any violation of traffic regulations, the motorist has to engage in the logic of bribery. This is because the rules are confusing, while punishments or penalties or fines for infractions can be excessive or extremely unclear. However, over the decades, the "bite" as it is popularly known, has evolved. In order to reach an agreement, the language and form of communication is full of euphemisms. The police officer usually complicates matters and warns the motorist (in this example a male) of the problem he has got himself into. It is at that point that the motorist can request the "help" and understanding of the police officer. In response to the signal sent, the police officer usually responds that he will have to think about it or ask for authorization. He pretends to speak or communicate with someone from his official car. He returns, says it is difficult to help him and that he will have to pay the fine or go to court. At that point, the motorist knows that he must insist: "Please, help me, you know what the situation is like". The police officer usually pretends to hesitate. He gives the matter thought. And then, with a great sense of "solidarity", he agrees to "help". And the transaction takes place. All this social melodrama leaves both parties in an ambiguous zone that avoids the use of words like bribery or illegality or bites. This dynamic has reached such a level of cynicism and simulation that some police say they receive that money and that they will deposit it in the motorist's name as the fine he must officially pay.

BOX 1.2 THE PRESIDENT AND THE CONTRACTOR

During the administration of President Enrique Peña Nieto, a piece of news made the headlines: his residence had been acquired through a loan. The loan was granted by one of the most important contractors in his administration. The president argued that this loan could not influence his trial because he never participated in the contests through which the contractor had won the aforementioned contracts through legal tenders. The contractor, the president argued, had known him long before he was a politician, governor, and then president. But that does not automatically make it a conflict of interest because, apart from the fact that he could not "get rid" of his acquaintances, he did not intervene legally in any decision. In addition, the loans were paid by his wife, a well-known, wealthy soap-opera actress in the country. An investigation carried out by a subordinate of the president's, reached the conclusion that no conflict of interest could be proved. The case opened the debate in Mexico regarding the entrenched, normal nature of the conflict of interest in the country and the lack of instruments to understand it.

In-depth understanding of the social and political logic of corruption seems to be an important step to take. The so-called anticorruption industry has made important efforts and advanced strongly in recent years to position the issue on the international agenda, as a serious problem to be addressed. However, it has also done so with a bias: a bias which, rather than studying the social roots of corruption in depth, has simplified it as an act of people who decide to be corrupt for the sake of convenience. It is one which is basically created in governments, rather than in other spaces such as companies. It especially takes place in developing countries (overlooking the roots and dynamics of corruption in developed countries, as shown by Caiden, Dwivedi, & Jabbra, 2017 and Cockroft & Wegener, 2017). Their formulas and recipes are usually based on a rhetoric of economic liberalization, state reduction, change in development strategies, and social protection (as Kajsiu, 2014, p. 11 has shown for the case of Albania).

Beyond whether this rhetoric of liberalization has been positive or not, in this case we are simply left with the need to go further and understand that a vision of this kind is neither innocuous nor neutral. And, therefore, there is a need to return to the debate on the social logic of corruption as a first step to understanding its roots and the logics of interaction and reciprocity. Understanding this social density of corruption will also allow us to remember that the battle against corruption is ultimately

48 Corruption as a Dense Social Relationship

a political battle, a battle advocated by agents with interests, which places costs on certain actors and groups. After all, it is worth remembering or at least discussing how countries now considered to have very little corruption such as Sweden or Denmark got where they are, which was not through the favorite strategies of the anticorruption industry (Mungiu-Pippidi, 2013; Rothstein & Teorell, 2015).

If the battle for the definition of corruption matters, it is precisely because people, groups, and societies need to understand how the forms of relationship, reciprocity, and exchange that are generated on a daily basis have enormous importance in justifying and giving meaning to their acts. Corruption is normalized in a society precisely because the roots of what is considered proper or improper end up being "negotiated", interpreted, and justified. And this is consolidated in real practices, in the everyday relations between people and authorities, whether governmental or otherwise. And whoever manages to impose or agree on a definition will be affecting many normal or normalized relationships and links. And forms of punishment and enforcement will be created, with differentiated costs and benefits. All this makes it fundamental to elucidate more the discussion about corruption, its forms, its logics, its deep social processes. All this has a single purpose: to allow a more transparent social and political debate. Not one that automatically places the good ones on one side and the bad ones on the other (Brioschi, 2017), alienating people and organizations and reducing the possibility of opening up the social mechanisms beneath corruption to discussion, several of which are regarded as normal or at least not illegal or illegitimate.

In the next chapter an attempt is made to build a vision of corruption that is socially dense. That is, one that will make it possible to understand the social roots of the exchange, interaction, and reciprocity that feed the logic of corruption in different societies. In other words, interaction and reciprocity are the glue that keeps society together. This glue is consolidated on a daily basis, in all kinds of interactions, including those that can be seen in certain societies as potentially immoral or frankly illegal. The fact that they are does not imply that they do not require or are unable to be institutionalized; that is, to become repetitive and to a certain extent, logical and involved in practices, languages, and symbols that give them meaning. Let us now turn to the dense social logic of corruption.

Bibliography

Aaronson, S., & Abouharb, R. (2015). Corruption, conflict of interests and the WTO. In J. B. Auby, E. Breen, & T. Perroud (Eds.), *Corruption and conflict of interests* (pp. 183–197). Cheltenham, England: Edward Elgar.

ACFE. (2016). *Report to the nations on occupational fraud and abuse.* Austin, TX: ACFE.

Anechiarico, F., & Jacobs, J. (1996). *The pursuit of absolute integrity.* Chicago, IL: Chicago University Press.

Argyriades, D. (2001). The international anticorruption campaign: Whose ethics? In G. Caiden, O. P. Dwivedi, & J. Jabbra (Eds.), *Where corruption lives* (pp. 217–226). Bloomfield, NJ: Kumarian.

Corruption: The Battle for Its Definition 49

Aroca, D. (undated). *Corrupción, elites, democracia y valores.* Retrieved from https://prensa necochea.wordpress.com/2008/09/17/corrupcion-elites-democracia-y-valores/.

Asencio, H. (2018). The effect of ethical leadership on bribing and favoritism: A field research study. *Public Integrity.* doi:10.1080/10999922.2018.1468204.

Ashforth, B. E., & Anand, V. (2003). The normalization of corruption in organization. *Research in Organizational Behavior, 25,* 1–52.

Baez-Camargo, C., & Passas, N. (2017). *Hidden agendas, social norms and why we need to re-think anti-corruption.* Basel, Switzerland: Basel Institute on Governance.

Bauhr, M. (2017). Need or greed? Conditions for collective action against corruption. *Governance: An International Journal of Policy, Administration and Institutions, 30*(4), 561–581. doi:10.1111/gove.12232.

Berdal, M., & Serrano, M. (2002). *Transnational organized crime and international security: Business as usual?* New York: Lynne-Rienner Publishers.

Berkovich, I. (2015). The corrupted industry and 'the wagon-wheel effect': A cross-country exploration of effect of government corruption on public service effectiveness. *Administration & Society, 48*(5), 559–579. doi:10.1177/0095399715607287.

Blundo, G., & Olivier de Sardan, J. P. (2001). Sémiologie populaire de la corruption. *Politique africaine, 3*(83), 98–114.

Boll-Stiftung, H., & Schonenberg, R. (2013). *Transnational organized crime.* Amsterdam, the Netherlands: Clausen & Bosse.

Bratsis, P. (2003). The construction of corruption, or rules of separation and illusions of purity in bourgeois societies. *Social Text, 77*(21–24), 9–33.

Brioschi, C. A. (2017). *Corruption: A short history.* Washington, DC: Brookings.

Brown, E., & Cloke, J. (2011). Critical perspectives on corruption: An overview. *Critical Perspectives on International Business, 7*(2), 116–124. doi:10.1108/17422041111128203.

Bukovansky, M. (2006). The hollowness of anti-corruption discourse. *Review of International Political Economy, 13*(2), 181–209.

Burke, R., Tomlinson, E., & Cooper, C. (2011). *Crime and corruption in organizations.* Aldershot, England: Gower.

Caiden, G., Dwivedi, O. P., & Jabbra, J. (Eds.) (2017). *Where corruption lives.* Bloomfield, NJ: Kumarian.

Chibnall, S., & Saunders, P. (1977). Worlds apart: Notes on the social reality of corruption. *The British Journal of Sociology, 28*(2), 138–154.

Cockroft, L., & Wegener, A. C. (2017). *Unmasked: Corruption in the west.* London, England: I-B-Tauris.

Comer, M., & Stephens, T. (2013). *Bribery and corruption.* Aldershot, England: Gower.

De Graaf, G., Wagenaar, P., & Hoenderboom, M. (2010). Constructing corruption. In P. de Graaf, P. von Maravić, & P. Wagenaar (Eds.), *The good cause: Theoretical perspectives on corruption* (pp. 98–114). Opladen, Germany: Barbara Budrch Press.

Della Porta, D., & Vannucci, A. (2012). *The hidden order of corruption.* London, England: Routledge.

Depuy, K., & Neset, S. (2018). *The cognitive psychology of corruption.* Oslo, Norway: U4 Anti-corruption Resource Center. Chr. Michelsen Institute.

Eicher, S. (2009). *Corruption in international business.* London, England: Routledge.

Fleming, P., & Zyglidopoulos, S. (2009). *Charting corporate corruption.* Cheltenham, England: Edward Elgar.

Foucault, M. (2010). *The birth of biopolitics: Lectures at the Collège de France 1978–1979.* Los Angeles, CA: Picador.

Goffman, E. (1981). *La presentación de la persona en la vida cotidiana.* Buenos Aires, Argentina: Amorrortu.

50 Corruption as a Dense Social Relationship

Guerrero, E., & Talledos, O. A. (2018). *¿Cómo entender el fenómeno de la corrupción?* Mexico City, Mexico: OPA.

Gupta, A. (1995). Blurred boundaries: The discourse of corruption, the culture of politics, and the imagined state. *American Ethnologist, 22*(2), 375–402.

Heidenheimer, A. J., Johnston, M., & LeVine, V. (1990). Terms, concepts and definitions: An introduction. In A. J. Heidenheimer & M. Johnston (Eds.), *Political corruption: A handbook* (pp. 3–14). New York: Transaction Publishers.

Heissner, S. (2015). *Managing business integrity.* New York: Springer.

Hine, D., & Peele, G. (2012). Integrity issues in the United Kingdom: An emerging debate. In D. Tanzler, K. Maras, & A. Giannakopoulos (Eds.), *The social construction of corruption in Europe* (pp. 59–86). Oxon: England: Routledge.

Holmes, L. (2015). *Corruption: A very short introduction.* Oxford, England: Oxford University Press.

HuntingtonS. P. (2006/1968). *Political order in changing societies.* New Haven, CT: Yale University Press.

Iyer, N., & Samociuk, M. (2006). *Fraud and corruption: Prevention and detection.* Aldershot, England: Gower.

Jancsics, D. (2014). "A friend gave me a phone number" – Brokerage in low-level corruption. *International Journal of Law, Crime and Justice, 20,* 1–20.

Kajsiu, B. (2014). *A discourse analysis of corruption: Instituting neoliberalism against corruption in Albania, 1998–2005.* Farnham, UK: Ashgate.

Kennedy, D. (1999). The international anti-corruption campaign. *Connecticut Journal of International Law, 14,* 455–465.

Klitgaard, R. (1988). *Controlling corruption.* Berkeley; Los Angeles, CA: University of California Press.

Kobis, N., van Prooijen, J. W., Righetti, F., & Van Lange, P. (2017). The road to bribery and corruption: Slippery slope or steep cliff? *Psychological Science, 28*(3), 297–306. doi:10.1177/0956797616682026.

Lord, N. (2014). *Regulating corporate bribery in international business: Anti-corruption in the UK and Germany.* London, England: Routledge.

Malem Seña, J. F. (2002). *La corrupción: Aspectos éticos, económicos, politicos y jurìdicos.* Barcelona, Spain: Gedisa.

Manzetti, L., & Wilson, C. (2007). Why do corrupt governments maintain public support? *Comparative Political Studies, 40*(8), 949–970. doi:10.1177/0010414005285759.

Marquette, H., & Peiffer, C. (2015). Corruption and collective action. Research paper 32. U4-DLP. Birmingham.

Moeen, A. (2010). Why does corruption persist in democracies? Retrieved from www.siasat. pk/forum/showthread.php?38854-Why-Does-Corruption-Persist-in-Democracies.

Mukherjee, S. (2011). *The emperor of all maladies: A biography of cancer.* New York: Simon & Schuster.

Mungiu-Pippidi, A. (2013). Becoming Denmark: Historical designs of corruption control. *Social Research: An International Quarterly, 80*(4), 1259–1286.

Mungiu-Pippidi, A. (2015). *The quest for good governance.* Cambridge, UK: Cambridge University Press.

Nichols, P., & Robertson, D. (2017). Introduction and overview: Bribery and the study of decision making. In P. Nichols & D. Robertson (Eds.), *Thinking about bribery: Neuroscience, moral cognition and the psychology of bribery* (pp. 1–30). Cambridge, England: Cambridge University Press.

Noonan, J. (1984). *Bribes: The intellectual history of a moral idea.* Berkeley, CA: University of California Press.

Nuijten, M. (2004). Between fear and fantasy: Governmentality and the working of power in Mexico. *Critique of Anthropology*, 24(2), 209–230.

Nye, J. (1967). Corruption and political development: A cost benefit analysis. *American Political Science Review*, 61(2), 417–427.

Olivier de Sardan, J. (1999). A moral economy of corruption in Africa? *The Journal of Modern African Studies*, 37(1), 25–52.

Philp, M. (1997). Defining political corruption. *Political Studies*, 45, 436–462.

Rocham, A. (2015). *Why corruption matters: Understanding causes, effects and how to address them. Evidence paper on corruption*. London, England: UKAID.

Rose-AckermanS. (2006). *International handbook on the economics of corruption*. Cheltenham, England; Northampton, MA: Edward Elgar.

Rose-Ackerman, S. (1978). *Corruption: A study in political economy*. New York: Academic Press.

Rotberg, R. (2009). *Corruption, global security, and world order*. New Delhi, India: Pentagon Security International.

Rothstein, B., & Teorell, J. (2015). Getting to Sweden, Part II: Breaking with corruption in the nineteenth century. *Scandinavian Political Studies*, 38(3), 238–254. doi:10–1111/1467–9477.12048.

Sampford, C., Shacklock, A., Connors, C., & Galtung, F. (Eds.). (2006). *Measuring corruption*. London, England: Routledge.

Sampson, S. (2010). The anti-corruption industry: From movement to institution. *Global Crime*, 11(2), 261–278. doi:10.1080/17440571003669258.

Schluter, W. (2017). *Soft corruption*. New Brunswick, NJ: Rutdgers University Press.

Tanzler, D., Maras, K., & Giannakopoulos, A. (2012). The German myth of a corruption-free modern country. In D. Tanzler, K. Maras, & A. Giannakopoulos (Eds.), *The social construction of corruption in Europe* (pp. 87–105). Oxon: England: Routledge.

Torsello, D., & Venard, B. (2016). The anthropology of corruption. *Journal of Management Inquiry*, 25(1), 35–54.

Transparency International. (2009). *The anti-corruption plain language guide*. Retrieved from www.transparency.org/whatwedo/publication/the_anti_corruption_plain_langua ge_guide.

Transparency International. (2015). *Impact report*. Retrieved from www.transparency.org/ whatwedo/publication/2015_impact_report.

Vogl, F. (2016). *Waging war on corruption: Inside the movement fighting the abuse of power*. Lanham, MD: Rowman & Littlefield.

Von Alemann, U. (2004). The unknown depths of political theory: The case for a multi-dimensional concept of corruption. *Crime, Law & Social Change*, 42(1), 25–34.

Warren, M. (2015). The meaning of corruption in democracies. In P. Heywood (Ed.), *Routledge handbook of political corruption*. Oxford, England: Routledge.

Wedel, J. R. (2009). *Shadow elites*. New York: Basic Books.

Wedel, J. R. (2012). Rethinking corruption in an age of ambiguity. *The Annual Review of Law and Social Science*, 8, 453–498.

Williams, P., & Savona, E. (1996). *The United Nations and transnational organized crime*. London, UK: Frank Cass.

Williams, W. J., & Beare, E. M. (2000). The business of bribery: Globalisation, economic liberalization, and the 'problem' of corruption. *Crime, Law and Social Change*, 32(2), 115–146.

World Bank. (1997). *Helping countries combat corruption: The role of the World Bank*. Washington, DC: World Bank PREM.

World Bank. (2006). *Anticorruption in transition: Who is succeeding and why?* Washington, DC: World Bank.

Wu, R. (2016). How do firms survive crime and corruption on and off the record? An empirical and cross-regional examination among global developing economies. *The Journal of Developing Areas*, 50(4), 253–273.

Zyglidopolos, S., Hirsch, P., de Holan, P-M., & Phillips, N. (2019). Expanding research on corporate corruption, management, and organizations. *Journal of Management Inquiry*, 26(3), 247–253. doi:10–1177/1056492617706648.

Zyglidopoulos, S., Dieleman, M., & Hirsch, P. (2019). Playing the game: Unpacking the rationale for organizational corruption in MNCs. *Journal of Management inquiry*. doi:10.1177/1056492618817827.

2

CORRUPTION AS A CULTURAL AND SOCIAL PROCESS

Corruption as a Social Relationship

Corrupt acts involve an interaction between at least two people although, generally speaking, we can say that an interaction can include several people in different logics: within an organization, between organizations, or from an organization affecting its clients or citizens. Whenever we speak of an interaction then, we have to discuss the specific social, normative, cultural, and specific context in which this relationship is generated and reproduced. The policeman who is bribed by a motorist links these two actors in a context of language, symbols, and rules that define and frame a specific group of risks, gains, and expectations that make the exchange possible or not. And the same happens in a case of fraud between suppliers of two companies in the private sector, or the exchange of gifts or money between politicians and citizens to obtain votes: it occurs in a specific framework of rules and symbols within which the transaction is intelligible for the people in the concrete situation they are experiencing. When the situation occurs, the relationship has some likelihood of being carried out. Even those frauds where an actor deceived others by hiding information and distorting the data imply a relationship in a context: The deceiver is in a position to know the detail and specific routes of how to successfully conceal certain critical issues. That is, in the end, even in a fraud, there is an interaction and a machination and fabrication that involves understanding the dynamics and the formal and informal rules of an interaction.

Accordingly, corruption implies knowledge, relationship, and exchange, not only of resources or money, but of signals, codes, and expectations. It requires building a certain type of link: one that allows the parties to calculate in some way the possibilities of risk and the degrees of understanding of the normative and cultural context in which this link occurs. It is worth stressing the fact that even in the event of a fraud where one of the parties deceives the other, there is a context of an implicit link, since it is necessary to understand the formal ways and logics that allow a person, with a certain calculated risk, to assume that the other person can be deceived when the other person is likely to have ways of discovering the deception.

All ties are therefore social, and corruption is no exception. Routines within organizations, institutional forms or rules, etiquette customs and norms, all occur in a context and provide meaning for people to understand how interactions between people in different situations and localities are carried out. Forms, routines, and customs enable social interactions to stabilize, allowing the constant repetition of actions and reciprocities: constituting the glue in any society. This glue for society is of the same material as the glue that produces corruption (Uslaner, 2017). Corruption is not only or not always hidden or based on fraudulent deception: it requires communication, codes; it can be justified, normalized, and be an ingredient involving many exchanges that solve specific problems for people in specific situations (Bauhr, 2017, p. 564; Walton, 2013, p. 178).

The social network of relationships and reciprocities become stable and repetitive thanks to the construction of relatively shared interpretations of which codes and transactions are allowed or seen as socially adequate, as well as those that are not. More sophisticatedly, existing codes and practices in a community or society allow people to understand under what circumstances an adequate interrelation becomes inadequate, and vice versa. What is established as adequate tends to have high social plasticity in any case: something suitable in a moral sense can have many subtleties when defining what is appropriate in a practical sense given the details and particularities of the actual interrelationships between flesh-and-blood people dealing with specific objectives and interests. Thus, paying a bribe may be morally inadequate, but adequate if the bribed subject feels he/she is in a social trap and has little power to escape from it and have another alternative (Rothstein, 2005).

Routines, imitation, customs, and traditions are social mechanisms that allow people in society to repeat constant interactions without having to calculate and foresee each and every one of the vicissitudes that may occur in an exchange. Without these routines and customs, social interaction would be extremely difficult: any communication would be slow, costly in terms of time, and potentially riskier. These social mechanisms come into action in both legitimate commercial exchanges and in those that can be considered illegitimate, such as bribes, embezzlement, and fraud. Corruption in its different forms implies an interaction: the fraudster, the bribe-giver, the embezzler, those who participate as accomplices, those who unknowingly participate, those who are affected, deceived, or those who are forced or driven to take part in the corrupt exchange. Corruption is a social act. Moreover, it generally implies knowledge: those who engage in various acts of corruption generally attempt to find out about the routines and forms of organizational relationship, processes, rules of etiquette, times, and customs (De Graaf & Huberts, 2008). Corruption is rarely an isolated interaction between two self-contained rational subjects (that is, they only think of their own rationality without considering the situations and particularities of the others with whom they are interacting). A very abstract view of the concept of corruption suggests exactly the opposite: that people interact making very direct and simple calculations of benefits and risks, in a classic, game theory style. It is necessary to say that this perspective of corruption, with individuals interacting in a game theory style game, has produced an enormous wealth of analysis which, although will not be focused on in this book, is essential to study (Andvig & Moene, 1990; Cameron, Chaudhuri, Erkal, & Gangadharan, 2005; Colombatto, 2003; Djawadi & Fahr, 2015; Engel et al., 2018; Guerrero & Rodríguez-Oreggia, 2008; Jain, 2001, 1998; Reja & Talvitie, 2012). Although it is a very important body of literature, it is also possible that its simplicity (in an effort to use and defend a comprehensive theory that will explain corruption) is a major limitation of this perspective. Those who interact in a relationship of corruption are generally part of a grid, a network of people linked by various social ties, a grid that is composed of both routines and formal and informal rules of action and meanings. Thus, the person who was defrauded probably trusted the person who let him down as a result of the routines and processes that cemented the interaction over time. Conflict of interest is established by a long history of contacts, friendships, and favors that were established in the past yet may be colliding with the logic of general interests or organizations in the present. They also require someone to notice this normative collision of interests, which did not exist before. It is exceptional in society for there to be processes substantively based on routines that are explicitly based on links almost exclusively of distrust (in a prison, at certain times, probably). What is common is for routines and customs to seek to facilitate interaction, make it stable and easy to interpret and therefore ensure the reciprocity expected by both sides of the relationship. In other words, the interaction between people tends to be more durable and more dense than a game theory style calculation by individuals.

Corruption generally involves a form of relationship and bonding that is built over time, and cemented through the interaction itself. And it is therefore no surprise that most of the time it occurs in a social context full of meanings, routines, customs, and ways of stabilizing these relationships. Understanding this is crucial to getting to probably the most interesting aspect of corruption: it occurs in a wide border between "acceptable" and "unacceptable" routines and customs, a border that is usually extremely permeable, dynamic, and changing (Cameron et al., 2005). Imagine a continuum where relationships and links are fully socially "acceptable" at one extreme. And at the other, those that are frankly and unambiguously "unacceptable". This second case clearly refers to spaces of organized crime, mafias that use violence to impose their conditions, for example. Well, even this last case refers to the sale of "protection" (Gambetta, 1993), which requires effective organization to cooperate with and coordinate members of the organization. Paradoxical as it may sound, organized crime and the mafia are built on the basis of codes of behavior, loyalty, and the creation of hierarchies that imply obedience and control codes, and therefore with the interaction of people who need to build a reputation. In other words, we are talking about the need and capacity of organized crime to technically manage and implement efficient coercion. Even

56 Corruption as a Dense Social Relationship

at this end of the continuum, the organization of corruption requires creating rules, norms, and routines in order to successfully and effectively control the organization: a mafia organization requires the honesty of its minions to carry out orders, keep silent, and hide what is necessary to hide. They also need to be able to impose on their victims the orders and promised consequences of their action or inaction. Furthermore, although it sounds paradoxical, the mafia organization requires its members to honor the agreement established with those who have been coerced: if I "sold" you protection, I must honor that contract and be effective in granting that protection. Even more paradoxically, the mafia organization, which teaches its members to lie, threaten, and cheat, requires preventing these same practices from being repeated within the organization, under the penalty of experiencing constant instability (which, in general, is a major concern of the "managers" of this type of organization).

Returning to the continuum that goes from "completely" ethical to "completely" unethical practices (extremes of a continuum that are difficult to imagine in the real world, at least in a "pure" way), it is simply necessary to imagine the richness of the social dynamics at intermediate points on the continuum, where the symbolic combinations of inadequate and adequate logics and acts are more diverse and confusing. For example, it is possible to speak of economic gangsters (Fisman & Golden, 2017) who are people who act formally in the legal and open world of business and government yet take advantage of the loopholes and limitations of norms and institutions, to abuse them while appearing as agents who obey laws. They do so either through argumentative and discursive smoke screens that seek to justify and rationalize their actions, or even through relatively organized mechanisms to abuse their power at the expense of other people.

That is to say, in every human and social interaction, there are explicit, open elements, and others that are hidden and ambiguous, unsuspected by the actors, or overtly used strategically in the interaction. Goffman (1981) extensively studied the forms, strategies, and customs of concealment and presentation of people in everyday life. Concealment and acted or even manufactured presentations are all essential dynamics for ensuring that the interaction between people is created and stabilized. Each person presents himself/herself to others and what he/she seeks is to control what he/she wants the other person to see. And, very importantly, what one person does not want the other to know. The critical thing to understand is that this is real and possible not only in the interactions we usually classify as adequate or legitimate. It happens in the most common chiaroscuro of all those relations that can be a combination of acts that are neither completely open or closed nor completely adequate or inadequate, nor totally transparent or opaque.

In this respect, understanding corruption involves analyzing how two different parts of the aforementioned continuum are linked: frankly corrupt acts that strategically use information and communication to achieve existence and acts that are on the border between "what is adequate" and "what is not adequate", which are confused and ambiguous. Corruption forms part of these reciprocal interactions that make significant efforts to conceal or at least make the corrupt act itself less "undesirable" in the eyes of the participants. There is a broad literature in psychology regarding the cognitive and behavioral processes of how people, even in cases of possibly improper acts, rationalize and transform events and relationships into less uncomfortable situations, giving them meaning and justification (Belle & Cantarelli, 2017; Darley, 2005; Depuy & Neset, 2018; Rusch, 2016).

In other words, corruption in this respect can be seen as a social exchange that generally makes the border between being a frankly inadequate act or an "almost adequate" one ambiguous. More than a "black or white" judgment, a social reality is not a continuum but only two extremes of what is appropriate and what is inappropriate, what is proper and what is improper. What one has is a "prism" where the same act or situation can have several aspects and forms that need to be interpreted by different people in a particular society (de Zwart, 2010, p. 39). In other words, it involves the construction of what Olivier de Sardan has called "moral economy" (1999, p. 37): the social processes of interpretation, negotiation, and agreement that lead to an act that is inadequate or appropriate, depending on the position of the agents in question and the specific situation in which they find themselves. It is appropriate at the end of the day thanks to a process of rationalization that justifies or socially envelops an act as ambiguous or justifiable in practice through interpretations and arguments. Socially and meaningfully constructing the end of the continuum that speaks of "a totally adequate or legitimate act" is a highly abstract, difficult task. Social relations are an amalgam of interpretations, intentions, values, and expectations of very different people, in social contexts that can be very specific and with actors who act out their communication and their presentation to others.

We could say then that, most of the time, the different forms of corruption appear and are located somewhere on the continuum between the appropriate and the inappropriate, in a mixture of both logics. In other words, corruption can be a by-product of other types of ties based on mutual aid, informal or semi-formal exchange practices, and even resistance to an autocratic or unjust government (Zaloznaya, 2014, p. 190). It is this mixture that makes taking actions regarding, understanding, and addressing corruption as a social relationship so difficult: the informal logic of exchanges and relations is ultimately an extremely rich, generalized and, one could almost say, universal construction. Understanding and finding ways to affect the profound social reasons why people maintain stable social practices, which are at the same time possibly illegitimate or even illegal at different moments and in different aspects, seems to be a well-established need (Hoffman & Patel, 2017). It is worth mentioning the work of several researchers led by Professor Ledeneva (2018 and www.ucl. ac.uk/ssees/research/funded-research-projects/global-informality-project) to build a broad encyclopedia of the multiple social practices of informal exchange and favors by creating a list of dozens of interaction practices performed in the continuous complex of improper and proper acts, which occur in a wealth of options encompassing continents, epochs, and developed and developing countries (Williams & Bezeredi, 2017).

58 Corruption as a Dense Social Relationship

A good example of this amalgam of social logics of appropriateness and appropriateness can be found in the way in which bribes in many societies are reconstructed as "gifts". Influence trafficking can be symbolically involved and understood by people as an exchange of favors (where even reciprocity between actors is neither immediate nor monetary). And within this continuum, there is the possibility that acts fully assumed as "appropriate" or socially accepted at a particular time may become suspicious as a result of a small change in perspective or a new interpretation at another particular time: this is the case of the apparent conflict of interest when no exchange actually takes place between a public servant and a businessmen whom he knows. But a third actor, say a citizen, may be uncomfortable, suspecting that this relationship "could" have led to some undue interference. This suspicion arises purely as a result of the friendship between those two people.

Unraveling this social process would appear to be very important to understanding the logic of corruption in practice. It is common for studies attempting to study this intricate logic of relationships, reciprocities, interpretations, and justifications to end up being attacked as "defenders" or justifiers of corruption. This could be construed as a failure to understand the objective: the point is not to reduce attempts by societies to break the vicious circle of corruption and its socially negative effects. The point is precisely to highlight and explain social density, the permeable border between the appropriate and the inappropriate in the practices and routines of people in their everyday lives. Understanding and highlighting the fact that permeability, that socially constructed ambiguity between the appropriate and the inappropriate, will make it much more possible to promote changes, engage in collective efforts to transform practices, and demand changes in the routines and values not only of government or political, but business and social, actors too. This may clarify the reason for the discussion in the previous chapter, criticizing the Manichean language of "battle" and "war" against the "cancer" of corruption. It may now be clearer why this language of battle often obscures and hinders the understanding of the deep social and interpretative meanings that relationships between people in any society imply (Sissener, 2001). Corruption is ultimately a social relationship, with logics of reciprocity, understanding, secrecy, presentation, routines, and customs. If, in actual fact, the aim is to reduce corruption, one key is to reveal the links these acts have with the construction of the reciprocities, customs, and languages that support it. Revealing the social dynamic that gives it stability will undoubtedly place one in a better position to explain and reach a consensus that there are currently acts, routines, and languages regarded as acceptable, logical, or necessary, which should not be.

Accordingly, in this chapter we will construct the bases for understanding corruption as a social relationship with the elements it involves: reciprocity, exchange, logic of meaning, communication, and stability. To this end, we will rely on the analysis of the relationship between social forms of exchange and favors and corruption. And the chapter will show how in various societies, these logics of exchange of favors have obtained such stability that they have become universal in

Corruption as a Cultural and Social Process **59**

their political and cultural contexts. They are not only universal, in the sense that they are institutions or customs communicated by word of mouth from childhood. They also acquire significant names that make them highly effective, known, understood, and socially and culturally assumed social instruments. As we shall see, this shows that, deep down, people in those societies may suspect there is a thin line separating these acceptable customs from acts and consequences that are at least not so acceptable.

Social Relations, Reciprocities, and Exchanges

Every social relationship implies the search for reciprocity, in a concrete sense or in many abstract senses. The social dilemma is how to ensure that the reciprocity obtained is what one expects. If human interaction involved immediate reciprocity with no risk, the world would be completely different. It is precisely the uncertainty of reciprocity that makes the social world so vivid and dynamic. Reciprocity can be simply a pecuniary exchange, of mutual interest, which, when performed, implies the termination of the relationship. An extreme case involves two people who meet, take part in an exchange (without even needing to think anything particular about the exchange), leave, and assume they will never meet again, so it is not necessary to add any additional symbol or particular communication beyond the exchange itself. It is difficult to find an example of this extreme because even two pedestrians who cross in a street may follow certain conventions such as walking on a different side to the other person (moving to the right or left, depending on certain customs) in order to achieve reciprocity (in this case, moving forward without bumping into the other person). In most social relations, the exchange implies a past, a present, and a potential future of the relationship. And that is why the reciprocity sought is possible if a mesh or grid linking the actors in the interaction has been constructed. This grid provides links precisely to create a logic that lends shared meaning to the interaction. If the interaction is going to take place and reciprocity is going to be achieved, it is because both parties share an interpretation of what is happening, know the consequences of failing to carry out the exchange, and are able to calculate the consequences of today's exchange for the future. They may even try to determine what has happened in similar exchanges in the past and whether the other party has a well-known, reliable reputation. In short, even the simplest social relationship can be extremely rich in meanings, calculations, interpretations, and expectations.

Because of this dynamic logic of exchange in social contexts, it has been extremely productive to study them in terms of transaction or exchange. An exchange tends to involve not only objects, but also meanings that "bind", linking people in a network or web of interactions and meanings. Those meanings that bind become safe, making the next transaction easier, faster, and more reliable. In other words, many times in an exchange of things or objects, they are "wrapped" or embedded in a more abstract, important reciprocal exchange: an exchange of favors. In its simplest case: the actor delivers an object or thing, not in order to obtain

60 Corruption as a Dense Social Relationship

something in return immediately, but to generate a link, a fact of trust or "good manners", in such a way that it generates a positive and future propensity in the recipient of the gift to reciprocate at another time, probably in a context or situation that is not explicit or even clear at this moment. Even this simple case implies a very broad social density: who are those who exchange? What social position or power do they enjoy in what social structure of hierarchies and stratification? What is the structure of the relationship in which they find themselves (accidental and therefore ephemeral, or familiar or organizational, and therefore not ephemeral)? Answering these questions in some way implies approaching a contextual vision of corruption, one where contingency, social or regional specificity, structure, and social stratification can be key elements for understanding the dynamics and what makes corruption so stable in various circumstances (De Graaf, 2007). In any case, what should be clear is that the exchange between people is often full of past and future meanings, expectations, implicit messages, and agreements that go beyond black and white contracts. In several situations, corruption is often involved precisely in this social density of the exchanges of favors and expectations. This will be made clearer later, but I hope that at this moment this possibility is already becoming clear as a possibility in the reader's mind.

In order to understand the dynamics of the exchange of favors, Torsello (2014) proposes three models based on the different logics of reciprocity and bond formation that underpin the exchange:

1. Marcel Mauss proposes seeing social exchange dominated by the omnipresence of the gift. The gift is a substantive piece not of unilateral delivery of an object or value but of a hope of reciprocal exchange, which seeks to strengthen certain bonds that give meaning to the exchange beyond the object itself (the spirit of the gift). This is what makes exchange relationships of this kind lasting, since they tend to stabilize and become almost eternal in gift–reciprocity–new gift chains.
2. In this respect, Lévi-Strauss proposed observing the varied forms that exchange can take. The case with which this model of exchange is illustrated is marriage (even between families), which shows how the creation of social exchange links is created, from which something is expected in exchange in the group where it is carried out.
3. Malinowski added that the notion of social interdependence is based on differences in social status and political power, where the spirit of the *gift* has an effect depending on the economic and political conditions of the exchange. In other words, the position of people in the social structure is crucial to understanding the dynamics of the exchange at certain times.

(Torsello, 2011, 2014)

The social relationships that are in a context of exchange that is more complex than one that is immediate, explicit, and direct are therefore constructed in a

Corruption as a Cultural and Social Process 61

dynamic where a series of elements coexist that envelop and give meaning to the exchange: It is not necessarily immediate, but it can be expected to repeat itself over time, creating expectations of continuity. Although it is generated with an idea of exchange, it may be that the exchange occurs in the future and is composed of many possible types of exchange (as in the logic proposed by Lévi-Strauss). And lastly, the reciprocity constructed by the exchange makes sense in a social structure, in a logic of different positions of power and influence, which are precisely what can form the basis of the exchange.

As Olivier de Sardan (1999) has shown, the dynamics of exchange are extremely rich since they are involved in everything from calculation issues such as negotiation and bargaining to more social issues and tact and tempo as the most reasonable definition to define the form of the delivery of the gift: for example, is it delivered open or semi-hidden or even hidden? Moreover, it is necessary to define (and not always explicitly) whether reciprocity is granted immediately and promptly or whether, on the contrary, it is necessary to let a certain amount of time elapse in order to avoid its being interpreted as a "payment". The plasticity of exchanges of favors or gifts can be truly amazing.

Every day, individuals are exposed to negotiation processes, not only in terms of relations of price, quantity, or merchandise they acquire or exchange in the most commercial areas. The negotiation to which the logic of favors and exchange refers contemplates the mental process (Rothstein, 2011) in which the individual negotiates the limits of the rules that seem to be accepted by their society. Negotiation is, therefore, a decision by the individual acting on the limit—which he/she can cross it suits him/her—of a set of values expressed in the rules that surround him/her (Olivier de Sardan, 1999); in other words, individuals are constantly exposed to negotiating since what is played is not just the exchange itself, but another equally important thing: one's reputation and the possibilities of expanding and maintaining it over time. Exchange also involves influences: when people form relationships to exchange favors or gifts, they tread a very thin line of instrumentally using another person (their resources, acquaintances, influence, or power) in order to achieve something in particular. But if it is a favor or a gift, the frankly instrumental disclosure of the use of the other person can be downright insulting. In that case, this instrumental exchange of favors can be seen (by the actors themselves or by society in general) as practically as a bribe, a relationship which is obviously unethical.

Let us then calmly break down the intricate relationship that the exchange of favors or gifts implies. Gift-giving is understood as the action of generally providing a good—whether monetary or in kind in gratitude or in response to a past or future favor the other person is expected to perform in a certain circumstance of agreement or promise. Torsello (2014) has pointed out that in the logic of *gift-giving* the exchange is endorsed with elements of influence among the people involved. In other words, the person requesting the favor or service requires the influence, acquaintances, or benefits of the position of the recipient of the request for the favor. In exchange for what? A monetary payment, direct and without

62 Corruption as a Dense Social Relationship

restrictions, can be the most direct and effective, but there is usually something in the social context that distorts or limits the possibility of direct exchange. The most typical case is that what is required of the person is that they use their acquaintances and influence to reach the right people in positions or with suitable resources to solve a certain situation. The exchange is often therefore determined by a relationship of interpersonal dependence: what is at stake is the use of relations between people, of acquaintances who have different types of influences, positions, and powers, and who can potentially exchange those positions and influences. The richness of this social dynamic is that it plays with potentialities and expectations: the influences and powers of one actor can be useful for another actor who has other influences and powers. Neither of them necessarily knows when they may require each other or for what purpose. Moreover, the network of acquaintances and influences of each of the actors is an asset that can be triggered in very different situations and contexts. In other words, the instrumentality and usefulness of the influences an actor possesses may only become evident when an attempt is made to solve a particular problem. It is extremely interesting: obtaining the maximum benefit from influences and acquaintances, the basis of the exchange of favors, is something that generally requires cunning intelligence to hide or veil, for example, the instrumentality of the interaction. The construction of relationships and acquaintances is in itself an activity, a social necessity: influences and relationships require "maintenance"; they need to be nurtured. Hence, a fundamental paradox appears: influences and acquaintances are potentially instrumental but making them obviously instrumental can cause anger or insult the same people if they feel or realize they are blatantly being used. Exchange can involve things, objects, or money, but the machinery that allows the exchanges themselves is profoundly social and cultural: it implies the weaving of relationships, the use (rather than the blatantly instrumental use of) acquaintances, and the influences this creates in certain contexts. Relationships between people who expect or assume that these are not only instruments of use and change, but relationships of empathy, rapprochement, and belonging. Therefore, assuming that these relations of acquaintances and the exchanges of favors can be reduced to patron–client logics can be misleading. Although there are expectations of reciprocity in these relationships of exchange that can be very instrumental, in the end they survive better over time if it appears, in the eyes of society and of the participants themselves, that they are not. Or in any case, if it is useful to analyze them as patron–client relationships, they prove to be extremely intricate and complex (Eisenstadt & Roniger, 1984; Smith, 2007, p. 56).

We can say then of the fact that relations involving the exchange of favors and gifts are the tip of the iceberg of a potentially wide-ranging set of relations between people and acquaintances who exchange influences and social relations. In many cases we can really talk about "social capital" (Putnam, 2000), networks of solidarity and exchange (not only of things, it should be said, but of social relationships and acquaintances). These networks effectively become frameworks with very broad meanings: people in the network can expect mutual assistance—usually favors—(Olivier de Sardan, 1999), sometimes seen as an obligation (at least moral) or a duty: acquaintances protect and support each other for very different reasons. In other words, in certain spaces and contexts, a kind of community or network of people is constructed which, among other things, share the various influences and networks of acquaintances, in a relatively open and explicit manner. These networks can or tend to start in the immediate family circle and, like an electric current, flow from the "acquaintance of the acquaintance of the acquaintance", empowering the network itself so that even the people in the network do not necessarily have full knowledge of all its members. And in certain logics and with certain rules, the idea that there is a moral obligation or a duty to "lend" or share the influences of some actors to other members of the network can even be expected to be consolidated in the network or group.

The dynamism of the logic of acquaintances, support networks, and exchange of favors leads us to suspect that a vision that is over-reliant on the rational calculations of an interaction such as corruption is of little help in understanding what happens in practice when we talk about the phenomenon. In other words, a vision that is over-confident about a logic of rational individuals who calculate gains and costs can quickly lose its usefulness for explaining a phenomenon in which the plasticity of the exchanges and symbols that sustain them produces a logic of very heterogeneous relationships. Torsello (2014), for example, has identified at least three different types of reciprocity in these dynamics:

1. Generalized reciprocity, which is a form of positive reciprocity, in which altruistic forms of exchange take place. It is usually generated among relatives, but it can be extended to other members of the network, depending on the proximity and levels of solidarity that have been constructed between different members.
2. Balanced reciprocity, where constant, stable reciprocity is expected in the exchanges, although not necessarily immediately. This reciprocity is then seen as the glue in the interaction and therefore as the basis for the codes of union in the network itself. If someone fails to reciprocate under the codes and times of the network, there is a possibility that there may be a greater or lesser reprimand, depending on the circumstances.
3. "Negative" reciprocity, where relationships within the network have degenerated into disproportionate shares of power in favor of certain people, creating a network that is less informal and where exchanges of favors begin to be constructed as obligations. This dynamic is classic of networks of acquaintances that end up being dominated by certain actors that even make belonging to the network obligatory, based on the logic of outright extortion.

It is important to observe how the plasticity of the exchange relationships is so broad that the logics of organization can be of several types: more open or closed, more equitable or unequal, more informal or formal, socially legitimate or verging on illegality. This last point is critical because it shows how the borders between

64 Corruption as a Dense Social Relationship

overtly illegal relationships and legitimate ones can be extremely blurred in the context of the social dynamics that give life to it.

These first brushstrokes of the logic of the exchange of favors allow us to begin to draw a much denser and more dynamic vision of corruption. Corruption can be, for example, one of the forms of exchange of favors and gifts. In many ways, the origin of corruption lies in this source of interrelation and exchange of favors and influences. The exchange of favors begins and is interpreted and rationalized as informal practices or mechanisms that work alongside formal institutions and are possible due to a multiplicity of social relationships that people construct in society. These relationships of reciprocity, whether professional, familial, friendly, interested, community, or dependent imply the same thing in every society: the network of relationships and protection everyone needs to survive in society.

Obviously, these networks of relationship do not end up being either equitable or balanced for everyone. Many of these relationships serve precisely to provide a solution to needs in unjust systems dominated by a few powerful or bureaucratic systems that restrict the possibilities of different people and groups in a given reality. But since they are dynamic social relationships, friendships and acquaintances and their use in solving problems can go from being an emergency solution or an exception to a customary, necessary, and omnipresent solution. And nothing prevents them, in the end, from being captured by certain people and groups, and becoming mechanisms that paradoxically reproduce the unfair, unbalanced logic they were originally supposed to solve.

Exchange relationships, particularly those involving the exchange of favors, are therefore highly ambivalent social "creatures": they are composed of practices that constantly shift between the legitimate and illegitimate, the legal and illegal, the beneficial and the harmful, the individual and the collective (Gupta, 1995). While it may be clear that accessing public goods or services by skirting or ignoring formal rules and processes constitutes an act of corruption, this is not always so clear or uniform, in practice and everyday life.

What is this dynamic plasticity like? The elements are clear: people, groups, exchanges, and the social context they construct in their everyday interaction. We can begin to understand this dynamic with the help of three basic ideas:

1. In contexts of formality and institutional rigidity, the presence of these mechanisms for the exchange of favors has the function of adjusting or making socially functional structures and organizational processes that allocate or distribute public goods and services (Lomnitz, 1990; Maynard-Moody & Mosheno, 2003; Verbeke & Kano, 2013). In other words, the mechanism of the exchange of favors can be explained, in some cases, as an expression of resistance against the impersonal, inefficient, or "excessive" rationality of bureaucracy.

2. There is a set of relationships and social values that play a central role in the activation, functioning, and continuity of these mechanisms, which mainly involve solidarity, collective identity, and trust (Danet, 1990; Lomnitz, 1990;

Rehn & Taalas, 2004). In other words, they are relationships with a great deal of symbolism at stake: codes of conduct, logics of tempo and etiquette, widely shared by various social sectors (if not practically all of society). Probably one of the most surprising factors that generally escapes corruption analysts is that these practices create ties and organized forms of interaction that can explain the resilience of corruption by sustaining and reproducing themselves through interactions that are rich in identifiable codes of ethics and of proper behavior and reciprocity (as Smith, 2007, p. 42, 2018, has noted in Nigeria).

3. There is a significant attempt to achieve redistribution and even justice. Relationships involving exchange can be quite instrumental but are generally wrapped in symbolic arguments of mutual support, favors, and flexibility thanks to the links (whether direct or indirect) that ultimately allow the exchange to take place (Barozet, 2006; Verbeke & Kano, 2013). Even in the most instrumental exchanges that are closest to illegality, participants often use euphemisms and rationalizations to justify their actions (even if merely to avoid cognitive dissonance). This justification can often be implicitly or explicitly sustained in an argument of justice: formal rules would be followed if they worked and were implemented in the way they are supposed to be. But since various powerful actors have captured their own formal rules, it is fully justified to find alternate ways and parallel paths to solve problems in practice, in real actions.

It is clear in this respect that the social context, the social and political structure of a society, ends up being crucial to understanding in depth these dynamics involving the exchange of favors and the importance of acquaintances in obtaining satisfactors or solving problems. In other words, the general logic of the exchange of favors acquires specific life in highly intricate contexts where history, culture, institutions, and laws, all specific to each society, end up giving meaning and reality to these practices. Moreover, these practices generally form a substantive part of political regimes, maintaining mechanisms of coopting, control, and maneuver, indispensable for the balance between the political forces of a society and the practical functioning of formal and informal institutions (Baez-Camargo & Passas, 2017; Muir & Gupta, 2018).

In the following section, we will explore several of these social constructions, focusing particularly on those of Latin America, specifically what are known as *palancas* in Mexico.

The Logic of Favors and Exchanges in Various Countries

In this section, we will discuss the most salient features of various mechanisms for the exchange of favors, paying particular attention to one that is extremely widespread in Latin America: *palancas* (levers), understood as such (with nuances) mainly in Mexico, Cuba, and Colombia among other countries. In order to frame *palancas* in a more general international context, we will also briefly analyze certain practices

66 Corruption as a Dense Social Relationship

or mechanisms of exchange that have been fairly extensively studied and therefore acknowledged in various circles of anthropological and sociological studies: *blat* in Russia, *guanxhi* in China, *protekzia* in Israel, *pituto* in Chile, and *jeitinho* in Brazil. The idea of this brief presentation is precisely to observe the universality of the dynamics of the social relations involved in the exchange of favors, and their profound historical and cultural specificity. The common element, as one will see, is extremely important: the way they spread through society and culture until they become a constant and an understanding shared by virtually everyone in these societies.

The chapter ends with a description of an empirical study conducted to understand one of the classic, most widespread mechanisms in Latin America: the case of the Mexican *palanca*. It shows how this empirical study breaks down the social logics and contradictions created by *palancas* as a social mechanism for solving problems.

Logic of Reciprocity: Favors

The theory of gift-giving in the study of corruption has generally focused on establishing a clear, operational distinction between gifts and bribes, due to the difficulty in certain contexts of differentiating an unacceptable act of corruption from another which could be on the verge of being a potentially corrupt act yet one that is acceptable in certain contexts (Graf Lambsdorff & Frank, 2010; Graycar & Jancsics, 2016).

However, the study of the mechanisms involving the exchange of favors may have a different and much more powerful and productive contribution. Favors and gifts are one of the key social pieces for understanding the ties and implicit logics of reciprocity that become stable and generalized at a social level, as discussed in the previous section.

Thus, the literature on gifts, arising primarily from the work of Marcel Mauss, has made it possible to explore the forms and reasons for the exchange of gifts not only in "archaic" societies (as Mauss emphasizes) but also in contemporary ones. The point or critical contribution of this literature has been to identify the obligations and duties that are flexibly constructed between various people and groups thanks to gifts and the exchange and expectations of reciprocity constructed. The logic of the *vis-à-vis* exchange of favors, multiplied on a social scale, leads to an intricate map or mesh of relations that are informally institutionalized: they become repetitive and common, obviously capable of permanently being reproduced on a large scale. Mauss rightly highlights the role critical issues such as honor and prestige can play in a dynamic of this kind. Wealth, prestige, power, and conflict are all critical ingredients for understanding these networks of exchange and reciprocity. The author also identifies the value (spirit or energy) that accompanies any gift and allows the construction of more extensive, highly socially stable chains or networks of reciprocity (Mauss, 2002, pp. 11–14).

Corruption as a Cultural and Social Process **67**

In line with the arguments of Mauss and other scholars of gift-giving, it is possible to further appreciate the function of the exchange of favors in the game of social relations: it makes it possible to maintain relations of reciprocity in time; to ensure the well-being (and, to a certain extent, survival) of the group or network of "trusted" people who share and distribute benefits to each other; it makes it possible to institutionalize the mechanism despite (and sometimes thanks to) the formal processes of public and private organizations that concentrate goods and services; and protects or advances the power and social status of people who exchange favors.

The most interesting aspect is how different societies, comprising different political systems, histories, and cultures, have created their own versions of relationships based on the exchange of favors. The need is the same, however: the use of an informal network of acquaintances and highly intricate links to obtain services or products which would be more difficult to achieve via formal institutions. Not only products or services, but protection and scope for maneuver among the most diverse problems (fair or unfair) people can face in their lives. Faced with a legal, economic, or social problem, there is nothing better than having the peace of mind that there is a network of acquaintances who will possibly be able to help with other acquaintances, until they reach the critical link that can help. Let us look very briefly at some of the most frequently studied social mechanisms.

The Russian Blat

As happens with many terms in virtually all languages, *blat* has no exact translation; the closest translation is the "use of connections or contacts" (Ledeneva, 1998, p. 12). *Blat* has changed profoundly in time, since its emergence seems to be intimately linked to the consolidation of the communist regime. In its origins, it seems that it was a very particular form of using the social relations people found for coping with the centralized, bureaucratized dynamics of the USSR. Faced with the expectation of having to wait months or even years to obtain certain services or products, *blat* provided an important solution to over-centralization and shortages in goods and service provision. We say that it did, because although *blat* may still be alive in Russia today, many people suspect that *blat* may be more easily identifiable with bribery, a concept that is generally regarded as illegitimate in contemporary Russian society. *Blat* was undoubtedly an exchange of influences, but one generally seen as necessary, reasonable, and perhaps even legitimate (Ledeneva, 2018, p. 41).

Quite simply, *blat*, as a constitutive element of relationships and even of friendship, was identified with the acceptance of the exchange of favors through the network of acquaintances, often with a logic of immediate reciprocity. An acquaintance secured a doctor's appointment more quickly and the exchange involved a gift to the doctor (and sometimes to the contact itself, although that gift or favor could be requested later rather than immediately). The gift was seen as a token of appreciation, although it could evidently be a payment for speeding up

68 Corruption as a Dense Social Relationship

the process or solving the problem. So why was it not simply seen as a bribe? The answer is complex but has to do with the social construction that allowed the gift or the exchange to be symbolically regarded as gratitude rather than payment.

Let's analyze the dynamics of *blat* in slightly greater depth. The political context is essential to understanding it: the Soviet system that centralized decisions and defended that system as almost perfect. Failures or delays were denied: it was anti-patriotic and anti-communist to criticize the system in any way or complain about its inefficiency. But problems really existed, and people had to address and solve them in everyday life. *Blat* was becoming an effective way of finding a solution: it was an essential and subversive instrument, so to speak. It was essential because it provided a path that produced real results. It was subversive because, in the end, it was a veiled, controlled covert criticism of the inefficiency and social inequalities produced by the Soviet system (Aliyev, 2013, pp. 106–110). However, as will be seen, *blat* was not only subversive but, paradoxically, an escape valve of the system.

In order to understand this paradox, the key is to observe that *blat* exists through the construction of interpersonal bases of trust, which, in theory were not necessary according to the ideological argument of the perfection of the communist system. That is, on the one hand, in the formal world, the communist system was perfect, egalitarian, effective, and efficient. In actual fact, things were different, but to say so was improper and perhaps even dangerous. *Blat* was therefore an extremely *palanca* social outlet: without having to formally contradict the ideology of the system, people could resort to networks based on trust, networks of acquaintances. The central point: first, everyone might sometimes need help (Aliyev, 2013; Ledeneva, 1998; Ledeneva, 2011; Rehn & Taalas, 2004;); and second, *blat* would also penetrate the formal paths, because via *blat*, what many solutions did in particular was to achieve the unthinkable: ensuring that formal paths, in certain circumstances and for the right people with the right *blat* networks, worked effectively.

The Soviet system was characterized by robust bureaucracies with the power to distribute essential resources, such as food and medical services. In the USSR, the authorities defended the superiority of this system as a fact—superiority in every respect: practical and moral. Since society was jointly responsible for this belief, it was not correct to criticize or complain about the failures of the system. These flaws did not exist, formally. But they were obvious and actually very serious. This kind of social and collective schizophrenia is one of the possible reasons why Soviet society gradually built up a practice of interaction that ended up defining a solution that was non-legal but legitimate, which would make it possible to continue formally claiming that everything was fine and that institutional channels worked well, while many of the solutions came from a social channel based on networks of protection for family members, friends, and acquaintances (Rehn & Taalas, 2004, p. 242). *Blat* made it possible to solve problems relatively quickly and obtain satisfactors that would otherwise require many months or years. Never perfectly, never with absolute certainty, but always with an important degree of confidence that there were possibilities of finding a solution via the informal route. At least *blat* created the hope that there was a way to solve problems that would otherwise be virtually impossible to solve. *Blat* is therefore not a legally established path, but one in the gap between the legal and the illegal. In other words, *blat* was not socially perceived as legal, or as illegal either. But it was often regarded as indispensable.

In certain situations, and moments, the shortage of resources and the extreme bureaucratization of the Soviet system could be a source of family and group distress. The lack of protection and uncertainty people experienced at certain times was as real as the ideological argument that no one should complain about a system that had to be perfect. Without breaking the rules, without taking major risks, *blat* made it possible to create shortcuts and achieve prompt responses to problems. The system it created worked so well that in certain processes, it was linked to the formal system: in other words, bureaucrats and officials understood that they were part of *blat* networks and offered solutions on the basis of this understanding of relationships and acquaintances. A way of making the formal, bureaucratic, and slow system become fast and efficient had been found. In other words, in many ways, *blat* was functional for the system itself, at least for public servants who were able to build their own *blat* networks (and probably profit from them). *Blat* was therefore also useful for the system: the authorities reaffirmed their power and disguised the granting of goods as gestures of friendship (Ledeneva, 1998). This was done in such a way that *blat* became so effective that under its logic, not only informal people or groups interacted, but they also affected processes of organizations which, in theory, were efficient and worked following efficient and just orders but in practice were affected by the relations of exchange in *blat* to distribute goods and services "more efficiently".

However, *blat* created practices, languages, and symbols that enabled it to be reproduced as any form of relationship involving the exchange of favors: *blatmeisters* (Ledeneva, 2018, p. 40) eventually appeared and became a substantive piece in this respect. *Blatmeisters* were people with skills, abilities, and cunning intelligence who had a knack for building contacts, establishing networks, and approaching those with power. They therefore became effective brokers, very special nodes in the network. The network was therefore neither homogeneous nor horizontal, but capable of creating new logics of hierarchies in which certain people obtained various benefits by having the ability and resources to become known and respectable brokers.

The paradoxes of these social practices are perhaps one of the most fascinating characteristics, as we will see in the other practices existing in other countries: exchange networks solve problems or situations that official or formal mechanisms are unable or unwilling to solve. But these informal mechanisms, however, encourage rule breaking and even create new forms of power used by certain actors that acquire relevance thanks to the situational management of networks and favors.

Before the fall and disappearance of the USSR, one might have thought that *blat* would have to disappear. And this has happened, to a certain extent. But it is also likely, as some analysts have observed, that what is happening is that the mechanism has been modified and adapted. Following the modernization, privatization,

70 Corruption as a Dense Social Relationship

and opening up to the free market, contacts or favors lost a certain type of relevance: those that made it possible to get round the bureaucratic communist system or enabled one to find the right link or way to make it work properly. But, given the oligopolistic and concentrating results that occurred in the distribution of government resources and companies, new concentrating logics soon emerged. A modified *blat* appeared: for example, in the exchange of sensitive information or networks to affect public policy and public servants in their decisions, especially in policies that would affect certain industries and companies (Ledeneva, 1998). This change in objectives has encouraged the continuation of the mechanism, which evolved from the delivery of public goods to the exchange commitment, when necessary.

Whether in the dynamics of the USSR or of contemporary Russia, trust and solidarity networks are still needed: *blat* is based precisely on the tacit understanding that "at some point, all participants will need help" (Rehn & Taalas, 2004, p. 242). This means that there is a social understanding that endorses a kind of support for compensation actions among individuals in a society in situations where formal and legal logic are not sources of real solutions. These solutions must appear and be constructed in the gap between the formal and the real: not legal but not illegal either. The path is clear: the construction of known networks in an intricate logic of favors and exchanges (which can range from a simple thank you to involving a lot of money or goods) (Hardin, 1993). *Blat* builds a dynamic of "social capital" in a strict sense. In the case of *blat*, its operation is strongly conditioned to the type of social relationship (Aliyev, 2013, p. 93) as in kinship, which is the strongest kind and normally does not demand reciprocity; or *blat* which, based on friendship, seeks to grant favors to those who "deserve it" with the hope of some kind of retribution.

Because of the way *blat* was consolidated—as a mechanism of redistribution in the face of the shortage of goods and services, and the monopoly of the latter by the government—it is the strongest case in the economic logic of the exchange of favors. To some extent, it continues to have a negative connotation (for some people, *blat* may come from the word *blatnoi* meaning "criminal"). This may help explain why, after the collapse of the USSR and the opening up of the Russian economy, with the highly contested process of privatization and opening up to the free market it implemented, *blat* has not entirely disappeared (Anderson, 2012). Contacts or favors became less important for access to services in the sense of the state monopoly, for example. However, the exchange of information through the use of *blat* in industries and companies became relevant and useful (Ledeneva, 1998). It did not stop here, however: Ledeneva (2008) reports that *blat* has been monetarized, making it more difficult to hide the contradiction between the exchange of legitimate favors and outright corruption. Let's say that the reasons for the existence of *blat* have shifted to a logic closer to being an instrument that encourages ambition and a calculating and selfish *ethos*. For this reason, perhaps, *blat* has lost much of its original ambiguity and has increasingly come to be clearly identified as a kind of bribe in contemporary Russian society.

Chinese Guanxi

In China, there is an ancient tradition based on the ethics of Confucius, which suggests the need to establish relationships of solidarity, hierarchies, and reciprocity in order to engage in mutual obligations, which ultimately contributes to the maintenance of the social order (Liang-Hung, 2011). This practice, known as *guanxi*, is translated as *guan* (bridge) and *xi* (connection): a bridge consisting of acquaintances and social networks (Torres, Alfinito, De Souza Pinto Galvao, & Yin Tse, 2015). Or simply: a relationship (Yang, 1994, p. 1). *Guanxi* consists of forming long-term relationships to achieve common goals through the exchange of favors. Reciprocity and trust are values that play a fundamental role in this practice.

The interpersonal relationships in *guanxi* are based on the solidarity that involves repaying one favor with another one, so in a certain sense it is usually seen as an accepted, normalized social action (Torres et al., 2015). This practice is regarded as a social lubricant for formal processes and operations to be carried out effectively (Luo, Huang & Wang, 2011). Its relevance and permanence have led to its being a mechanism famous for being used in both business and relationships with public administrators that facilitate the procedures, goods, and services provided by the government (Liang-Hung, 2011).

Unlike *blat, guanxi* has a less negative social connotation, because of the popular references to the family and the ethics involved in repaying a favor. At the same time, like *blat, guanxi* is a contradictory practice in several ways. In various discourses, formal authority is defined as an undesirable practice which should be considered illegitimate. Due to its informal and ambiguous connotations, in official discourse it is simply regarded as a practice that entails legal or normative risks, for example, due to its proximity or similarity to bribery. However, in popular logic, *guanxi* can be distinguished from bribery with some ease, at least in people's everyday conversations or dialogues. But if people are asked to formally distinguish between *guanxi* and bribery, it is requested in such as way that people, say in an interview, will find it more difficult to construct precise arguments on how to differentiate them (Yang, 1994, p. 62). Some authors like Yang in various field studies have managed to show that the key argumentative point is probably that bribes can be distinguished from *guanxi* by the selfish reasons that define the former: in bribery, there is no chain of reciprocities that honor the act of giving something for a favor. *Guanxi* implies reasonable demands of people in a network: members of a network who "understand" the legitimacy of the need of one of their close relatives or acquaintances, and therefore regard it as legitimate to move the gears of personal relationships to meet this need. In bribery, the relationship between people is ephemeral, instrumental. In *guanxi*, a pre-existing relationship is assumed and created—not always directly, but with someone from the *guanxi* network. And the exchange therefore occurs beyond two people: it occurs in the logic of chains of reciprocity in a network. Thus, what many attack as illegitimate or illegal about the *guanxi*, one could say, is actually an attack on a "badly done" or poorly executed *guanxi* or, worse still, one that is hypocritically sought. Indeed,

72 Corruption as a Dense Social Relationship

guanxi is a mechanism which, "properly used", implies honesty and honor, at least in the logic of the network of reciprocities and duties (in the sense of honoring the promise) of reciprocating that is generated among the members.

This is why its extensive use leads to the de facto construction of advantages in business circles, for example. *Guanxi* is a generalized social form that builds lasting social relationships based on respect. It therefore does not only exist in an underground way in relationships *vis-à-vis* isolated people but is widely used in the business and government elites, based on the fundamental principle of chains of favors. It is also a skill, something that must be developed and even studied and learned, as an art in itself (*guanxixue* or the study of *guanxi*, Yang, 1994, p. 3).

Thanks to *guanxixue* and the ability to develop relationships and chains of favors, obligations, and duties, a multiplicity of problems can be addressed. In a society such as socialist China, with a huge, intrusive bureaucratic system, but with a very strong tradition of social strata, *guanxi* is seen as a necessary mechanism that connects high strata with low ones, linking bureaucracy with flesh-and-bone people.

At bottom, *guanxi* repeats something we find in *blat*, which we will find in the other mechanisms for the exchange of favors: the key is that relationships link, bind, and create commitments. These ties and commitments are based on a strange, contradictory combination of obligation and duty. In other words, *guanxi* links two paradoxes and makes them congruent: it is a mechanism of "disinterested and instrumental generosity, of voluntary and coerced reciprocity" (Yang, 1994, p. 8). How is this double paradox possible? Like any informal relationship mechanism, *guanxi* is based on a series of rules of etiquette: who asks for what, how, and at what times are fundamental rules. Making the favor appear purely instrumental is rude and insulting. For *guanxi* to be seen as a respectable mechanism, its essence lies in its being a favor—a favor with the implicit promise of reciprocity. It is not known when or how. But it is known that it should be reciprocated. That is why it is ultimately instrumental: the chain of favors creates a network and that network is based on the effectiveness of the mechanism. But not a *vis-à-vis* explicit instrumental effectiveness. The risk is clear: reciprocity has its own logic; the person who does a favor expects to receive a favor with the same or similar degree of importance or weight. But not necessarily immediately or with a label that reveals its *quid pro quo* nature, which would unmask the instrumentality of the mechanism and therefore jeopardize the argument and feeling of people that it is a legitimate, valid way to achieve things through reciprocity (not through crude, outright interest) (Bourdieu, 1977, p. 5). The key seems to be that, although there is an expectation of reciprocity and exchange, this does not happen automatically as if it were an accurate calculation of profits and costs. It occurs as a result of the fact that whoever receives a favor becomes morally indebted. That is why it is both voluntary, at the individual level, and coercive, socially speaking (or at least in the network). It is coercive from a "soft" perspective, so to speak: it is a debt of honor, which expands over time, not only to the person who granted the favor but in fact to the network itself. In other words, reciprocity is sought not because of the object, service, or money that was delivered, but in order to respond politely to a favor and thereby

Corruption as a Cultural and Social Process **73**

maintaining honor with it for the participants. It is assumed that a favor does not necessarily seek something in return (which would bring it dangerously close to bribery or blackmail). It is a matter of honor, however, to show gratitude, repaying the debt of honor and therefore reciprocating.

This is why *guanxi* is an art, *guanxixue*. It is essential to know the different rules of the game applied in different circumstances for different situations, with different people. Not everyone has those skills. You can learn, but there are also people who are "born" to be skilful at *guanxixue*. They possess *shili yan* or what can be translated as an "eye for power". These are people with cunning intelligence, no doubt, a skill that is also reproduced. The more you use *guanxi*, if you know how to do so, the stronger your network will be and constantly grow. And to this end, *guanxi* should be constantly exercised, which means asking for favors, while at the same time knowing you must reciprocate. When and how? It is not explicit or general for any circumstance; it cannot be because the naked instrumentalization of the mechanism destroys the magic of the circuit of a network of acquaintances who are bound by reasons of friendship or honor and who constantly reciprocate by maintaining and increasing their prestige, as a result of which they are perceived to be reliable.

One of the most fascinating issues regarding the mechanisms for the exchange of favors is its contradictory nature. On the one hand, it can be viewed positively, even in terms of economic efficiency. For example, according to the Transaction Cost Economics (TCE) approach, the exchange of favors is not necessarily an *ex ante* negative practice, but rather a component of the contractual relationship that contributes to economizing given the existence of a limited rationality and reliability (Verbeke & Kano, 2013, pp. 409–431). According to Verbeke and Kano, the exchange of favors is a common business practice that consists of the informal exchange of goods, services, and opportunities based on expected future reciprocity. In particular, the authors argue that legal contracts—and formal norms—almost never accurately reflect the true social relationships that are operating in practice (Verbeke & Kano, 2013, p. 409). *Guanxi* is one of the examples of business practices, sometimes questioned, but widely allowed because of its distributive function. Moreover, the role of *guanxi* as a social and cultural "complement" to contracts and transactions makes it one of the strongest practices.

However, concerns also exist about its negative effects not only in legal or normative, but even ethical, terms. It is clear for people in general that *guanxi* is a practice that makes it possible to obtain favors from government agents, by creating collusions between companies, building entry barriers, or seeking to influence the decision making of organizational or governmental policies (Luehrmann, 2012). It is therefore considered by some to be a practice that must be reviewed due to its possibly illegitimate and even illegal facets. Like all these mechanisms for the exchange of favors, their legitimacy depends greatly on the form, times, and moments when *guanxi* is used, always in particular circumstances, on a case-by-case basis (or context-specific basis, as explained by Ledeneva, 2008, p. 120). In other words, socially speaking, there are ways to evaluate *guanxi* and argue about its

74 Corruption as a Dense Social Relationship

illegitimacy. It depends on the circumstances, time, form, and even the rules of etiquette followed. This ambivalence is classic in all the mechanisms for the exchange of favors reviewed in this book, which is very important for understanding the enduring nature of these practices.

Protekzia *in Israel*

This Israeli practice, *protektzia*, is defined as the mobilization or management of personal ties to obtain recommendations or support from a person of influence in obtaining public goods or services that would not otherwise be granted. This necessarily involves circumventing or manipulating official standards and procedures, although it usually excludes the involvement of money since the dynamics of *protekzia* emphasize links or bonds of solidarity, trust, and group identity (Danet, 1990; Etzioni-Halevy, 1975; Even-Shoshan, 1983; Galnoor, Rosenbloom & Yaroni, 1998; Werner, 1983; Zelekha & Werner, 2011). The term comes from Slavic (and Eastern European) migration to Israel; it originally referred to both the exchange of favors and bribery, but in Israel it refers exclusively to the former (Danet, 1990, p. 913).

As is common in the practices of chains of favors, *protekzia* is promoted through the creation of an obligation or informal duty between people in response to a situation of solidarity required when dealing with a social reality where the rules in everyday life become obstacles rather than helping people. This very concrete problematic and frustrating situation felt by a flesh-and-bone person is also shared by many people. And this socially shared frustration triggers a kind of feeling of solidarity that makes it justifiable to attempt to solve the problem through informal mechanisms, even if it "bends" formal rules. Given this situation, solidarity implies helping in order to get round the rules (only slightly, it is assumed, although establishing how little is always difficult to define). These formal norms can even be socially accepted; they are real and compulsory for everyone. However, at the same time, in certain situations, it is socially accepted (not publicly but in *vis-à-vis* contacts between people) that it is necessary and even acceptable to bend them (Danet, 1990, p. 914). They are formal norms at the end of the day, but contextually inadequate because they are too "abstract" and incapable of helping in the thousands of variations of concrete situations. In some extreme cases, people in various societies suspect that this inadequacy may even be a construction on the part of the authorities themselves, in order to reproduce their power over others and even obtain income from it.

In the case of the activation of personal *protekzia* connections, it regularly involves more than two people since brokers are usually included in the relationship. The most commonly used relationships are obviously found in school friendships, shared experiences in a kibbutz—an agricultural commune used to create settlements for Jews in the new territory of Israel and in occupied territories—having served in pre or post-State military corps, or in the *milums* (reservations)—migration within the same country, membership of the same political

Corruption as a Cultural and Social Process **75**

party, neighbors, etc. (Danet, 1990, p. 914). Lastly, a very particular feature of *protektzia* is that it does not involve negotiating conditions to return the favor or what is known as direct reciprocity. This reciprocity is legitimized because it is not for a person but, it is argued, for "the group". Duty and collective courtesy are quite explicit in *protekzia*, with a different logic than in *guanxi*. This is apparently more explicit than in the case of *blat*.

The history of Israel is a fundamental context for understanding *protektzia*. The various waves of migration, and the fact that the population is under permanent military alert, have forced it to quickly build ties and dynamics of integration which, together with a certain bureaucratic rigidity, has been the breeding ground for these bonds of trust and reciprocity (Danet, 1990; Rostila, 2010, p. 321).

It is therefore easy to identify several elements that are becoming common in the chains of reciprocity and favors: a rigid structure of rules, a perception of difficulty in obtaining, through the formal rules of the game, what is needed, and the need for informal reciprocity. The constants are also found in group dynamics: the construction of ties, the effort to prevent the instrumentalization of the relationship, the skill required to build the informal but effective dynamics of the relationship. In this case, the role of brokerage is quite strong, because the existence of skilled people who have managed to create broad, effective networks of solidarity or reciprocity at least, becomes very explicit. This can be explained by the enormous importance of the context, of concrete, everyday situations that must be addressed and which require intelligence and skill, cunning intelligence, to find the specific methods that are really effective. No two cases are the same and *protekzia* routes must be found on a case-by-case basis. This concrete situation people experience on a daily basis is critical to understanding how cunning intelligence is required to understand and make intelligible the logic, communication, and engagement codes required to deal with the events people must cope with.

As one can see, these three practices involving the exchange of favors, in three highly dissimilar contexts, share common features. The political and cultural context is substantive. But the general patterns seem to be quite common. We will now examine three examples of the Latin American context. We will examine the cases of Brazil and Chile, where specific characteristics of the Latin American context emerge: the weight and quasi-legitimization given to the development of the personal ability required for chains of favors to be sustained and effective. Being proficient in the art of bending the rules is therefore a socially appreciated skill. These two cases will allow us to explore in greater detail the Mexican case, which has probably one of the most widespread, sophisticated mechanisms of reciprocity in the region: *palancas*.

Brazilian Jeitinho

In Brazil, *jeitinho*, literally "little road" (De Paiva, 2018, p. 43; in other words, finding the way or route to solving a problem), refers to a creative, skillful, and intelligent way of finding a solution to specific problems, usually caused by

76 Corruption as a Dense Social Relationship

bureaucratic rules and procedures. Doing so implies being able to find a fast and effective way to reach a successful conclusion: doing things "the Brazilian way" as it is called colloquially (Castor, 2002; Duarte, 2011; Smith, Huang, Harb, & Torres, 2012). *Jeitinho* implies having a great capacity to "get round the rules" and the difficulties they impose: obstacles may seem impossible to overcome, but with skillful and intelligent *jeitinho*, "nothing is impossible". *Jeitinho* immediately and unambiguously implies skillful and cunning intelligence; those who can develop this ability become *"pistolao"* or "big shots". They are people with the social weapons that allow them to use their great astuteness and capacity, to solve insoluble problems (which are only insoluble for those who do not have *jeitinho*) (Castor, 2002).

Jeitinho involves intelligently cheating. "To give a *jeitinho*" means being able to not see formal rules and to be able to skirt them, disobey them, but with the best intention of finding a solution that is expected not to harm virtually anyone. It is, therefore, a solution to help relatives, friends, and acquaintances, with, discursively speaking, good intentions. It is important therefore to link these two elements: the intelligence required to get round rules and the importance of networks of acquaintances. The first implies a highly specific characteristic of Latin American cases: the explicitly socially rewarded pride in being able to solve a problem, even if it violates the rules. The second is the common feature of the social relations underlying favors, which we have ana-lyzed: the use of personal relationships and contacts formalized over time. In this case, though, Brazil emphasizes one of its particular aspects: the importance of charisma in being able to perform *jeitinho* successfully (Duarte, 2011). *Jeitinho-pistolao* is widely used in all social sectors in Brazil and for some, it is even regarded as an essential part of the culture of this South American country (Dos Santos, 2014). Various analysts seek to find their roots in the colonial relation-ship of this country with Portugal and the existing dualism between what it implies to accept a rule imposed by the colony, and yet one which the locals can obey flexibly (de Sousa, 2012). This social mechanism can be seen as a game involving values such as solidarity, trust, affection, reciprocity, and sym-pathy, because in the end, part of the legitimacy of *jeitinho* lies in the "good intentions" a person has in bending the rules (Ashton & Lof, 2015; Guerra, Cortez, & Diogo, 2016; Marinoni & Becker, 2003).

Usually, also in the case of Brazil, there is a recurrent element that has already been dealt with extensively in this chapter: bureaucratic rigidity (Maynard-Moody & Mosheno, 2003), which creates a straitjacket of formal rules and procedures that make it difficult or complicated to obtain services and goods, authorizations, and licenses. To a certain extent, this characteristic is repeated in many Latin American cases: not because of the omnipresence of the state as in communism, but because of a contradictory situation in which the power of the state and bureaucracy is due precisely to the capacity to impose restrictions and obstacles on the population, forcing it, paradoxical as this may sound, to negotiate with the state. Thus, *jeitinho* in Brazil may, in many respects, be functional for both the bureaucrat and the citizen since it is a mechanism that creates balance and even social harmony. A distinctive aspect of the Brazilian case appears to be that *jeitinho* is embedded in a logic of charisma and good attitude (Torres et al., 2015).

The existence of mechanisms of favors as a reflection of bureaucratic dysfunction in Latin American countries is closely related to governments and public administrations that are perceived as alien to the society in which they operate, due to the history of colonization and economic domination this region has suffered as much at the hand of Europe as more recently from the United States. Mechanisms of reciprocity are even seen by some people as a means of resisting bureaucratic impositions alien to the local culture. It is impossible to refer to *jeitinho* in Brazil without considering that in Portuguese colonial times, the rules of access to public goods and services were dictated by Europe, which was more concerned with the welfare of the empire than that of the locals.

As for charisma, trust, and solidarity as ingredients of the social legitimization of *jeitinho*, it is important to note that they are the basis for identifying those capable of successfully undertaking the complex process of bending the rules yet doing so without destroying the established formal order. *Jeitinho* implies charm, sympathy, and even empathy. Some authors like Castor argue that the archetype of the "affable Brazilian" is partly rooted in *jeitinho*: the imaginary that becomes national identity in the kind, hospitable, and courteous Brazilian. Over time, this remarkable cordiality, expressed through charm and sympathy, was consciously used to obtain certain favors in an alternative way. Thus, beneath this social image that has been constructed over the centuries, certain strategies tend to be adopted to use charm, such as smiling, flattering, speaking with a friendly tone and even, in a slightly darker sense, "seducing" and manipulating in order to obtain what is wanted (Duarte, 2011). The use of sympathy and charm to obtain favors is a way to offset the acute economic inequalities and power asymmetries often attributed to the political and economic order in Brazil. This is a skill that becomes indispensable and justifiable, even with another collective imaginary: that of keeping the peace and avoiding disputes or confrontations in an eternally "chaotic, overcrowded and noisy" context (Duarte, 2011, p. 31). In this respect, *jeitinho*, together with its differentiating elements (sympathy and charm), is perceived as part of the Brazilian identity.

Finally, with respect to the logic of reciprocity of *jeitinho*, it can be argued that it has some differences from *guanxi* and *blat*: using jeitinho does not necessarily imply waiting for the exchange of a future favor. The exchange or reciprocity is diffuse (De Paiva, 2018, p. 44). Although reciprocity is expected, it may be the case that gratitude alone and the strength of charisma are reason enough to do favors without a clear chain of reciprocity. For example, approaching a friend, bureaucrat, or boss will be easier if you have the charisma and the tact to make the relations of reciprocity flow in a much more "fluid" or ambiguous way, where the promise to give back or respond is seen as something more closely related to the bonhomie of the relationship itself. In other words, the instrumentality of favors is much more opaque; this does not mean that this more instrumental reciprocity does not

78 Corruption as a Dense Social Relationship

actually happen, but merely that it takes place on the basis of the idea of the "happiness" provided by solving problems.

Pituto *in Chile*

Pituto (colloquially known as cronyism or favors) is a mechanism of exchange of favors that seeks the redistribution of wealth and the preservation or differentiation of the Chilean bureaucratic middle class. Its origin is linked to the structural and administrative changes undergone by the Chilean state at the end of the 19th century (Lomnitz, 1994). Thereafter, the Chilean state undertook a process of bureaucratization, corporatization, and expansion of the state structure that led to the birth and strengthening of a new social class (Barozet, 2002; Barozet, 2006; Lomnitz, 1994).

During this period, the increase in state functions also expanded the labor force of the state structure—even in times of crisis and particularly in the entities responsible for the provision of social services (Barozet, 2006, p. 78). Thus, a body of more-or-less homogeneous bureaucrats was consolidated, together with a social group linked to it, characterized by its educational achievement and social capital. This body strengthened its social status through a system of perks and direct state benefits that translate into subsidies and advantages related to the power of the state and its processes (Barozet, 2006). In other words, society understands the importance of accessing this group. The group is obviously not formal, nor does it have clearly established boundaries. But its existence is expressed precisely in the ability to use networks and acquaintances to access the benefits this group appears to enjoy. When, through contacts and acquaintances, a person achieves access to the network of benefits (real or imagined) the group enjoys, it is clear that they somehow belong to the group and can use *pituto*. In other words, *pituto* is developed in a group of people in a semi-closed circle, which you have to know how to access. Achieving this implies having access to options for services or goods that would otherwise be extremely difficult to access. Belonging to this group, relating to this group, implies developing skills for the exchange of favors, since contacts and links become the means determining whether or not one has access to the status of this group. It is a curious circle that appears contradictory: to use *pituto* effectively, you must belong to the group and in order to belong to the group, you must show skill in using *pituto*, by offering the group some thing or advantage. Reciprocity is maintained in the gray area between duty and obligation. There is no immediate exchange, but rather a symbolic debt that marks the relationship.

In a way, all of the mechanisms we have studied up to now create a logic of collective imaginary: the ability to play the rules of reciprocity is essential to creating, accessing, and increasing the exchange network. They all to a certain extent create a circle that requires certain capacities and rules to play in the sphere of this network. In *pituto*, one can say that the role of the construction of a particular, relatively well identified group, which becomes a circle to which it is necessary to belong, is fairly obvious. Some critics have observed that this view of a

Corruption as a Cultural and Social Process   **79**

fairly closed *pituto* group has promoted more clearly than in other spaces the emphasis on practices of reciprocity and class solidarity, and political loyalties, as opposed to social values such as competitiveness and merit (Barozet, 2002; Barozet, 2006; Durston, 2005; Lomnitz, 1994).

In the case of *pituto*, a strong relationship with elements such as cronyism and nepotism is socially understood, especially in government issues and bureaucratic circles. A very basic clientelistic logic is developed, so to speak, where the rules are bent to encourage the delivery of services to certain people or groups. A "good civil servant" takes care of his "beneficiaries", helping and supporting them on a regular basis. This is useful for the civil servant because it broadens his network of political influence and his control over certain agendas (Barozet, 2006; Durston, 2005).

Mauss and other scholars of gift-giving posit that it is possible to further appreciate the function of the exchange of favors in the game of social relations: it makes it possible to maintain relations of reciprocity over time, ensuring the well-being (and, in a certain sense, survival) of the group or network of "trusted" people who share and distribute benefits to each other. *Pituto* makes it possible to institutionalize the practices that can happen and even coexist relatively smoothly with formal processes, bending them but not necessarily breaking them. Therefore, setting *pituto* in motion implies an instrumental logic: Reciprocity is "important and compulsory" because it establishes a "symbolic debt" in the exchange of favors (Barozet, 2006, p. 71).

In this practice, if a person refuses to return a favor, they will be removed from the contact network as punishment. Through *pituto* "[officials] capitalize [on the favors they do for their friends] in order to obtain other elements in return and consolidate their social position and status" (Barozet, 2006, p. 82). Thus, trust and reciprocity act hand in hand to exercise redistribution. This social mechanism is powerful and prevails because it is a way of accessing positions that would not be expected to be held except by the group to which the individuals belong. The instrumentality of *pituto* is quite direct, compared with other cases. Its binding power lies precisely in belonging to and having loyalty to the group of "privileged persons" who build that circle which controls resources and influences. Ambition and the prestige of belonging or relating to that circle is a sufficient reason, affording prestige, intelligence, and status.

Pituto is the most suitable preamble for approaching the analysis of *palancas* in Mexico and understanding the way they operate.

Toward a Semiosis of Palancas *in Mexico*

The logic of *palancas* is in many ways similar to the mechanisms we have analyzed so far. In Mexico, *palancas* refer to the help or informal exchange of favors (usually in bureaucratic issues) that takes place between people who are able to use their contacts to help others or themselves. In a world of highly discretionary, opaque bureaucratic processes people face in the request for public or private services, informal networks of trust increase the likelihood that what is sought in the

80 Corruption as a Dense Social Relationship

intricate bureaucratic network of procedures will be achieved. Since bureaucracy is highly discretionary and corrupt, *palancas* are a way to avoid the problems and uncertainties of any formal process. *Palancas* can be sought directly or through intermediaries: friends of friends.

As in the previous mechanisms, the *palanca* is an ambiguous mechanism, socially speaking. It is not clear whether or not it involves corruption (Lomnitz, 1990; Tapia Tovar & Zalpa, 2011; Zalpa, Tapia Tovar, & Reyes, 2014): a judgment that can only be made (according to the people in this society) on a case-by-case basis, depending on the very specific circumstances. *Palancas* differ from bribes in assuming that the people involved enjoy trust and a certain equity with respect to the other; that is, there is respect and the point is to "help". However, it often involves a commitment of reciprocity that ensures the exchange of equivalent services in the future (Lomnitz, 1990). Accordingly, there may be cases of *palancas* that led directly to a bribe or which substantially contributed to fraud. But in many cases, *palancas* ended up helping people in trouble, bending the rules, but in an area that is not necessarily seen as illegal. In other words, there are *palancas* that are not corruption but only seen as a slight bending of the rules (which are probably regarded as rigid and even unjust).

Like all mechanisms involving the exchange of gifts, the *palanca* suffers from strong contradictions: it is an "adaptive mechanism" which, in its attempts to satisfy the unmet needs of people due a rigid and inefficient system, may, as we will see later, paradoxically reinforce the excessive rigidity of the formal system (Lomnitz, 1990).

In Mexico, the bureaucratic system has characteristics of rigidity that have been the perfect breeding ground for *palancas*. As examples of this we have arguments that speak of formal processes of public administration that are too complex (Nuijten, 2003, p. 226), the slowness of problem solving by the bureaucracy (Tapia Tovar & Zalpa, 2011) and the existence of excluded groups that are unimportant for the government apparatus. Accordingly, the *palanca* is an alternative and highly expanded mechanism among the population of every stratum and level which makes it possible, in the collective imaginary, to level and facilitate the distribution of public services or the relationship between citizens and governments and private bureaucracies in general. In other words, "bending the rules" through contacts and granting favors is justified as a way to skirt inefficient and inequitable government procedures. Specifically, without the use of the *palanca* mechanism, the costs and opportunities to obtain goods and services can be illogically high (Lomnitz, 1990). Using and having *palancas* is a generalized mechanism in all spheres of activity and among all strata of the population.

Part of the explanation for the omnipresence of the *palanca* dates back to colonial times. The imposition of rules from the metropolis was seen as extremely illegitimate at various times by the population. By the 18th century, a visitor described the basis of the widespread mechanism of favors for leapfrogging the rules (Villarroel, 1785/1994). And since then, the dynamics of the *palanca* has usually been regarded as positive by society because *palancas* are rationalized as legitimate, or at least necessary, instruments facing the often irrational limitations imposed by an unpopular authority. If one adds a historically rigid, unprofessional, and slow bureaucracy, then all the elements are in place for the success of a social relationship such as *palancas*.

However, *palancas*, like the other mechanisms we have studied, are contradictory, and even paradoxical. *Palancas* are a response to an unfair and unpopular regime and a slow, inefficient bureaucracy. But empirical studies have shown that the *palanca* is fundamental and exists even in intra-bureaucratic relations: people within the same ministry, in different areas, use *palancas* to help them perform their work and with performance objectives (Arellano-Gault, 2018). In other words, a mechanism that helps solve relationship problems between people and bureaucracies or authorities has expanded as an organizational mechanism which, in certain situations, helps them to work.

The omnipresence of *palancas* suggests that they are the rule rather than the exception. The *palanca* is a mechanism that allows the reproduction of the very thing it supposedly fights. In other spheres, it has been argued that Mexican bureaucracy is not exactly the embodiment of the Kafkaesque (Arellano-Gault, 2018). The reason is that bureaucracy in Mexico can be effective and even efficient because socially and historically, even structurally, the relationship between people and authorities can be resolved thanks to the always possible presence of paths and parallel solutions. These parallel paths, and informal or even twisted solutions (but ultimately solutions), are formally the exception, but in everyday practice, they are the norm. The Kafkaesque monster of Mexican bureaucracy is controlled. Or rather, controlled, only to be unleashed when people cannot or do not have the resources to gain access to parallel routes. Thus, in the context of bureaucratic rigidity constructed, the *palanca* is a phenomenon that happens through chains of reciprocity. It is based on knowing people who in various circumstances are in position of (or in turn know people who are in position of) intervening to solve a particular situation or problem in exchange for some form of reciprocity, which may be material or of another type.

In addition, since it is a widespread practice, attempting to act without using *palancas* entails agreeing to pay costs ranging from not getting what you want—given that in many situations, the normal, rational way is through *palancas*—to being stigmatized, paradoxically, as someone who is unsuccessful and ineffective (even disloyal to their families for making them pay the cost of the effects of not using *palancas*). The paradox is impressive: in this logic, the stigma is not due to bending or breaking the rules, but rather to not being *cunning* or intelligent enough to obtain suitable, powerful *palancas*.

In Mexico, in everyday life, *palancas* are assumed to be a legitimate, necessary act (in many cases) to benefit and generate reciprocity. *Palancas* occur when an individual possessing a certain sphere of influence has the possibility (in some cases even the faculty, given its scope and organizational hierarchy) to influence a decision, a distribution, or access to certain assets, resources or scenarios of action/strategic decisions. To activate it, society has created codes, symbols, insinuations, words,

82 Corruption as a Dense Social Relationship

and attitudes, but above all, mechanisms that create hope for exchange that help maintain the practice.

Specifically, *palancas* in Mexico operate as a mechanism that considers the following attributes: scope (the framework in which it is activated and in which the aim is to obtain something in the public or private sector), context (the procedure whereby the person identifies, constructs, and requests the *palanca*), actors (the role in which they participate: public servant, citizen, or entrepreneur), contact mechanism (access directly or through an intermediary), information inputs and means of communication (personal contact, by phone or email, documents, electronic files, or simply a dialogue), type of benefit created (money or time saving, which encourages something to happen or allows access to strategic scenarios or extraordinary goods/ services).

Palancas are usually seen as the solution to a bureaucratic system that is crammed with often obscure and opaque rules that interfere with accessing public services or goods. But in fact, it seems that this rigidity and occasional surrealism in Mexican bureaucracy is part of a well-oiled system. Bureaucratization in Mexico does not appear to be a pathology or misfortune that happened by mistake. *Palancas* are so widespread and are so old that it sometimes seems that this rigid, surreal logic was put there intentionally. *Palancas* find quasi-legitimate, socially quasi-acceptable paths to escape the constraints of formal rules. The Kafkaesque nature of bureaucracy is therefore probably not an accident then. It makes sense since it has a particular logic of exercising power. In order for the Kafkaesque monster not to run loose, Mexican society has built an effective but also perverse bridge with authority. In other words, a logic of relationships, reciprocities, and exchanges: *palancas*.

For Mexicans, the art of *palancas* is learned from an early age because they live with them on an everyday basis. The *palanca* is a seemingly universal expression in Mexico. Everyone has heard of it and probably all of them have participated or have at least heard of its dynamics and logic. The *palanca* is a complete ritual with rules of etiquette, language, and proportionality. Using a *palanca* improperly can lead to an offense and to the breaking of the chain of acquaintances that is activated to meet a particular need. The art of *palancas* is to keep the network of acquaintances in a dynamic of such trust that its instrumentalization will not end up being so obvious as to destroy the illusion that direct or pecuniary interests are the glue that keeps the interaction together. However, *palancas* have several dark sides. For example, for those who do not take part in the exchange yet realize that someone benefited from having *palancas* and rather than merit. It may even be that people did not witness or have evidence that someone benefited in this way, but the suspicion may remain there, marking people's interpretation of the merit with which such benefits were obtained. In other words, while for many people, having *palancas* is a symbol of intelligence and cunning, for many in concrete situations it can be seen as an unjustified privilege. The *palanca* can also apparently be used for innocuous issues, but in fact the *palanca* also applies to "major" favors, for true political or economic conspiracy, influence peddling, collusion, and fraud. At one extreme, *palancas* are so universal that there are popular sayings that if someone is rich or powerful, it is surely because, at some point, they are corrupt. There is not much space under this logic to think that someone socially or economically successful has achieved this through their own merits and legitimate efforts.

Understanding mechanisms such as *palancas* seems essential if one wishes to understand the logic of corruption permeating Latin American countries. The *palanca* is an excellent example that warrants studying in depth: a widespread, successful, widely used mechanism for the exchange of favors. It is one which has its "experts" and users, rules, and languages. And it can go from being a legitimate mechanism socially speaking for small favors and reciprocities, to being linked to major events involving exchanges and favors that are already illegal and corrupt. Scale is probably one of the most negative factors of *palancas*: it serves both for minuscule favors and major collusions. An important point to be emphasized in this respect is that scale not only refers to the severity of the rule violated, or the privileges obtained, but also to the long chain of *palancas* required to obtain these kind of privileges. The *palanca* is not an exceptional act, but a style and indispensable practice in social relations which permeates organizations and the most diverse interactions. It is a true *modus operandi* which is already a *modus vivendi*.

Next, we will discuss an empirical study on *palancas* in Mexico, in order to understand the dynamics and codes of this relationship of reciprocity and the scope it can have.

Studying the Mechanisms for the Exchange of Favors: The *Palanca* as a Double-Edged Sword

Oddly enough, the study of *palancas*, understood as an informal, generalized, and stable social mechanism, is underdeveloped (some important analyses can be found in Lomnitz, 1990; Lomnitz, 2000; Nuijten, 2003; Zalpa, Tapia Tovar, & Reyes, 2014;). This has partly to do with the difficulty of studying a mechanism that basically involves obtaining and using or trafficking in personal relationships, especially if it is an empirical study, which entails various difficulties and challenges. This section focuses on discussing the quest for understanding the semiology of the *palanca*. Semiology implies understanding how people lend meaning to something, in this case, to behaviors and relationships. It involves an approach to the discovery of the signs and symbols with which people obtain and assign meaning to the action or to a certain social relationship. It requires as a study logic avoiding the assignment of *ex ante* values or, worse, a normative or moral judgment of the matter under analysis (Chandler, 2002).

In this way, inspired by semiotic studies of corruption (Blundo & de Sardan, 2001), several advantages of undertaking a particular study of *palancas* were considered. A semiotic method has several advantages in this case, because a concept such as the *palanca*, which can be related to acts with a negative moral charge—such as the use of privileges and even corruption—can be analyzed more effectively if what is sought is to understand what people assign to the *palanca* as a symbol without assigning them *ex ante* judgments (as usually happens in corruption

84 Corruption as a Dense Social Relationship

studies). It therefore tries to understand that people express themselves in the least stressful way possible: through an exchange of anecdotes and reflections.

To carry out this study, several focus groups were implemented using the idea of experts in the Delphi method (Varela-Ruiz et al., 2012, p. 94). The Delphi method can be used in various ways (Blasco, López & Mengual, 2010; Varela-Ruiz et al., 2012) but basically it is carried out through different groups of "experts" or people with first-hand knowledge of what they are going to talk about. The idea is to make selections according to very specific criteria that serve to understand several variations of the matter to be discussed. The coordinating group of researchers is responsible for promoting communication and dealing with the information collected.

In this case, three groups of experts of between five and seven members each were formed, who from their diversity of occupations, contexts, and relationship with organizations of heterogeneous sectors were able to achieve a conceptualization and explanation of the symbols and practical meanings of *palancas*. The people who were invited to participate were told that the study involved attending a Gessell chamber (explaining the logic of the chamber). They were assured of the anonymity of their responses and of the protection of the information they gave, whose purposes were exclusively academic.

For its part, the coordinating team consisted of a moderator who interacted directly with the experts in a Gessell chamber, while three assistants on the other side of the mirror collected the information that was produced, and offered advice using a microphone to communicate with the moderator via earphones. The purpose of this double interaction was to encourage the balanced participation of the experts, to redo questions, generate timely feedback, and determine when a minimum level of information saturation was reached and when a satisfactory minimum response variation had been reached (Blasco, López, & Mengual, 2010).

The logic of the focus groups generated was then used to discuss the *palanca* and its dynamics in three different areas: as a worker in a company or organization, as a civil servant at the managerial level and as a citizen (at this point university students were selected as a group that could be considered representative of society in general). The idea of asking operative workers was designed to understand the common sphere of people with apparently fewer economic or social privileges. The group of civil servants at the senior management level sought exactly the opposite: the experience of people supposedly with privileges above the social average and who also have, in this case, access to resources and relationships in various areas. Finally, the students considered themselves a proxy of citizens in general: a vision from the field of the common life of a young person in the Mexican urban environment. The duration of each session—with different groups of experts—was approximately 120 minutes, which included two rounds of questions, the feedback process and the integration of a brief final questionnaire to be answered individually by each expert, once a certain level of shared information had been reached. We attempted to achieve, as far as possible, the same gender proportion per group and a relatively homogeneous intra-group age range.

It should be noted that one of the first possible results of the study was in the call for applicants itself. The participants were told that the topic of discussion was *palancas* in Mexico. There was not a single participant who asked for more information about it or any explanation of what that category meant. That is, the *palanca* is apparently part of the tacit knowledge any Mexican obtains from an early age and in its most intimate circuits such as family and school.

The following is a summary of what has been discussed in these focus groups, which provides an initial understanding of the logic of the *palanca*, its meaning, and its social form of expression.

The Palanca, a Permanent Companion of Mexicans

The moderator always began the focus groups with a phrase that referred to the *palancas* being discussed in Mexico. The first relevant fact is that, invariably, the people who participated in the three groups immediately showed their knowledge of the term. No one asked, what is that? Or what is a *palanca*? All the participants apparently knew the term and did not feel it necessary to obtain more information. The *palanca* is a seemingly universal expression in Mexico. Everyone has heard of it and probably all of them have participated or have at least heard of its dynamics and logic.

The *palanca*, as a first approximation, is an aid, a help that comes from people who know each other and who have information or knowledge. A worker explains:

> Well, I think more than anything it is a friend, right? A friend or a family member. That is, there are things, say, related to my car or things like that, so, I trust him because I know it's part of his job. That is, if this person is familiar with the subject, maybe you trust him because he has more knowledge than you. And he knows more about what you're talking about than you do. That is, you trust him, you know that he is a person who maybe knows more than you, right? And you approach that kind of people.

Relations with people, acquaintances, are important sources of knowledge and help. But the *palanca* can go beyond a list of favors between friends and acquaintances. The instrumental element of the use of the *palanca* appears clearer, as one civil servant said:

> For me, the *palanca* has a fundamental element and is the exercise of power that would not be accessed in a formal institutional way. It may involve cronyism but not necessarily.

That is, there is implicitly a logic of utility in the social relationship. It can be a social relationship that is fundamentally not instrumental: the goal of the relationship is not that everyone gets something, at least in principle. But that social

86 Corruption as a Dense Social Relationship

relation is not tied mainly to an explicit obtaining of benefits; it may, under certain circumstances, be instrumental. Let us return to the group of workers:

> It depends because the government is very bad, so if I go to the town hall and I have a very big problem and I file a complaint, they tell me: "Wait, the lawyer is not there" or "the judge is not there" and you say: "Ok"; but important people arrive with their lawyers saying that something has just happened and they say: "Yes, come this way". So you say: "Do I have to have someone to make you listen to me?"

There are situations, then, where relationships become a source of support, a way of looking for solutions to problems that cannot be solved in formal ways. Having an acquaintance who has acquaintances or "influences" is highly effective. The same worker points out:

> He is a friend of the family; I had to look him up, I do not like doing that, but I was very desperate and had to look him up. He did not have to come in; that is, he sorted everything out from his home. I told them that even in the government, in the town halls, they have to have an acquaintance or someone inside to listen to us. We are citizens and we all have the right to express ourselves and why do not they do so? I think the government has always been like that.

To a certain extent, the social relationships everyone has and obtains throughout life can fulfill several different purposes: from simple company and friendship to help in cases of need. Social relationships are often protection networks and when the person has a need, a social relationship that has never been instrumental (to obtain something) can become so. In the words of a citizen:

> I was going to say that I think it's not right, but it also crops up when there's a need. If nobody really needed a *palanca*, there would not be all the contacts and I think there are people who, I'm with both sides, there are people who use it as a last resort, but I know many people for whom *palancas* are the first port of call and they are surrounded by contacts and their world is divided into contacts.

How instrumental can a social relationship be? In principle, many social relationships can be affected at the time when the expected reciprocity is explicit or direct. But it can also be that this same instrumentality can become part of the strategy of people's social existence. A citizen explains: *"Even universities. The students who go there are chosen because of the contacts that are going to be there and according to where they want to go"*. In other words, social relations can be constructed explicitly as *palancas*, as a strategy that certain actors seek to build and nurture in an overt, conscious way. The *palanca* is obviously a mechanism to correct injustices, but it can also be

Corruption as a Cultural and Social Process **87**

an individual and group strategy for success. *Palancas* that balance and *palancas* that speak of privilege are two seemingly contradictory but clear logics that appeared in some of the focus groups.

The *palanca* can be useful in other more formalized areas, for example, in the relationships between different government agencies, as in the case of the federal government. A civil servant explains:

> For example, especially in issues where there are different institutions, dependencies, sitting at the table; there are times when you have to obtain things which by normal processes are not going to meet the deadlines that are being demanded, so if you know you have someone you know in the area that can get them to receive you earlier, or you can get your issue placed further up the agenda and dealt with earlier, or you can make something that involved a process that was not going to work, work.

This topic is very interesting because it speaks of the omnipresent *palancas*, not only in the relationship between people or between people and bureaucracy, but within bureaucracy itself, and not for minor issues but for high-level negotiations. Another public servant explains:

> We need to deposit resources in the states, we need to publish the rules of operation. The process is terribly convoluted; you have to go through the Treasury, for everything, ten thousand windows, the deadlines have expired, you need to publish in the official gazette. I am already in the final phase and you need to publish in the official gazette, but I cannot deposit, because the Treasury window closes. First, a telephone call, I say that I am from the main office and I say: "Do not close the window on me".

So, in highly formalized spaces such as government bureaucracies, however, the construction of informal relationships is crucial. The *palanca*, that request for favors to avoid negative consequences or achieve important objectives, works in a normal, substantive way in formal organizational dynamics. The paradox is interesting: in order to sort out what formal rules complicate, informal dynamics such as *palancas*, with their codes and forms, are required even in the context of highly formalized relationships.

The *palanca* is therefore omnipresent, multifunctional, and there is a fairly developed knowledge in people about its logic, dynamics, and need, in very different situations.

The **Palanca**, *Its Usefulness, and Rules of Etiquette*

Every social relationship implies a logic of reciprocity. The way people present themselves (Goffman, 1981), languages, words, poses, are crucial to creating the basis of a certain likelihood of successful reciprocity. In other words, any social

88 Corruption as a Dense Social Relationship

relationship, including *palancas*, implies a certain degree of uncertainty and therefore certain logics of secrecy, masks, and fabrication. This is particularly the case in *palancas* where exchanges of favors of great monetary or political or social importance may be involved, and even a certain "bending" of the established formal rules. Thus, clumsily requesting a *palanca* can reveal the fact that one sees the other person as a purely manipulable instrument. And that, in many cases, can jeopardize the likelihood of success. *Palancas*, then, have informal but important rules about meetings, labels, and tempo. In the words of one worker:

> It's like a gun: why use cartridges unnecessarily? You should always know how to use them. Because for example I already know who I have to communicate with in the Mexican Social Security Institute because I have my contacts right now, but if I go in for studies and they tell me to do them in three months, why am I going to use a cartridge when I can save it for something else?

There are rules of "decency", and tempo: it is not a primarily instrumental relationship (at least in the logic of etiquette). *Palancas* are nurtured, cared for, and irrigated like gardens so that they continue to exist in time. Another worker: *"I think if you feel committed to that person, right? Because he is helping you. There is always a payment, whatever it is, there is going to be a payment, so unconsciously we all expect payment in return"*. The instrumentality of the *palanca* implies a promise, albeit implicit, of mutual commitment. Mutual exchange can take place in time; it is not something that is necessarily "charged" immediately. This logic of tempo in its use (that is, the implicit rules of reasonableness and steps and processes for using the *palanca*) and the reciprocity that can be displaced in time are probably two of the most complex and interesting issues of the *palanca*. In this sense, a citizen clearly explains:

> ...so when you have the help of a *palanca*, you already know that in advance you have to return the favor at some point. It is not, "Oh, I did you this favor", unless it is a close friend and that only happens in extreme cases because nobody gives you anything for free.

How are *palanca* favors repaid? The rules of etiquette vary. They probably depend on the size or risk involved in using a palanca. Reciprocity may not be provided in a single act, but in several acts diluted over time. A civil servant gives an example of these codes of maintenance (in this case an invitation to lunch), rather than of "payment":

> The meal itself is unimportant: it is something symbolic, it is the oil that makes the machine work, it is not the energy, it is not the motor that moves the machine, it is merely the oil. It is the social relationship, the person who knows you, the one we see, the person with whom you always have to be present.

Corruption as a Cultural and Social Process **89**

The way *palancas* are handled is critical. It is a social relationship that requires art. A civil servant explains:

> I am struck by that as a woman, seeing how many things are handled and I am very analytical, when I see high-level groups, if I am seeing that and if I believe that there are skills and that it is an art, and that there are different forms of communicating, even through body language when favors are being asked; there are gestures that make the use of the *palanca* more effective.

There may be many words, codes, and polite phrases. Some examples from a civil servant:

> So I think that there are some classic forms, which include: "I owe you one"; I think that this is a fundamental characteristic. It can be explicit or it can be implicit but normally, instead of saying "thank you", thanks are given by saying: "I owe you one".

The following discussion is interesting, where the *palanca*, in the government, can have implications of imposition, rather than an exchange of favors:

> I think I have another connotation there too, sometimes it is the use of my position; that is, I give a slap and it's over. "I'm going to tell my boss: I'm going to use your name", I call and say: "I'm calling on behalf of... and he wants it tomorrow, he told me". It's a *palanca* and I'm not expecting any favors, I'm intimidating; I'm not expecting any favors, I'm giving an instruction; it's a *palanca*, I went and used my boss's name.

MODERATOR: And do you expect a favor there too?
CIVIL SERVANT: From my boss. Even though I solved the problem for him.

> [Laughter in the room]

MODERATOR: Even though you used his name?
CIVIL SERVANT: Well, I said: "Boss, do you want me to move things along?" He said yes, "So I'll use your name". I called and said that those were the Secretary's instructions. I moved the *palanca*.

Palancas are a social relationship commonly used in very different contexts and for different objectives and logics. It is no surprise that it is necessary to distinguish between *palancas* that more closely resemble improper actions or to bend the rules "unduly" from those that may be done (in people's eyes) for "good reasons" or for "a greater good". A civil servant had the following to say in this respect:

90 Corruption as a Dense Social Relationship

> In fact, that's why I said at the beginning of the discussion that there are *palancas* for private benefits and *palancas* for public benefits. I can talk about the second ones that sometimes have to be solved; the first ones are almost issues that you do not discuss anywhere in my position, because they are going to… they are going to do you a favor, but here in the arm and they are going to tell you that it is heavily frowned upon to get someone.

According to this same logic, another civil servant said:

> …because you have to be clear about who you ask, what you ask, and if you are the *palanca*, how far can you do or not do it, without doing something illegal or outside the shared values of what is right or wrong? I think you have to think it through properly.

Palancas have to be analyzed by people. In that respect, there are many things that should remain implicit, hidden, in the space of spoken and body language. Otherwise, the "magic" of the *palanca* can be diluted or even counterproductive. Because at the end of the day, it is an exchange that expands over time: a good *palanca* is one that lasts and is sustained over time by its prestige and reliability. The instrumentalization of the *palanca* is precisely the border that brings it closer to the violation of the rule, to corruption perhaps, to bribery or influence peddling. What prevents it from looking like this is precisely the fact that it is embedded in a social logic that gives it a different meaning: a nobler or more justifiable, less reprehensible one. The borders are, of course, very malleable, and can fall or be strengthened between one situation and the next.

The fact that the *palanca* is an "open secret" is its strength: it involves bending the rule for good, justifiable, necessary, and indispensable causes. Clumsy handling of the *palanca* can also reveal everything bad that exists in the hidden activity: that rules are violated, that processes are skipped, that something is obtained through influences rather than by merit. Clumsy handling reveals the worst elements of the *palanca*: secrecy becomes conspiracy, reciprocity illegal exchange, a necessary good a private business that violates the established rules. In addition, the *palanca* might realize she or he has been used. She or he then goes from being an acquintance to become a mere instrument (something that is sold and bought). If the *palanca* is made explicitly instrumental, then the charm is broken, the ambiguity that allows people to live with *palancas* without feeling bad, reducing the cognitive dissonance its use can cause (Festinger, 1957). In other words, thanks to its ambiguity, people hide the fact that it is an instrument and hide the fact that the *palanca* may involve an exchange of objects and benefits. So are *palancas* bad? Reducing cognitive dissonance, in this case, means hiding the instrumentality of the potential exchange that takes place between the person who provides the *palanca* and the person who uses it. The art of *palancas* is that secrecy, influence, and reciprocity remain justified and justifiable, socially speaking.

The **Palanca,** *Its Dark Side*

It seems, however, that there is a clear awareness that the *palanca* is located in a weak and complex border. Necessary perhaps, but always risky. In the words of one worker: *"However you look at it, it is corruption. Because for this, there are certain rules and when you break them you are already corrupting something. So it is a model of corruption".* Another worker, somewhat uncomfortably, tries to clarify the issue: *"You're not being honest, you know that asking for that favor is wrong. But we're going back to the same thing; it depends on your situation".* In response, another worker retorted: *"The thing is, when you do it, when you use a* palanca, *it's fine; when others do it and they make you wait longer, it's wrong. Because then you are only thinking of yourself and we always think like that".*

It is clear in the different groups, thanks to the discussion that developed around each one of them, that *palancas* are an exceptional mechanism; they are a mechanism for getting round rules and difficulties, although in order to justify them they are made more obvious. At this point in the session, there was palpable discomfort in the air. Some tried to make sense of that contradiction. One worker argued:

> And there are people who are rich and have possibilities and are worse than us. I feel that when we are poor we are ignored, so we have to choose whether to be honest or not. We have to find someone to pay attention to us or listen to us.

However, the contradiction remains. One citizen said: *"The fact that a* palanca *benefits you does not mean it was fair, because you avoided the whole process, the time, the filters, etc."*

This led to a discussion in the group as to whether *palancas* are fair. Another citizen felt the need to explain herself better: *"I do not want you to misunderstand me, what I meant is that there are nuances."* Another citizen said: *"They are necessary because sometimes the system does not work the way it should work and that's why we use them".*

The *palanca,* viewed from a social rather than a personal perspective, seems to be more problematic. A citizen pointed out:

> I do believe that people that do not have *palancas* might feel angry or upset. Maybe it is because, I do not know, maybe they feel repulsed by the authorities. If they do not have palancas, their paperwork is stuck and won't be resolved any other way... A little while ago I was thinking about the phrase, "If you don't cheat, you won't get anywhere" [a Mexican popular saying]. *Palancas* do not involve cheating, but in the end they cause the same thing.

Regarding this same logic of the necessary, albeit illegitimate, nature of *palancas,* one citizen said:

> I believe that the essence is what are you going to use it for? You are going to put pressure on someone to make something happen, to give you something,

92 Corruption as a Dense Social Relationship

to solve something, or to do something illegal for you. The fact that they put my file on top of someone else's means that I am already hurting someone.

The possible relationship between *palancas* and corruption emerges clearly in this last discussion. Individually, it can be a necessary and justified mechanism, although socially, when it has to be discussed (for example, in a focus group such as this one), the justification becomes more difficult and the link with issues such as corruption emerges more clearly at various times.

A discussion among citizens: *"They are illegitimate, because in the end they are skipping the process, they are giving privileges, they are giving space benefits… it is being given to a specific person and not to others; it also benefits the person who is doing something like that"*. Another citizen answers: *"But I don't think that makes it illegal"*. He responds to a previous citizen: *"It's not illegal but it is illegitimate"*.

There seems to be a generalized consensus about the inevitability of *palancas* in social relations in Mexico. Workers react to the inefficiency of services. Public servants believe that the bureaucratic organization itself, within it and in its own logic, needs it. A public servant highlights the fact that:

> You don't always have all the relevant agents sitting where decisions are going to be made, often because you do not even manage to see them all. My point is, the fact that the system is so rigid, because one thing is that your boss tells you what to do and you go to the operating rules and there you do not have to use one *palanca*, you have to use twenty thousand to get one thing done. For example, you have to know someone who convinces the Treasury to modify them and in another agency you have to know someone who will make a decision as quickly as possible so that you can make the modification and your boss doesn't care about that.

Probably the best way to summarize the importance and role of *palancas* in a country like Mexico is provided by a public servant: *"Life is all about getting palancas"*.

Palancas: The Social Density of Relationships between Acquaintances

Palancas can be understood as a mechanism of countries, such as Mexico, that have experienced entrenched political processes where the authorities are supposed to be impartial, but are not in fact impartial (Morris, 1999). And people know this and see it every day. Mexican society is perfectly capable of understanding the schizophrenia and hypocrisy of the political and governmental system: where the formal language of the authorities speaks of legality and impartiality, but this discourse is known to be false. The authorities are substantively partial and disrespectful of the formal rules and legality itself. People know it and the authorities know it. How is it possible to understand and live in this kind of dual world? A world with legal and impartial language but where everyday life is quite the opposite. What Mungiu-Pippidi calls particularistic societies (Mungiu-Pippidi, 2015), Kurer discriminatory societies (Kurer, 2005), and Rothstein and Varraich (2017) societies where the principle of impartiality fails.

In these societies, there is little point in believing that the authorities will be impartial, even if they repeat this in their laws, speeches, and official documents. The rules of the game are that they are not. This schizophrenic duality therefore opens the doors to a social game of masks, poses, and skills that must be acquired, developed, and maintained: the game of influences. This is a common element shared by *palancas, guanxi, blat,* and *jeitinho*: everyday life unfolds through influences. In the social arena, there is therefore an arena of networks of influence, with the condition that, strictly speaking, everyone can participate in the game. Everyone can hope that, with the right influence, even people living in poverty or disadvantage can get what they need.

It is in this context that *palancas* have probably flourished in Mexico. Precisely because it is a game that allows people to have hope (as Nuijten [2003] convincingly shows in his study of rural Mexico): you can get services and benefits from the authorities, even if you do not belong to their closed, privileged circle. How does one access these services and benefits? Through the proper use of networks of acquaintances. The use of these networks implies reciprocal dynamics that range from being highly instrumental (becoming practically logics of bribes) to other more ambiguous dynamics of reciprocity: you scratch my back, I'll scratch yours, for example. The *palanca* is justified and legitimized, uncomfortably so, but legitimized. The border between *palanca* and bribe or influence peddling is ambiguous and reconstructable. But the point is that it is a structural part of the relationship between people and between the latter and power, which involves emotional elements even (Breit, Lennerfors, & Olaison, 2015), even in a relationship such as the *palanca*, even when it leads to improper or corrupt acts. Relationships between people, relationships involving the exchange of favors, imply understanding the social processes that are created: a corrupt act may not have begun with corrupt acts. The border between what some have called "soft" corruption (Schluter, 2017) and serious corruption may be an issue that depends on the point in the chain of events being analyzed. Improper and proper actions, different conceptualizations among different people regarding the legitimacy or otherwise of a particular act, the situationality of each act, and the emotions involved in the interactions mean that in many countries, generalized interaction networks are the basis of a logic endemic to corruption, which is extremely difficult to address because it takes place in everyday common and indispensable social practices.

This intricate logic of reciprocity constitutes a dynamic, broadly effective circle: a circle that is repeated and reproduced. The different logics of reciprocity, many of them ambiguous, extend the tangle of languages and codes learned in practice and shared in groups, creating different options for their use, all specific to certain circumstances and sectors.

94 Corruption as a Dense Social Relationship

This obviously means that there are islands with different degrees of formalization of *palancas*. In other words, in certain circumstances and with certain actors, *palancas* can be quasi-organized. They do not become formal, but they may be close to becoming so. The logic of the reciprocity of various *palancas* can be properly established and sophisticatedly organized. Its reproduction is therefore more solid and permanent.

This logical chain of *palancas* that people know and explain in the focus groups is a good indication that the clue that links this social practice to corruption seems solid. Nuijten and Anders (2007) have advanced the hypothesis of how, in various social realities dominated by particularism, logics such as *palancas*, influence peddling, and corruption end up being highly functional, socially and politically (Fisman & Golden, 2017, p. 27). The *palanca*, with its dynamics, rules, and stability, gives people the hope that through skill and tenacity, the most diverse problems can be solved. It is possible to find the most suitable ways of bending the rules: many of them are seen as unfair or frankly intentionally constructed to force people precisely to look for a parallel path. More perversely, *palancas* not only serve to give people from the lowest strata of society hope for a solution to their problems. The *palanca* is also an instrument of people with power and resources: it is a path open to conspiracy and collusions that can be extremely productive and efficient for enriching and expanding their power. Through *palancas*, politicians and businessmen find parallel ways to bypass anticorruption and anti-fraud regulations, build alliances, and obtain contracts.

The *palanca* is a social and cultural construction that is extremely widespread and much appreciated in Mexico (and we have seen that there are similar mechanisms in other countries in Latin America and the world). The fact that it is so highly valued socially is probably due to the fact that it is an equalizing mechanism available to everyone: the collective imaginary appears to assume that having *palancas* is a matter of intelligence and skill. In a context where authorities, of all kinds, are seen as distant and clearly an elite separated from people in general (Lomnitz, 1996), *palancas* are therefore apparently a democratic mechanism or at least one capable of generating justice: anyone can have *palancas* and use them to escape the trap of Kafkaesque bureaucracy. But in fact, *palancas* are paradoxical: using *palancas* is a logic of privilege to escape the privileges of a few. *Palancas* are probably a social mechanism providing a false solution; in other words, they end up perpetuating the logic of privileges. Hence the intricate and dangerous relationship between *palancas* and corruption: corruption is not an accident or a disease of the system. *Palancas* feed a logic of the informal, of parallel paths, of the legitimacy of bending the rules and turning them around. This has been conceptualized in psychology as "perverse rules": rules that are broken in any way are accepted by people, are well known, but are not obeyed, so to speak (Fernandez-Dols, 1993; Fernandez-Dols & Oceja, 1994). And, therefore, in keeping with that rationality, corruption can be part of an underground but normalized reality, socially accepted as essential, or at least justifiable in certain circumstances. If the world of the informal is a way out of the unjust world of the formal, corruption forms part of particularistic practices that are justified on a case-by-case basis. That is, obeying rules is ultimately appropriate and correct. But in a messy world, things have to be measured, socially speaking, on a case-by-case basis. *Palancas* are not justified in general, but on a case-by-case, need-by-need basis. Corruption, in this respect, thrives on this very particularism: it can be undesirable for anyone; in the abstract it is a deplorable matter for anyone. But in practice, in everyday situations, an event may be transformed to be justified. Justified and rationalized. The same event that is corrupt can be rationalized as necessary, as justifiable in a particular case. There is an obvious dilemma: the *palanca* is a mechanism that tries to get around the privileges of a few in an unequal society, but ends up reproducing the very logic of the privileges it deplores. The most skilled, the most "cunning" people end up having more *palancas* and therefore having access to more privileges. The *palanca* is an illusion: the hope produced by *palancas* that there is always a way to solve problems. But it builds the social basis of the violation of rules, or at least of bending them, justifiably. And it ends up being the social basis of corruption, which makes it stable, acceptable, and resilient. It is worth continuing along these lines.

It is worth including a final argument that gives a slightly different meaning to the role of social mechanisms such as *palancas*. Taking the point that the mechanisms of the exchange of favors are socially "dense" to an extreme, what would it imply to think that more than a mechanism, the logic of exchanges of favors, in certain countries and cultures, is a substantively rational means of obtaining certain ends? In other words, thinking that mechanisms such as *palancas* are merely the symptom of a highly rational way of achieving the most precious social objectives within a society that defends or is based on certain ends and values, which may be different from those of the classical instrumental, prototypical rationality of the West. Dealy has attempted to construct precisely this conceptualization (Dealy, 1977). In short, Dealy argues that understanding the aims of particularist societies in the style of Latin American countries helps enormously to understand the logic of the strategies for relating in these societies. The purpose of these societies, probably derived from their solid Catholic tradition, claims Dealy, leads to a form of socialization based on people's search for public relevance, as an end. Just as the classic Western person seeks to accumulate wealth through work, the public man (as Dealy calls him) seeks to accumulate contacts, acquaintances, and friends. This is because what makes a person in these societies is their role and importance in the public space: who knows you, and how many people know you, is a sign of your worth. Particularism is therefore rational: it knows the right means for achieving the goals and values that are respected and sought (Dealy, 1977, p. 10). Cultivating friendships and contacts is critical and necessary; the public man is a person surrounded by other people as a sign of success. The implications of this extreme argument are clear: mechanisms such as *palancas* are not pathologies in these societies, but functional, effective arrangements. Cultivating and maintaining friendships and acquaintances acquires a much greater instrumental sense than the exchange of favors: the cunning acquisition and cultivation of friendships constitutes the basis on which power and influence are socially created and distributed.

96 Corruption as a Dense Social Relationship

If this is so, corruption appears as a concept that requires a very important social and cultural transformation for its delegitimization. This should begin with the fact that the normative definitions of corruption make very little sense in this type of society: the improper use of a power granted for private benefit forces us to assume that there are fairly precise boundaries of a separation understood and accepted between the private and the collective. These are two spheres really assumed as distinct (Bratsis, 2003). This is a strange question for a society where the private cannot be constituted without being intimately intertwined with the collective, because it is ultimately in that collective that the game of influence, friendship, and the bonds between acquaintances and people is played out in a sphere, the collective sphere, which is where a person's worth is defined. Abusing the collective for private purposes, in a society of the public man à la Dealy, would be quite different: it might involve abusing friendships and relationships without offering some form of reciprocity or hope of reciprocity for favors. But in this type of society, trying to influence and affect, for example, the processes of government bureaucracies and their decisions, does not appear as a contradiction, since anyone who seeks to nurture and improve their prestige and influence must be able to prove the ability to influence in that way. The contradiction is obvious: a fight against corruption that posits abstract concepts of a clear, substantive separation between the collective and the private would find it difficult to make sense in societies such as this one.

This last statement is obviously extreme: it implies an ideal type of society of the public man that probably no longer exists. In other words, it would be more possible and useful to think that contemporary Latin American societies are a hybrid: a social logic that continues to be supported by a particularistic dynamic of the public man, but in a context that has constantly and systematically promoted and introduced the strange idea of a possible, sharp and clear separation between the collective and the private. This hybrid probably produces more intricate dynamics, with an increasingly difficult coexistence of mechanisms such as *palancas* or *pituto* or *jeitinho*, together with normative frameworks that tend to make these practices increasingly less accepted or legitimized, at least in the formal or normative sphere. Legally, more and more acts can be classified as improper or even illegal, reducing the scope, although not completely, for informal practices that make a great deal of sense for solving real problems. In any case, it seems important to maintain this extreme vision of the sociality and density of social practices, which is still so highly valued in these countries, and the rude shock involved in the introduction of concepts as abstract and normative as those that the fight against corruption generally uses to justify and propose solutions.

The Logic of Favors and Exchanges and Their Relationship with Corruption

After this brief account of the various social mechanisms based on the logic of favors and exchange, it is worth focusing on understanding how the logic of favors and exchanges relates to corruption. Indeed, it is possible to appreciate in all the literature consulted that there is no clear line that can indicate when these practices go beyond the illegal line and become acts of corruption. However, there is a tacit recognition of the ambiguity of these mechanisms since there are various negative and positive conceptions of this type of practice in all the cases we have discussed here. On the one hand, the values identified evoke positive practices and solidarity, trust, as well as resistance to excessively rigid processes. On the other hand, the use of these practices can encourage differences between those who do or do not have contacts, which creates or reinforces differences in access to goods or services and perpetuates social inequalities based on personal relationships rather than factors such as merit and personal effort.

Exchange between people in a society is a matter of contact, often face to face, where the familial, labor and social context, matters, affects, and is considered. They can be extremely dense and deep, requiring efforts to obtain more information, affected by logics of empathy, and emotions. They can be carried out through processes such as negotiation, gift-giving, solidarity, or reciprocity, which includes the abuse of power and redistribution. The effects of these relationships can be very durable and intense, given that people act in environments of values and rules with fuzzy borders between what is socially appropriate and inappropriate. People need to interpret, make sense, and rationalize the processes of exchange in which they are inserted—sometimes rationalizing in a conscientious way and at other times less so.

Corruption is a form or mechanism of exchange. And as such, it is permanently connected with other forms of exchange. Perhaps because of this first relationship, the theory of social exchange tends to study corruption on a small scale. Despite the great capacity for explanation of the analysis of the logic of favors or social exchange, it tends to over-emphasize "small-scale" corruption and, in this respect, explains corruption "on a large scale" to a lesser extent (Torsello, 2011, 2014). And it may also give clues as to why anticorruption reforms in societies with systemic corruption fail (Mungiu-Pippidi, 2006, p. 87; Persson, Rothstein, & Teorell, 2012)

The logic of negotiation assumes that in acts of corruption there is a negotiation of the rules, in the sense of their relevance and their interpretation, which may include a rhetorical dimension in the use of language to circumvent the norm, as in the case of *palancas*. Therefore, negotiation is a logic that cannot be separated from improper practice, so much so that if this practice has been trivialized in society, it becomes part of everyday negotiations (Olivier de Sardan, 1999). It should be said that this opens up the possibility of directly relating the degree of vagueness of the rules of a society with the practices of corruption, with a bargaining background that is broader the less concrete the rules are.

There is a spectrum of action of individuals in which the relationship between the logic of *gift-giving* and corruption coexists. This spectrum is expanded or reduced by the prevalence of a "moral duty" that societies incorporate into their logic of exchange: "there is a very thin line between corruption and the practice of gift-giving in everyday life. The multiplication of 'presents' in everyday practice provides scope for hiding [drowning] illicit presents in the great mass that exists of them" (Olivier de Sardan, 1999, p. 40).

98 Corruption as a Dense Social Relationship

Corrupt relationships can literally be socially transformed into relationships of a different kind, which are less morally and socially questionable. This is achieved through practices of secrecy or camouflage, or agreements that justify acts to make them more "normal" (Alatas, 1999). Corruption is socially constructed from a process of transfiguration of acts that make them more "acceptable" or as Darley (2005, p. 1185) would say: people are ethical, but they are so intermittently. The relationship between the logic of solidarity networks or reciprocity and corruption has to do with a growing intervention of the networks on behalf of the people who comprise them. Interventions are progressively normalized. They become ways of acting and are trivialized. When personal favors are found in most social aspects, there is a risk of falling into functional dysfunctions of the network, either because people act on the outer limits of what is established in the framework of social rules or because the need to be reciprocal with the members of the network is superimposed. Again, the line between what is appropriate and inappropriate in the favoritism for a group to which one belongs can fall into an area of ambiguity if one acts in the normative sense, or in the sense of favoring social capital. The foregoing is also a function of the vagueness of the norms and the values societies have developed. As has been shown experimentally at least, in contexts where exchange practices are linked to corruption, people tend to perceive that normatively, that interconnection is valid or at least acceptable, encouraging them to engage in corrupt behaviors as something normal (Kobis, Prooijen, Righetti, & Van Lange, 2015, p. 12).

The practices analyzed break or circumvent bureaucratic rigidity, strengthen social relations, and help distribute goods and services, while the cost of these functions translates into greater social and economic inequality. Confidence, solidarity, and reciprocity are strongly linked to group identity, which translates into dynamics of conditioning, exclusion, or marginalization for people who do not belong to these groups. That is, even in cases where we have rigid, inefficient institutions in the distribution of public goods and services—which represents an initial problem of access to the latter for the entire population—the implementation of the logic of the exchange of favors implies new conditions and criteria of access that never manage to include the entire population.

In the case of Chile, *pituto* has been considered as one of the factors that accentuates inequality and differences between social classes (Garretón & Cumsille, 1994, p. 2). In Brazil, there are negative perceptions that regard this practice as corruption, because it is outside the norm and produces negative consequences (Guerra, Cortez, & Diogo, 2016). Marinoni and Becker (2003) cite the example of litigant lawyers whose triumphs are determined by their connections and ability to obtain *jeitinhos*: lawyers who succeed by achieving connections outside the norm, which are usually the most expensive ones.

Guanxi has also been conceived as an element that affords an advantage and closes business circles. Since it is a mechanism that implies lasting social relationships, there may be business elites that take advantage of the chains of favors. Using favors from the government, not allowing the entry of new competition or influencing decision making are examples of negative actions surrounding *guanxi*, which are possible because of the informal nature of the way it is performed. Within this logic of favors, whoever gains access to high social levels usually points this out and his/her group observes that he/she has succeeded. However, there is a moral duty that indicates he/she should extend the benefit to his/her family, friends, or acquaintances, as in the Israeli case. This logic lends a social meaning to acts such as nepotism, for example. When a person fails to comply with particularist social obligations (such as giving preference to acquaintances or relatives), the social groups to which he/she belongs can either frown on this or label him/her a disloyal person. As noted earlier, a perverse logic comes into play: nepotism in the abstract or legally speaking can be socially deplorable, but the final judgment of the groups and therefore of society is de facto in the concrete situation, on a case-by-case basis.

The logic of the exchange of favors and their social practices have more "white" or "less harmful" expressions compared to more serious types of corruption. Many of the studies considered in this chapter begin by identifying the exchange of favors as a "white" or "gray" type of corruption that may be widely accepted by society. However, returning to the understanding of corruption as a social relation, many of the principles, logics, and practices involved in the exchange of favors facilitate or encourage other practices of corruption such as bribery, patronage, or the purchase of favors. The *spillover-effect of corruption* theory argues that accepting "white" corruption may end up making grayer or black forms of corruption acceptable or normal (Zelekha & Werner, 2011).

In the case of *palancas*, the same process of the social "slide" is observed: one where a logic of exchange between people that may be innocuous or innocent socially escalates to build a broad social base of acts that are rationalized and normalized, including corrupt acts. And this even includes clearly organized, large-scale acts of corruption, which reveal a hidden order of corruption that can be extremely stable and lasting (Della Porta & Vannucci, 2016).

Corruption can therefore be a by-product of other relationships, meaning that corruption does not actually start with corrupt acts (not always, at least) (Darley, 2005, p. 1180). Before activating a *palanca*, the petitioner and the *palanca* that will carry out the action requested already know or suspect whether what they will do is or is not legal. But the rules of etiquette, languages, and forms make it possible to hide or divert attention. People go into a special room, so to speak, where the rules of the game are different: they talk about favors, exchange, due to fidelity, friendship, and affinity. A kind of moral obligation is even constructed among participants to provide help and support: it is not only or mainly merely a sphere of calculation, but one of bonds and moral and relational obligations or duties (Baez-Camargo & Passas, 2017, p. 13).

Language helps a great deal: words such as skirting the rules are not used, but rather the ability to solve a problem quickly. There is no talk of bribery; there is talk of gifts. There is no talk of collusion, but of mutual support in a group of acquaintances. Emotionally, people can even protect themselves. Indeed, *palancas*

100 Corruption as a Dense Social Relationship

create a variety of different emotions: of solidarity and favors received and support obtained, creating bonds of gratitude, for example. These emotions therefore make it easier for people to rationalize, to create even moral reasons that justify their actions (Epley & Caruso, 2004, p. 181). In a scenario of continuous *palancas*, the rationale is to strategically follow a tactic of sowing links with influential friends and acquaintances, as well as to know when to use them and maintain a presence in them, in order to preserve confidence and willingness when support is required.

The use of *palancas* or *guanxi* or *jeitinho* comprises a very broad spectrum of shades where the exchange of support and favors can range from acts that can be framed as bribery and influence peddling to the sphere of "the normal, everyday chain of favors" between work colleagues, where rule bending is a recurrent alternative for resolving issues in the work and programmatic agenda of an organization. The complexity of this conceptually radial phenomenon shows that there is still a broad agenda of empirical studies remaining to be done to understand how interpersonal relationships, trust, reciprocity, and commitment among actors is a dimension in constant tension with doing the right thing and the function of impartiality, whereby the modern world demands that individuals act as servants or members of an organization. Thus, the logic of the reciprocity of various *palancas* can be well established and sophisticatedly organized. Its reproduction is therefore more solid and permanent.

Nuijten and Anders (2007) have advanced the hypothesis of how, in various social realities where particularism dominates, logics such as *palancas*, influence and corruption end up being functional (Fisman & Golden, 2017, p. 27), constituting normal, effective logics so that political groups can perpetuate themselves in the control of the arena of power. Accordingly, *palancas* and corruption are not therefore "dysfunctional" practices and behaviors. On the contrary, they are the center of the logic of the reproduction of power of various societies.

One of the most perverse aspects of the logic of the exchange of favors such as these is undoubtedly the vicious circle it constructs. *Palancas* are apparently available to everyone: the collective imaginary appears to assume that having *palancas* is a matter of intelligence and skill. Apparently, then, it is a democratic mechanism or at least one capable of creating justice. Anyone can have *palancas* and use them to escape the trap of Kafkaesque bureaucracy. But in fact, *palancas* are paradoxical: using *palancas* is a logic of privilege to escape the privileges of a few. *Palancas* are probably a social mechanism providing a false solution; in other words, they end up perpetuating the logic of privileges. Hence the intricate and dangerous relationship between *palancas* and corruption: corruption is not an accident or a disease of the system. *Palancas* feed a logic of the informal, of parallel paths, of the legitimacy of bending the rules and turning them around. Therefore, according to this rationality, corruption can be part of an underground but normalized reality, socially accepted as indispensable, or at least justifiable in certain circumstances. If the world of the informal is a way out of the unjust world of the formal, corruption forms part of particularist practices that are justified on a case-by-case basis. Moreover, this network of exchange relationships also explains and allows us to study one of the paradoxes that has most surprised various scholars of corruption: that it can be organized, that people can build systematic spaces that create stability and are sustained over time, in the long term, despite their apparent regulatory undesirability (Johnston & Doig, 1999, p. 14).

Palancas are not justified in general, but on a case-by-case, need-by-need basis. Corruption, in this respect, is part of a logic that is at the same time undesirable: it is undesirable in the abstract but justifiable on a case-by-case basis, in everyday life. An essential part of its logic, then, lies in a dynamic of privileges and social ways of accessing privileges through, in this case, an illusion: the hope produced by *palancas* that there is always a way to solve problems.

Bibliography

Alatas, S. H. (1999). *Corruption and the destiny of Asia*. Englewood Cliffs, NJ: Prentice Hall.

Aliyev, H. (2013). Post-communist informal networking: *Blat* in the South Caucasus. *Demokratizatsiya: The Journal of Post-Soviet Democratization*, 21(1), 89–112.

Anderson, L. (2012). Corruption in Russia: Past, present and future. In C. Funderburk (Ed.), *Political corruption in comparative perspective* (pp. 71–94). London, England: Routledge.

Andvig, J., & Moene, K. (1990). How corruption may corrupt. *Journal of Economic Behavior and Organization*, 13, 63–76.

Arellano-Gault, D. (2018). Government corruption: An exogenous factor in companies' victimization? *Public Integrity*. doi:10.1080/10999922.2018.1433425.

Ashton, V., & Lof, R. (2015). *Who wants to be a Brazilionaire? Deciphering the mystery of jeitinho and how it may influence Swedish companies doing business in Brazil.* (Unpublished doctoral dissertation). Linnaeus University, Sweden.

Baez-Camargo, C., & Passas, N. (2017). *Hidden agendas, social norms and why we need to rethink anti-corruption*. Basel, Switzerland: Basel Institute on Governance.

Barozet, E. (2002). *El intercambio de favores en las capas medias en Chile: Un marco antropológico para la reforma de la gerencia pública*. Centro Latinoamericano para la Administración del Desarrollo. Retrieved from https://studylib.es/doc/6380294/el-intercambio-de-favores-a l-seno-de-las-capas-medias-chi…

Barozet, E. (2006). El valor histórico del pituto: Clase media, integración y diferenciación social en Chile. *Revista de Sociología*, 20, 69–96.

Bauhr, M. (2017). Need or greed? Conditions for collective action against corruption. *Governance: An International Journal of Policy, Administration and Institutions*, 30(4), 561–581. doi:10.1111/gove.12232.

Belle, N., & Cantarelli, P. (2017). What causes unethical behavior? A meta-analysis to set an agenda for public administration research. *Review of Public Administration*, 77(3), 327–339. doi:10.1111/puar.12714.

Blasco, J., López, A., & Mengual, S. (2010). Validación mediante método Delphi de un cuestionario para conocer las experiencias e interés hacia las actividades acuáticas con especial atención al windsurf. *Ágora*, 1, 75–96.

Blundo, G., & Olivier de Sardan, J. P. (2001). Sémiologie populaire de la corruption. *Politique africaine*, 3(83), 98–114.

Bourdieu, P. (1977). *Outline of a theory of practice*. Cambridge, England: Cambridge University Press.

Bratsis, P. (2003). The construction of corruption, or rules of separation and illusions of purity in bourgeois societies. *Social Text*, 77(21–24), 9–33.

102 Corruption as a Dense Social Relationship

Breit, E., Lennerfors, T., & Olaison, L. (2015). Critiquing corruption: A turn to theory. *Ephemera: Theory & Politics in Organization*, 15(2), 319–336.

Cameron, L., Chaudhuri, A., Erkal, N., & Gangadharan, L. (2005). *Do attitudes toward corruption differ across cultures? Experimental evidence from Australia, India, Indonesia and Singapore*. Research Paper 943. Melbourne, Australia: The University of Melbourne.

Castor, B. (2002). *Brazil is not for amateurs: Patterns of governance in the land of jeitinho*. Philadelphia, PA: Xlibris.

Chandler, D. (2002). *Semiotics: the basics*. London, England: Routledge.

Colombatto, E. (2003). Why is corruption tolerated? *The Review of Austrian Economics*, 16(4), 363–379.

Danet, B. (1990). Protektzia: The roots of organizational biculturalism among Israeli Jews. *Social Forces*, 68(3), 909–932.

Darley, J. (2005). The cognitive and social psychology of the contagious organizational corruption. *Brooklyn Law Review*, 70(4), 1177–1194.

De Graaf, G. (2007). Causes of corruption: Towards a contextual theory of corruption. *Public Administration Quarterly*, 31(1/2), 38–86.

De Graaf, G., & Huberts, L.W. (2008). Portraying the nature of corruption using an explorative case study design. *Public Administration Review*, 68(4), 640–653. doi:10.1111/j.1540–6210.2008.00904.x.

De Paiva, F. (2018). Jeitinho, Brazil. In A. Ledeneva (Ed.), *The global encyclopedia of informality* (Vol. 1; pp. 43–46). London, England: UCL Press.

De Sousa, L. (2012). 'Above the law, below the ethics': Some findings on Portuguese attitudes toward corruption. In D. K. Tanlzar, K. Maras, & A. Giannakopoulos (Eds.), *The social construction of corruption in Europe* (pp. 245–264). London, UK: Routledge.

De Zwart, F. (2010). Corruption and anti-corruption in prismatic societies. In P. De Graaf & P. Wagenaar (Eds.), *The good cause: Theoretical perspectives on corruption* (pp. 34–46). Opladen, Germany: Barbara Budrch Press.

Dealy, G. C. (1977). *The public man: An interpretation of Latin American and other Catholic countries*. Amherst, MA: The University of Massachusetts Press.

Della Porta, D., & Vannucci, A. (2016). *The hidden order of corruption*. London, England: Routledge.

Depuy, K., & Neset, S. (2018). *The cognitive psychology of corruption*. Oslo, Norway: U4 Anti-corruption resource Center. Chr. Michelsen Institute.

Djawadi, B. M., & Fahr, R. (2015). "...and they are really lying": Clean evidence on the pervasiveness of cheating in professional contexts from a field experiment. *Journal of Economic Psychology*, 48, 48–59. doi:10.1016.j.joep.2015.03.002.

Dos Santos, M. (2014). *Cultura e identidad: Interacción y conflicto en la construcción de una cultura común brasileña* (Unpublished doctoral dissertation). Universidad Complutense de Madrid, Madrid.

Duarte, F. (2011). The strategic role of charm, simpatía and jeitinho in Brazilian society: A qualitative study. *Asian Journal of Latina American Studies*, 24(3), 29–48.

Durston, J. (2005). El clientelismo político en el campo chileno (primera parte): La democratización cuestionada. *Ciencias Sociales Online*, 2(1), 1–30.

Eisenstadt, S. N., & Roniger, L. (1984). *Patrons, clients and friends*. Cambridge, England: Cambridge University Press.

Engel, E. et al. (2018). *Report of the expert advisory group on anti-corruption, transparency, and integrity in Latin America and the Caribbean*. Washington, DC: IDB.

Epley, N., & Caruso, E. (2004). Egocentric ethics. *Social Justice Research*, 17(2), 171–187. doi:0885-7466/04/0600–0171/0.

Etzioni-Halevy, E. (1975). Some patterns of semi-deviations on the Israeli social scene. *Social Problems*, 22(3), 356–367.

Even-Shoshan, A. (1983). *The new dictionary*. Ha'milon ha'xadash, Jerusalem: Kiryat-Sefer.

Fernandez-Dols, J. M. (1993). Norma perversa: Hipótesis teóricas. *Psicothema*, 5, 91–101.

Fernandez-Dols, J. M., & Oceja, L. V. (1994). Efectos cotidianos de las normas perversas en la tolerancia a la corrupción. *Revista de Psicología Social*, 9(1), 3–12.

Festinger, L. (1957). *A theory of cognitive dissonance*. Stanford, CA: Stanford University Press.

Fisman, R., & Golden, M. (2017). *Corruption: What everyone needs to know*. Oxford, England: Oxford University Press.

Galnoor, I., Rosenbloom, D. H., & Yaroni, A. (1998). Creating new public management reforms: Lessons from Israel. *Administration & Society*, 30(4), 393–420.

Gambetta, D. (1993). *The Sicilian mafia: The business of private protection*. Cambridge, MA: Harvard University Press.

Garretón, M., & Cumsille, G. (1994). Las percepciones de la desigualdad en Chile. *Proposiciones*, 34.

Goffman, E. (1981). *La presentación de la persona en la vida cotidiana*. Buenos Aires, Argentina: Amorrortu.

Graf Lambsdorff, J., & Frank, B. (2010). Bribing versus gift-giving: An experiment. *Journal of Economic Psychology*, 31, 247–357.

Graycar, A., & Jancsics, D. (2016). Gift giving and corruption. *International Journal of Public Administration*, 1–11. doi:10.1080/01900692.2016.1177833.

Guerra, A., Cortez, D., & Diogo, H. (2016). Brazilian jeitinho and culture: An analysis of the films elite squad 1 and 2. *Revista Administración Mackenzie*, 17(3), 84–104.

Guerrero, M. A., & Rodríguez-Oreggia, E. (2008). On the individual decisions to commit corruption: A methodological complement. *Journal of Economic Behavior & Organization*, 65, 357–372. doi:10.1016/j.jebo.2005.09.006.

Gupta, A. (1995). Blurred boundaries: The discourse of corruption, the culture of politics, and the imagined state. *American Ethnologist*, 22(2), 375–402.

Hardin, R. (1993). The street-level epistemology of trust. *Politics and Society*, 21(4), 505–529.

Hoffman, L. K., & Patel, R. N. (2017). *Collective action on corruption in Nigeria: A social norms approach to connecting society and institutions*. London, England: Chatham House.

Jain, A. (1998). *Economics of corruption*. New York: Springer.

Jain, A. (2001). *The political economy of corruption*. London, England: Routledge.

Johnston, M., & Doig, A. (1999). Different views on good government and sustainable anticorruption strategies. In R. Stapenhurs & S. Kpundeh (Eds.), *Curbing corruption: Toward a model of building national integrity* (pp. 13–34). Washington, DC: The World Bank.

Kobis, N., Prooijen, J. W., Righetti, F., & Van Lange, P. (2015). "Who doesn't" – The impact of descriptive norms of corruption". *Plos One*, 10(6), e0131830. doi:10.1371/journal.pone.0131830.

Kurer, O. (2005). Corruption: An alternative approach to its definitions and measurement. *Political Studies*, 53, 222–239.

Ledeneva, A. (1998). *Russia's economy of favours: Blat, networking and informal exchange*. Cambridge, England: Cambridge University Press.

Ledeneva, A. (2008). "Blat" and "guanxi": Informal practices in Russia and China. *Comparative Studies in Society and History*, 50(1), 118–144.

Ledeneva, A. (2011). Open secrets and knowing smiles. *East European Politics and Societies*, 25(4), 720–736.

Ledeneva, A. (Ed.). (2018). *The global encyclopedia of informality*. Vol. 1 and 2. London, England: UCL Press.

Liang-Hung, L. (2011). Cultural and organizational antecedents of Guanxi: The Chinese cases. *Journal of Business Ethics*, 99, 441–451.

Lomnitz, C. (coord.). (2000). *Vicios públicos, virtudes privadas: La corrupción en México*. Mexico City, Mexico: Ciesas-M.A. Porrúa.

Lomnitz, L. (1990). Redes informales de intercambio en sistemas formales: Un modelo teórico. *Comercio Exterior*, 40(3), 212–220.

Lomnitz, L. (1996). El compadrazgo, reciprocidad de favores en la clase media urbana de Chile. In L. Lomnitz (Ed.), *Redes sociales, cultura y poder: Ensayos de antropología latinoamericana* (pp. 68–84). Mexico City: Flacso.

Luehrmann, L. (2012). Corruption in China: Red capitalists on parade. In C. Funderburk (Ed.), *Political corruption in comparative perspective* (pp. 95–116). London: Routledge.

Luo, Y., Huang, Y., & Wang, S. (2011). Guanxi and organizational performance: A meta-analysis. *Management and Organization Review*, 8(1), 139–172.

Marinoni, L., & Becker, L. (2003). *Influencia de las relaciones personales sobre la abogacía y el proceso civil brasileño*. Paper presented at the Congreso Mundial de Derecho Procesal, Mexico City, Mexico.

Mauss, M. (2002). *The gifts: The form and reason for exchange in archaic societies*. London, UK: Routledge.

Maynard-Moody, S., & Mosheno, M. (2003). *Cops, teachers, counselors: Stories from the front lines of public service*. Ann Arbor, MI: University of Michigan Press.

Morris, S. (1999). Corruption and the Mexican political system: Continuity and change. *Third World Quarterly*, 20(3), 623–643.

Muir, S., & Gupta, A. (2018). Rethinking the anthropology of corruption. *Current Anthropology*, 59(18), 4–15.

Mungiu-Pippidi, A. (2006). Corruption: Diagnosis and treatment. *Journal of Democracy*, 17(3), 86–99.

Mungiu-Pippidi, A. (2015). *The quest for good governance*. Cambridge, England: Cambridge University Press.

Nuijten, M. (2003). *Power, community and the state: The political anthropology of organization in Mexico*. Sidmouth, England: Pluto Press.

Nuijten, M., & Anders, G. (2007). *Corruption and the secret of law: A legal anthropological perspective*. Aldersoth, England: Ashgate.

Olivier de Sardan, J. (1999). A moral economy of corruption in Africa? *The Journal of Modern African Studies*, 37(1), 25–52.

Persson, A., Rothstein, B., & Teorell, J. (2012). Why anticorruption reforms fail: Systemic corruption as a collective action problem. *Governance: An International Journal of Policy, Administration and Institutions*. doi:10.1111/j.1468.0491.2012.01604.x.

Putnam, R. (2000). *Bowling alone: The collapse and revival of American community*. New York: Simon & Schuster.

Rehn, A., & Taalas, S. (2004). Znakomstva I Svyazi' (Acquaintances and connections) – *Blat*, the Soviet Union, and mundane entrepreneurship. *Entrepreneurship & Regional Development*, 16(3), 235–250.

Reja, B., & Talvitie, A. (2012). Observed differences in corruption between Asia and Africa: The industrial organization of corruption and its cure. *International Public Management Review*, 13(2), 112–141.

Rostila, M. (2010). The facets of social capital. *Journal for the Theory of Social Behaviour*, 41(3), 308–326.

Rothstein, B. (2005). *Social traps and the problem of trust*. Cambridge, England: Cambridge University Press.

Rothstein, B. (2011). *The quality of government: Corruption, social trust, and inequality in international perspective.* Chicago, IL: Chicago University Press.

Rothstein, B., & Varraich, A. (2017). *Making sense of corruption.* Cambridge, England: Cambridge University Press.

Rusch, J. (2016). *The social psychology of corruption.* Paper presented at the 2016 OECD Integrity Forum, Paris.

Schluter, W. (2017). *Soft corruption.* New Brunswick, NJ: Rutgers University Press.

Sissener, T. (2001). *Anthropological perspectives on corruption.* Bergen, Norway: CMI Working Papers.

Smith, D. J. (2007). *A culture of corruption: Everyday deception and popular discontent in Nigeria.* Princeton, NJ: Princeton University Press.

Smith, D. J. (2018). Corruption and 'culture' in anthropology and in Nigeria. *Current Anthropology, 59*(18), 83–91.

Smith, P., Huang, H., Harb, C., & Torres, C. (2012). How distinctive are indigenous ways of achieving influence? A comparative study of Gauxi, Wasta, Jeitinho and Pulling Strings. *Journal of Cross-cultural Psychology, 1*(43), 135–150.

Tapia Tovar, E., & Zalpa, G. (2011). La corrupción a la luz de los dichos y refranes. *Relaciones, 32,* 21–65.

Torres, C. V., Alfinito, S., De Souza Pinto Galvao, C. A., & Yin Tse, B. C. (2015). Brazilian Jeitinho versus Chinese Guanxi: Investigating their informal influence on international business. *Revista de Administração Mackenzie, 16*(4), 77–99.

Torsello, D. (2011). *The ethnography of corruption: Research themes in political anthropology.* University of Gothenburg: QoG Working Paper Series 2011:2.

Torsello, D. (2014). *Corruption as social exchange: The view from anthropology.* Bergamo, Italy: University of Bergamo.

Uslaner, E. (2017). *The historical roots of corruption.* Cambridge, England: Cambridge University Press.

Varela-Ruiz, M., Díaz-Bravo, L., & García-Durán, R. (2012). Descripción y usos del método Delphi en investigaciones del área de la salud. *Investigación en Educación Médica, 1*(2). 90-95

Verbeke, A., & Kano, L. (2013). The transaction cost economics (TCE) theory of trading favors. *Asia Pacific Journal of Management, 30,* 409–431.

Villarroel, H. (1785/1994). *Enfermedades políticas que padece la capital de esta Nueva España.* Mexico City: CONACULTA.

Walton, G. (2013). Is all corruption dysfunctional? Perceptions of corruption and its consequences in Papua New Guinea. *Public Administration and Development, 33,* 175–190. doi:10.1002/pad.1636.

Werner, S. B. (1983). The development of political corruption: A case study of Israel. *Political Studies, 31,* 620–639.

Williams, C., & Bezeredi, S. (2017). Evaluating the use of personal connections to bypass formal procedures: A study of vrski in Republic of Macedonia. *UTMS Journal of Economics, 8*(2), 169–182.

Yang, M. (1994). *Gifts, favors and banquets: The art of social relations in China.* Ithaca, NY: Cornell University Press.

Zaloznaya, M. (2014). The social psychology of corruption: Why it does not exist and why it should. *Sociology Compass, 82*(2), 187–202. doi:10.111/soc4.12120.

Zalpa, G., Tapia Tovar, E., & Reyes, J. (2014). El que a buen árbol se arrima…intercambio de favores y corrupción. *Cultura y representaciones sociales, 9*(17), 149–176.

Zelekha, Y., & Werner, S. (2011). Fizers as shadows of 'public servants': A case study of Israel. *International Journal of Public Administration, 34*(10), 617–630.

SECTION II

Latin American Anticorruption Strategies

Introduction to Section II

This section studies four cases of organizational and institutional efforts in Latin America. It is a region characterized by high levels of corruption and problems of inequality and poverty that are often related to extremely poor quality, clientelistic, and populist governments.

Corruption in Latin America has a long history: diverse analysts establish that the colonial logic, which is highly extractive and also creates a highly stratified society (Warf, 2019, p. 21), forms the basis of the creation of a political system that is highly dependent on clientelistic logics and strong personalities, which tend to dominate the political spectrum. It is a region which, in various countries in the 20th century, experienced military regimes which arrived via coups d'état, yet underwent a major process of liberalization and democratization at the end of the century. However, despite this process of strengthening democracy, corruption remains a serious problem for these societies. As mentioned earlier in the Chapter 1, the Corruption Perceptions Index (CPI) is an imperfect measure, yet useful in many ways, at least to provide a general idea of the situation many people believe applies in these countries. According to data from the CPI (2017), no Latin American country has an index above 80%, that is, where countries with a very low perception of corruption are located. The closest ones are Chile (67%), Uruguay (70%) and Costa Rica (59%), while those furthest away include Argentina (39%), Brazil (37%), and Mexico (29%) (International Transparency, 2017).

Latin America therefore faces an enormous challenge to address the high levels of corruption. Two variables are critical, according to what has been discussed in previous chapters: the first is precisely the low quality of governments and their limited ability to solve complex social problems such as inequality, poverty, and corruption itself. The second, as we saw in the first two chapters of the book, is

108 Latin American Anticorruption Strategies

that corruption in every society can be linked in different ways to entrenched, enduring social practices. Specifically, such practices involve the exchange of favors and influences that enable people to solve the most diverse problems they face with various types of authorities and organizations. Solving these problems takes place by bending the rules and turning around the often-motley illogical rules that are established by the state and private bureaucracies. Through the exchange of favors and influences, the actual treatment received by a person may be different from what is formally established: he/she does not have to follow the steps or processes, wait in line, or fully comply with the formally established requirements. The network of acquaintances and influences that can be used are extremely useful and often effective for people to solve their problems. It comes at a high social cost, involving reproducing a scheme that legitimizes the violation of formal rules, processes, and forms of order. Legitimation, as we saw in Chapter 2, is based on a justification. Otherwise, things do not work, and without those contacts, people would be unlikely to solve their problems. It is a vicious circle: without this exchange of influences, without connections, problems are not solved, but this implies bending the rules, which are probably designed to be difficult to follow, thereby generating a high degree of uncertainty in people who therefore need to resort to their networks of acquaintances to bend the rules. Bending the rules and creating a parallel world of informal relationships becomes a necessity. As we have seen, it even becomes a valued capacity that certain people develop better than others. The more connections and networks, the more problems can be solved. And the exchange of favors is constituted and crystallized, as a broad, socially extended grid, where those with the most influence are those who move best in this informal world of solutions and paths which, in practice, in everyday life, enable things to work.

There is a high social cost, of course: that of pretending that there is a formal world of important, necessary rules and norms, which must be followed, yet which, at the same time, are disobeyed and bent, precisely so that everyday reality is possible, works, and is socially accepted and legitimized.

In Latin America, these social exchange mechanisms have different names and logics, intensities, and capacities. *Jeitinho* in Brazil, *pituto* in Chile, *sociolismo* in Cuba, and *palanca* in Mexico are examples of the various mechanisms for the exchange of favors that exist in countries in the region. Although the extent and strength of these mechanisms, their indispensability, and their legitimacy vary widely from country to country, their presence is widely known by the Latin American population.

The dilemma of controlling corruption in the region must be understood in this double dynamic: that of incapable or poor-quality governments, and that of a series of societies that have constructed an extremely stable political and social fabric, from below, through practices and effective exchanges in everyday life. In its different forms and in different ways, corruption in these countries has very stable and widespread social and political support.

There is no stable or single or effective recipe. This is where the strategies of what we have called the "anticorruption industry" appear to be ineffective, at least in many countries of the region. Due to their economic and population size, Brazil, Mexico, and Argentina feature prominently in corruption levels. This is not to mention the current humanitarian disaster in Venezuela. Countries such as Peru, Honduras, and Guatemala have launched major efforts in recent years, in response to a view of corruption that has spun out of control and is clearly systemic, political, and socially sustained. Chile, Uruguay, and Costa Rica are cited as examples of Latin American countries that have managed to control corruption. Their strategies, history, size, culture, and context are usually mentioned to justify their results. But in fact, there is little understanding of why they can be considered countries outside the predominantly high corruption levels in the region. In any case, the aim of this second section of the book is to show that the strategies being tried are diverse and numerous, and that many of them are truly international innovations such as the CICIG in Guatemala and the National Anticorruption System in Mexico.

It has therefore been decided to study four cases: Argentina, Brazil, Mexico, and Guatemala. Argentina because it is the Latin American country that has a traditional anticorruption agency that has managed to survive the most diverse attacks and boycotts since 1999. The case of Brazil was selected not only because it is a country of great size and importance, but because, compared with others in the region, it has a clear institutional framework for controlling corruption, which is decentralized and has multiple organizational overlaps. It is also based on a strong civil service tradition. The case of Mexico was chosen for its daring and, at the same time, desperate attempt to control its rampant political and economic corruption with cultural bases, through an ambitious but elephantine National Anticorruption System. The system tries to connect an enormous amount of powers and organizations, at the federal and national level, as a means of reversing an ancient and resilient culture of corruption. And finally, Guatemala is studied, with its daring new anticorruption agency: a hybrid between an international organization and one with the capacity to act in the national sphere. This organization has been built, unlike the Mexican case (elephantine and redundant), as a more focused organization, with highly specific and sophisticated research capacities. It has strategically decided not to promise to reduce, far less eliminate, all corruption in the country, but rather to control it, to make it less important in the logic of the Guatemalan political system through a focused strategy.

These are obviously four very different cases. But they all have a specificity that makes it possible to observe the panorama and especially the challenges of controlling systemic, socially sustained, and politically functional corruption. This specificity can be regarded as the common thread. That thread is the need to build a legitimate, politically viable, and sustainable mechanism that can affect and change the very social and political dynamic that makes corruption a socially acceptable and politically useful practice. How can such a mechanism be built, with political legitimacy, if the political system itself must create and sustain it? And if society itself will see its dynamics of exchanges of favors, connections, and acquaintances affected. This common thread led to the study of these four cases, because in all of them, there is an attempt to solve the dilemma differently. Argentina has a traditional anticorruption agency that was almost immediately

110 Latin American Anticorruption Strategies

attacked by the very political system that created it. Mexico refused to create an agency that would suffer the same fate, given the perennial social and political logic of corruption the country experiences, instead creating an extremely risky innovation. Guatemala created a hybrid organization (international and national) giving it the best of both worlds: because it is international, it can in principle escape the pressure exerted by internal political agents on Argentina's anticorruption agency, but with a national capacity for research and accompaniment. It also boasts an enormous technical capacity to investigate cases. The Brazilian case is not an agency or a system, but a long, continuous effort to control corruption based on the decentralized professionalization of various agencies from the executive, legislative, and judicial branches that often end up coordinating under a functional rather than a predesigned logic. Despite this, Brazil also discusses how to coordinate efforts through a national strategy, since the effects the political system is experiencing as a result of the success in Brazil to dismantle corruption networks are already significant.

As an introduction to the four cases studied in this second section of the book, the following text will briefly outline the anticorruption agencies, their logics, and problems.

Anticorruption Agencies

Anticorruption agencies (ACAs) are usually organizations created by national governments granting them multiple, ambitious mandates. ACAs generally combine legal powers of investigation and prosecution with other preventive and political advice to the cabinet or the president. These institutions vary enormously as to how they perform these functions, and as to their resources and budgetary, technical, and legal capacities. In some cases, they focus on initiating research based on complaints received or evidence identified by the organization itself. If there is a case that warrants being tried, the matter is usually referred to the Office of the Prosecutor or a similar organization (Dionisie & Checchi, 2008).

Anticorruption measures began to be introduced into countries in the region in the late 1990s, under pressure from international organizations such as the Council of Europe, the OECD, the World Bank and, above all, the European Union. (Dionisie & Checchi, 2008). It seems important then to discuss, albeit briefly, these ACAs, given that in the cases that have been selected for analysis in this book, ACAs serve as a benchmark: either to continue this strategy (Argentina), not to follow it and look for options (Mexico), create an innovation (Guatemala), or continue on a more decentralized path (Brazil).

What Is an Anticorruption Agency?

An anticorruption agency is basically created to implement national anticorruption strategies or programs. These strategies can emphasize various combinations of preventive and repressive measures as well as being a response to pressures or recommendations resulting from the ratification of international instruments. There are several instruments of this type, the best known of which being designed by the United Nations, the European Union, or the OECD. In any case, ACAs are assumed to be organizations with various specialized capacities and competences: in research, prevention, monitoring, using sophisticated techniques, statistics, and indicators (Dionisie & Checchi, 2008). Likewise, some of these agencies have expanded their functions to include transparency, education, and accountability agendas.

Several options and models have been experienced, as summarized in the following table.

TABLE I.II.1 Types of Anticorruption agency models

Multi-purpose agencies with the power to enforce the law and preventive functions	Agencies, departments and/or units of application of the law	Prevention, policy development and coordination institutions
Strictly speaking, it would be equivalent to an "anticorruption agency".	This model adopts different forms of specialization in the field of research and processing or a combination of the two.	This is the most diverse model, comprising a variety of institutions with varying degrees of independence and organizational structure.
It combines a multifaceted approach in an institution.	It has three important elements:	Additional subcategories can be identified:
• Prevention.	• Prevention.	• Services responsible for conducting and facilitating research into corruption phenomena.
• Research.	• Coordination.	
• Education.	• Research functions.	
"Multi-purpose agency".	"Police agency".	• Reviewing and preparing the relevant legislation.
		• Evaluating the risk of corruption.
The model has attracted the greatest visibility and has sparked discussions in the international arena. When literature and reports refer to specialized anticorruption agencies, this is this model they have in mind.	What distinguishes this model from the first is the level of independence and visibility, since it is usually placed within the existing police force or the procedural hierarchy.	Be the focal point for international cooperation and the link with civil society; controlling institutions with responsibilities related to the prevention of conflicts of interest and the declaration of assets; commissions responsible for monitoring and coordinating the implementation and updating of strategic national and local anticorruption documents.

Source: Compiled by the author using data from the OECD (2008).

What Happens with Independence in an Institution?

When we speak of an institution specializing in the fight against corruption, independence is regarded as a fundamental element. The reasons why independence criteria are so high up on the anticorruption agenda can be summed up in one sentence: "Corruption in many respects amounts to the abuse of power" (OECD, 2008, p. 24).

The question of appropriate powers to request documents, and carry out inspections and hearings are also relevant for the preventive bodies, which have certain control functions in areas such as the prevention of conflicts of interest, the financing of political parties and the declaration of assets of public officials (OECD, 2008).

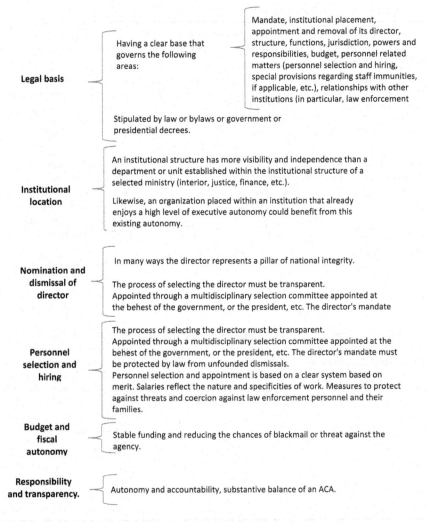

Legal basis — Having a clear base that governs the following areas: Mandate, institutional placement, appointment and removal of its director, structure, functions, jurisdiction, powers and responsibilities, budget, personnel related matters (personnel selection and hiring, special provisions regarding staff immunities, if applicable, etc.), relationships with other institutions (in particular, law enforcement

Stipulated by law or bylaws or government or presidential decrees.

Institutional location — An institutional structure has more visibility and independence than a department or unit established within the institutional structure of a selected ministry (interior, justice, finance, etc.).

Likewise, an organization placed within an institution that already enjoys a high level of executive autonomy could benefit from this existing autonomy.

Nomination and dismissal of director — In many ways the director represents a pillar of national integrity.

The process of selecting the director must be transparent. Appointed through a multidisciplinary selection committee appointed at the behest of the government, or the president, etc. The director's mandate

Personnel selection and hiring — The process of selecting the director must be transparent. Appointed through a multidisciplinary selection committee appointed at the behest of the government, or the president, etc. The director's mandate must be protected by law from unfounded dismissals.
Personnel selection and appointment is based on a clear system based on merit. Salaries reflect the nature and specificities of work. Measures to protect against threats and coercion against law enforcement personnel and their families.

Budget and fiscal autonomy — Stable funding and reducing the chances of blackmail or threat against the agency.

Responsibility and transparency. — Autonomy and accountability, substantive balance of an ACA.

SCHEME I.II.1 Factors that determine the independence of an anticorruption agency
Source: Compiled by the author using data from OECD (2008).

Main ACA Models

Model Number 1. Multi-purpose Agencies with the Power to Enforce the Law. Hong Kong Special Administrative Region: Independent Commission against Corruption

Hong Kong's Independent Commission against Corruption (ICAC) was established in 1974 as an independent multidisciplinary body. Its mandate is a combination of three main tasks:

- Persecuting the corrupt through effective detection and investigation.
- Eliminating opportunities for corruption through the introduction of corruption-resistant practices.
- Educating the public about how corruption is harmful and encouraging its support in the fight against the latter. (OECD, 2008).

SCHEME I.II.2 ACA mandates
Source: Compiled by the author using data from the OECD (2008).

It has powers such as arrest, search, access to financial information, and confiscation of property. From the beginning of its operations, the ICAC placed great importance on public trust and the establishment of the credibility and effectiveness of the institution (OECD, 2008).

One of the ICAC's first priorities was the arrest and conviction of an infamous high-ranking police officer suspected of corruption, who fled Hong Kong. A year later, the officer was extradited to Hong Kong, successfully prosecuted, and convicted. The following year, the ICAC successfully suppressed a corrupt trade union involving police officers.

The first successes of the ICAC boosted public confidence in its anticorruption work. In 1977, three years after the establishment of ICAC, the proportion of non-anonymous corruption reports (complaints about corruption) submitted to the ICAC exceeded the reporting statistics (OECD, 2008).

The ICAC has specific powers and legal tasks, which can be perceived through two other laws:

1. The Bribery Prevention Ordinance.
2. Elections Ordinance (corrupt and illegal behavior).

The following table shows the function of each law.

TABLE I.II.2 Laws that grant functions to the ICAC

Elections Ordinance (corrupt and illegal behavior).	*The Bribery Prevention Ordinance:*
Prescribes the duties of the ICAC Commissioner Establishes the parameters of the ICAC's research work, the procedure for handling a detainee and the disposal of property related to offenses. • It grants the ICAC the powers of arrest, detention, and granting of bail. • It confers on the ICAC the power to search and capture. • It gives the ICAC the power to take non-intimate samples of an arrested person for forensic analysis. • It empowers the ICAC to arrest persons who are referred to as pre-scribed officers who commit the crime of blackmail through misuse of their position, as well as any person who commits crimes related to or directly or indirectly facilitated by alleged offenses under the Prevention of Bribery Ordinance.	Bribery Prevention Ordinance • Specifies bribery offenses related to the government, public entities, and the private sector. • It grants powers to the ICAC, through a court order, to unravel and identify trans-actions and assets hidden in different ways by the corrupt. The powers include searching for bank accounts; searching for and confiscating documents; and requiring suspects to provide details of their assets, income, and expenses. • It grants the ICAC the powers, with the order of the court, to stop travel documents and restrict access to assets to prevent the corrupt from attempting to flee. • It gives the ICAC the power to protect the confidentiality of an investigation. • It prevents corrupt and illegal behavior in elections. • It specifies the crimes related to elections to elect the president.

Source: Compiled by the author using data from the OECD (2008).

TABLE I.II.3 Procedure for the investigation and prosecution of corruption offenses by the ICAC

1. The ICAC Report Center receives a complaint (on behalf of individuals, legal entities, regional offices of the ICAC or other government departments) about corruption.
2. The complaint is examined by the ICAC and categorized with a view to pursuing or not undertaking additional actions.
3. For complaints with recommended additional measures, investigations will be conducted by the Operations Department.
4. For complaints with justified evidence, the relevant details will be presented by the prosecuting institution to the Secretary of Justice and the head of the Department of Justice of the Hong Kong Special Government of the Administrative Region.
5. The prosecution of corruption will be undertaken by the two sections of the ICAC (public sector and private sector) of the Commercial Crimes and Corruption Unit, Prosecution Division, Department of Justice. It advises ICAC and handles its judicial processes.
6. The report will subsequently be submitted to the ICAC Operations Review Committee.

Source: ICAC, Department of Justice.

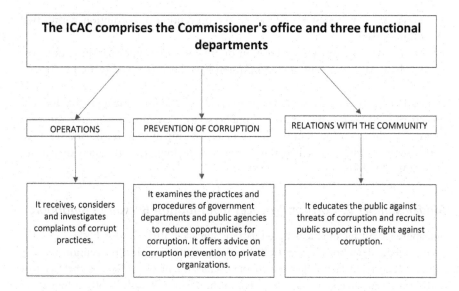

SCHEME I.II.3 Composition of the ICAC
Source: Compiled by the author using data from the OECD (2008).

Responsibility

The work of the ICAC is scrutinized by four independent advisors which are committees comprising community leaders or responsible citizens, designed by the Chief Executive of the Government of the Hong Kong Special Administrative Region. These are:

- The Advisory Committee on Corruption.
- The Operations Review Committee.
- The Advisory Committee on Corruption Prevention.
- The Citizens' Advisory Committee on Community Relations.

The committees, respectively, offer advice and proposals for the improvement of the Commission's policies, as well as the work of its three functional departments (OECD, 2008).

The ICAC produces annual reports, which are available on its website. It also publishes statistics that include corruption reports, reports of corruption related to the elections, as well as judicial actions available for public consultation (OECD, 2008).

All tasks are carried out within the "performance standards" to which the ICAC staff is committed:

- Respond to a corruption report within 48 hours.
- Respond to a report that does not involve corruption within two business days.

116 Latin American Anticorruption Strategies

- Respond to a request for advice on the prevention of corruption within two business days.
- Respond to a request for education or anticorruption information within two working days after reports of corruption have been received (OECD, 2008).

The ICAC community strives to personalize education campaigns for different objectives and groups, including the public sector. To further improve the promotion of ethics management in government departments, the ICAC and the CSB (Civil Service Office) launched the "Civil Service Integrity" Program in January 2004 (OECD, 2008).

Model Number 2. Corrupt Practices Investigation Bureau of Singapore

Singapore's Corrupt Practices Investigation Bureau (CPIB) was established in 1952 as an independent body responsible for the investigation and prevention of corruption. The main factor that led to the establishment of CPIB was the fact that corruption was perceived as a way of life in the 1940s and early 1950s in Singapore (OECD, 2008).

The CPIB was created by the government as an independent body, separate from the police, to investigate all cases of corruption. In the early days, the CPIB faced a series of difficulties. Anticorruption laws were inadequate, which had prevented the collection of evidence against corrupt individuals (OECD, 2008). Another problem was the lack of public support. Citizens did not cooperate with the CPIB since they were skeptical of its effectiveness and feared reprisals (OECD, 2008).

This situation changed with the new government that took power in 1959. Firm measures were taken against corrupt officials, many of whom were dismissed from service. Public confidence in the CPIB grew when people realized that the government was sincere in its anticorruption campaign (OECD, 2008).

In 1989, the Law on Corruption (Confiscation of Benefits) was approved. The law empowers the court to freeze and confiscate the property and assets obtained by corrupt criminals. In 1999, the Corruption Law (Confiscation of Benefits) was replaced by new legislation known as Corruption, Drug Trafficking and other Serious Offenses (confiscation of the Benefit Law). Moreover, new legislation against money laundering has been introduced to grant the same powers to the court for the freezing and confiscation of property and assets owned by criminals (OECD, 2008).

Legal and Institutional Framework

The CPIB is an independent governmental body. Its mandate is to investigate and prevent corruption in the public and private sectors in Singapore (OECD, 2008).

The main functions of the CPIB are:

Latin American Anticorruption Strategies **117**

- To receive and investigate complaints of corrupt practices.
- Investigate bad practices and misconduct of public officials suspected of corruption.
- Prevent corruption by examining practices and procedures in public service to minimize opportunities for corrupt practices. (OECD, 2008).

Model Number 3. National Anticorruption Directorate of Romania

The Romanian National Anticorruption Directorate (NAD) is a structure with a legal personality, within the framework of the Prosecutor's Office attached to the Superior Court of Appeals and Justice.

The NAD is responsible for the prosecution and investigation of cases of corruption when crimes cause material damages exceeding 200,000 euros, or a particularly serious disturbance of the activity of an authority, public institution, or any other legal entity (Dionisie & Checchi, 2008). Corruption cases are also investigated by the NAD when crimes are committed by high officials, deputies, senators, cabinet members, etc. (Dionisie & Checchi, 2008).

The NAD has special investigative powers such as the possibility of establishing surveillance of banks, accounts, and the interception of communications. Agency personnel consist of prosecutors, judicial police officers, experts in the economic, financial, banking, and customs spheres and other fields, special auxiliary personnel, and administrative personnel. In addition to law enforcement activities, the NAD also plays an important role in the prevention of corruption, as it has the responsibility to analyze the causes of corruption and the conditions that encourage it. It prepares and submits proposals with a view to eliminating corruption, and improving criminal legislation (Dionisie & Checchi, 2008).

The NAD is led by a chief prosecutor whose independence is guaranteed by law. The ordinance that establishes the NAD also establishes its independence from the courts of justice and offices of the prosecutor attached to the latter, as well as other authorities (Dionisie & Checchi, 2008).

Why Does an Anticorruption Agency Fail?

A fundamental risk in an anticorruption body, such as the ICAC, is that it becomes an instrument of political oppression, which makes it difficult to guarantee its use. To date, Hong Kong can be considered one of the least corrupt countries in the world.

In 1994, Botswana established its anticorruption agency with the responsibility of leading the country's anticorruption strategy that includes the same three elements of the Hong Kong strategy. For people like de Speville (the first ICAC director), the absence of just one of those elements will result in the failure of the entire strategy (de Speville, 2010).

The government sets up an anticorruption agency, believing that the problem will disappear. However, at least in the short term, the most likely scenario is that "corruption will bite back": the groups most deeply embedded in the logic of systemic corruption will attempt to hide their actions better, process their frauds more carefully or even attack the anticorruption agency in a legal or extralegal way (de Speville, 2008)

Finally, as has been widely discussed in the first section of this book, corruption is part of a network of exchanges and social practices that may be deeply entrenched and combines activities that are legal or regarded as socially legitimate, with acts that may be considered unlawful or at least improper. This suggests that in general, a society may be against corruption at the abstract level, but that its final evaluation of what is corruption and what is not, is generated on a case-by-case basis, through subjective criteria that are not very explicit or even properly reasoned. In the short term, attacking a network of corruption may create serious disruptions in public services or the delivery of certain resources to the population. Paradoxically, this causes people to be upset and think that the remedy of an anticorruption agency was not adequate. The causal connection between corruption and many of the ills of society is hard to see (de Speville, 2008). If one adds the fact that in many countries ACAs are created with exaggerated missions and expectations that are impossible to achieve, disillusionment with the virtues of the mechanism is likely to be high.

Table I.II.4 provides three examples of why an anticorruption initiative can fail.

Many political and economic actors are not really willing to accept the scrutiny of an anticorruption agency and are prepared to use many means to protect their power. Some evaluations highlight the fact that the agencies do not have in-built functional capacities, as is the case with the Kosovo ACA, where the law on asset declarations does not allow the agency to publish the declarations or make inquiries about the origin of wealth (Dionisie & Checchi, 2008). This agency also encounters several problems in establishing its position in the administrative framework and coordination with other agencies: for example, the agency is competent for administrative investigation and enforces disciplinary measures against public officials, but in this area its competence overlaps with the disciplinary committees present in the various public services (Dionisie & Checchi, 2008).

As one can see, the strategy of creating ACAs is interesting, but extremely intricate. Corruption is not an issue that can be resolved by a single instrument and the real effects of these mechanisms are not obtained immediately and often produce unexpected and unintended consequences.

Let us now move onto the case studies, where the various strategies and challenges, innovations, and risks that various Latin American countries are generating in order to change the tendency of these societies toward systematic, stable corruption will be seen in action. Addressing a social relationship such as corruption, one that is intimately embedded in social practices such as relationships involving the exchange of favors, involves paying attention to the rich and sophisticated reactions and counter-reactions that groups and people will create in order to cope with the changes anticorruption instruments will imply. Good intentions are

TABLE I.II.4 Examples of the failure of anticorruption initiatives

Characteristics of inappropriate initiatives	Minimum participation of the community	Lack of transparency	Insufficient responsibility	Loss of values in anticorruption agency
They are excessively complicated and unintelligible.	Little has been done to involve the community in the work of the agency, with the inevitable result that the public distrusts the agency and does not provide information about what is happening.	Part of the fight against corruption requires confidentiality in order to be effective. Strong investigative powers are needed.	Any government agency that receives public funds must be obliged to be accountable about the way it has spent that money.	It is not surprising that the morale of the agency's staff goes down. There is no pride in the institution or its work and the agency itself is corrupted in a short time.
The law applies only to public officials and not to the private sector, or only to the recipient of a bribe and not to the donor, or does not prohibit public officials from requesting or receiving gifts.	Without that information the investigative powers of the agency are useless.	The combination of strong powers and confidentiality easily arouse suspicion in the public.	An anticorruption agency that considers itself an exception is doomed to fail.	Corruption begins to spread in the agency itself.
A common mistake is not to make the anticorruption agency an agency responsible for investigating allegations of corruption. It expects other agencies to lend a hand: the police, the audit department, the income services, including the administration of public services.	In addition, educational work is likely to be ignored due to lack of public support.	The agency becomes secret. It will only rarely remain effective.	Anticorruption agencies are often tempted to be selective as regards allegations.	When that happens, it only remains to bury that particular anticorruption initiative, as soon as possible.

Source: Compiled by the author based on de Speville (2008).

120 Latin American Anticorruption Strategies

obviously not enough. Nor are instruments that propose a war, a battle that separates good from bad. The lessons observed and drawn from the cases analyzed can be of great importance and generate learning that is worth recovering, in order to continuously improve the understanding of how societies can emerge from the various social traps into which they have fallen.

Bibliography

De Speville, B. (2008). *Failing anti-corruption agencies – causes and cures*. Presented in the workshop, Empowering Anti-Corruption Agencies: Defying Institutional Failure and Strengthening Preventive and Repressive Capacities, Lisbon, May 14–16, 2008.

De Speville, B. (2010). Anticorruption commissions: The 'Hong Kong model' revisited. *Asia-Pacific Review*, 17(1), 47–71. doi:10.1080/13439006.2010.482757.

Dionisie, D., & Checchi, F. (2008). *Corruption and anti-corruption agencies in Eastern Europe and the CIS: A practitioners' experience*. Unpublished document retrieved from www.ancora ge-net.org/content/documents/dionisie-checchi-corruption_in_ee.pdf.

International Transparency. (2015, 2016, 2017). *Corruption perception index 2015, 2016, 2017*. Retrieved from www.transparency.org/news/feature/corruption_perceptions_inde x_2017#table.

OECD. (2008). *Specialized anti-corruption institutions:review of models. Anti-corruption network for Eastern Europe and Central Asia*. Paris, France: OECD.

Warf, B. (2019). *Global corruption from a geographic perspective*. Cham, Switzerland: Springer.

3

THE ANTICORRUPTION AGENCY
OF ARGENTINA

Limits of Anticorruption Agencies in Latin America

Latin America is a region that suffers from systemic, social, and culturally sustained corruption. Logics such as *palancas* or *jeitinho* are common and widely used as ancient and well-established social practices. After decades of economic crises and political disasters led by military juntas that come to power through sequential coups d'état, most of the region has enjoyed a degree of stability. However, corruption continues in all its facets, and is a constant, both politically and socially. Efforts to reduce or control it have multiplied in various countries. And their results and experiences are worth studying, because in fact little is known about them in the international debate.

The purpose of this first chapter devoted to studying some of the experiences that have arisen in the region deals with the case of Argentina. In particular, it seeks to study the vicissitudes and organizational complexities of establishing an anticorruption agency (ACA) as a strategy for addressing the problem of systemic corruption the country suffers. The case of Argentina, one could say, is the case of a "classic" anticorruption organization or agency: created by the central government in order to concentrate anticorruption efforts in a special, exceptional entity, with autonomy and political force with the goal of effectively transforming the political and administrative conditions that create the context of widespread corruption. And doing so from within the political system itself, that is, ultimately, the source of corruption itself. Under this logic, in this book, an anticorruption agency in Guatemala will be discussed in Chapter 6 on Guatemala, which is different: the CICIG in Guatemala is an organization that acts within the country in question yet was created by the UN as an exceptional international organization.

The fact that a political regime should consider the creation of an anticorruption agency can be considered a desperate act. It is desperate because it is talking about

122 Latin American Anticorruption Strategies

the moment when a society realizes that formal institutions and traditional organizations such as executive, legislative, and judicial power, their checks and balances, and monitoring mechanisms, are failing to stop corruption. Moreover, it is precisely in those institutions that corruption has been embedded, forming part of its dynamics and operation. Corruption ranges from the practices of the exchange of favors to their political institutionalization, creating endogenous corruption, organized politically and administratively. Given this situation, it seems that the argument supporting this type of strategy is that the only alternative that remains is to build a new organization, an exceptional one, which is given the power to act in parallel to formal institutions, outside the general process of checks and balances so to speak. It is an exceptional solution because it is based on several paradoxes. The first paradox is that it is created and must be sustained by the very groups and state apparatuses that must be watched and punished in the event they engage in corruption. The second paradox is that an agency of this type requires coordination with many of these same state organizations, which are those that formally have powers to control wrongful acts and punish them, yet which fail to do so, for various reasons. Having to build an organization that works in parallel with formal state organizations, which must eventually coordinate with, but also confront, them, and for this option to be seen as having the best chance of controlling or reducing corruption, is surely a truly desperate act.

Organized or systemic corruption is the term used to refer to the fact that not only social practices such as the exchange of favors have been maintained between society and government, as we analyzed in previous chapters. It is also possible to speak of societies that have established solid networks to organize corruption at a political level. In fact, many of the countries in the region could create flow charts on processes and relations to explain the interaction of corruption among parties, public servants, politicians, and businesspeople. These networks may even be able to effectively prevent its detection and evade the formal penalties that should be imposed on the actors involved. Thanks to the practices of the exchange of favors that have become cultural and institutionalized, the organization of corruption is strongly horizontally integrated, so to speak. In other words, there is interaction and mutual support between practices that have spread throughout society, such as *palancas*, and the political and administrative organization of fraud, embezzlement, and collusion, in this case organized by parties, government agencies, civil society organizations, and firms. This double integration between the practices of exchanging favors and the organization of corruption is what constructs the phenomenon that has come to be known as systemic corruption. Under this logic, it is possible to speak of a "systemic" phenomenon because a stable equilibrium is created, in which laws and norms, social practices, customs, languages, symbols, and organizations interrelate in an apparently virtuous manner; in other words, in a constant, repeated fashion, which is even socially accepted in different circumstances. This balance is accepted and actually defended: various people and social agents can develop mechanisms of resistance to confront or boycott any attempt to change the status quo of the system. Corruption, as has been mentioned throughout this book,

The Anticorruption Agency of Argentina   123

is not only an act of isolated individuals, but a fully established social relationship, with exchanges, networks, institutions, norms, and rules that can be stable and organized.

It is in the context of systemic corruption that dozens of countries have taken the step of founding ACAs as one of the options that can be effective, and with a multiplicity of designs, as seen in the introduction to Section II of this book.

In general, we can say that an ACA is "a permanent organization financed with public resources, whose specific mission is to combat corruption and reduce opportunities for corruption through prevention and punishment strategies" (Sousa, 2009, p.3). In other words, these agencies seek to do what formal organizations in the political system should do but are incapable of: from identifying, investigating, and punishing, to attempting to transform social practices and values to make corruption undesirable. Depending on the ACA, the combination of these factors varies widely. In general, however, they can be said to be agencies created with a broadly instrumental sense. Therefore, they are created with broad social expectations that they can quickly reduce corruption, with the promise that they have at their disposal specific instruments that will directly produce quick results. To a certain extent, it is logical that they should have been created with such high expectations: their creation implies extremely complex political negotiation between the political actors themselves, who will be subject to surveillance and punishment by the ACA in question. Moreover, the political actors who have decided to control themselves through an agency that will supposedly have autonomy and run parallel to the formal political logic, puts them in a high-risk situation, so they will focus on obtaining political gains from appearing to champion the initiative. Therefore, it is not surprising that they are generally created with the language and rhetoric of being technical agencies, with instruments for detection, investigation, and even punishment, which are strong and measurable and have an almost immediate effect. In effect, when they are established, they usually create very high expectations in society, which, given the complexity of the phenomenon of corruption, may become a problem for the agency itself. There is no doubt that it is a risky political bet: As we have discussed, corruption in many Latin American countries is embedded in social and collective practices, so to assume that it is a phenomenon that can be controlled instrumentally, at least in the short term, is a risky bet. However, these agencies usually obtain their legitimacy precisely from the promise and hope that the control of corruption is a basically technical matter. This involves a very high social expectation that creates a difficult circle to break.

ACAs usually emphasize their instrumental capabilities to affect the behavior of people and organizations so that they stop acting or engaging in improper practices. They tend to emphasize the use of incentives to change behaviors through economic incentives or simply punishments and penalties (Hodgson & Jiang, 2008; Rose-Ackerman, 2001). Given this instrumental expectation of ACAs, it often happens that the mix of instruments is highly heterogeneous, depending on each case, generating equally heterogeneous results (Charron, 2008; Fjeldstad & Isaksen,

2008; Otahal & Wawrosz, 2013). At the end of the day, ACAs do not cease to be political organizations which, from their inception, supposedly acting in parallel to the political system, necessarily end up looking for how to liaise with that same political system. It is a system that is supposed to monitor, investigate and punish, and at the same time, depends on the political system for its financing and above all its legitimacy. The paradox of these organizations is extremely interesting: their legitimacy lies in the hands of the very political system they are supposed to watch and punish. Which parts of the system provide support and resources, which ones end up being watched and handcuffed, which ones support it contingently or with interest and which ones boycott it? This is the organizational and political logic these agencies have experienced in practice, with differences and specificities in each case.

Knowing the political and organizational process these agencies undergo in practice, and knowing their forms of adaptation and legitimacy, can be extremely interesting. In the case examined in this chapter, an ACA in Latin America, political and administrative corruption is supported by a series of entrenched social practices such as *palancas*. In general terms, it can be argued that ACAs seek to be effective organizations for reducing corruption by gaining a high level of autonomy and showing a certain degree of effectiveness over time. In other words, before their birth with very high expectations, socially speaking, and at great risk, politically speaking, ACAs seek, like any organization, to acquire legitimacy and find a space that enables them to sustain themselves and be politically viable in time. However, achieving this capacity for autonomy and organizational power in an agency that must act in parallel with the formal bodies of a political system is the most difficult challenge to meet, for logical reasons. An anticorruption agency of this nature will almost immediately face resistance and counter-offensives, not only by the actors involved in acts of corruption, but also by formal organizations in the political system, which feel that their activities and even their legitimacy are affected by the existence of a parallel organization that monitors and sanctions them. The ACAs are therefore a very special organizational creation: they are an exceptional organization in a political system, whose legitimacy is based on acting autonomously and therefore in parallel to the formal powers of a state. They form part of the political system, but are expected, in a very particular way, to have an autonomous logic. They belong to a system which, however, they must monitor and punish. This can be seen as a contradiction or even as a paradox which these organizations must resolve in practice. In this respect, it is worth studying the Argentinean case: it is an organization whose fundamental success has been to survive, first of all, after being attacked, boycotted, and having its capacity reduced by various actors in the political system.

Precisely, the case of the Anticorruption Office of Argentina (OAA), created in 1999, makes it possible to longitudinally study the dramatic moments and challenges an ACA has to face in order to legitimize itself and survive in a context of systemic corruption. What is clear when longitudinally studying an ACA is that the process is full of contingencies and specific political–cultural considerations, which

The Anticorruption Agency of Argentina **125**

require the organization to constantly rethink the strategy so that it will be able to survive in a context that clearly opposes its mission.

Analyzing ACAs as dynamic organizations that change and constantly (re)define strategies in order to (and by) counter attacks and pressures from corruption networks, requires more than studying the functions and structures themselves. For this reason, the following guiding questions are posed: What were and continue to be the main challenges a situation of systemic corruption imposes on an ACA like the one in Argentina? And what are the strategies this Argentinean ACA has tried in order to survive, legitimize itself, and be able to address the conditions of systemic corruption in the country? To answer this question, this chapter states that in situations of systemic corruption like the one experienced in this Latin American country, an ACA is, in fact, an organization under constant siege by various actors across the spectrum of society (political, economic, and social). The case we will analyze shows how the real history of an ACA goes far beyond creating a technical agenda in order to have instruments that attack discrete, individual acts of corruption. An ACA like that of Argentina has had to prepare to operate against a network of corruption, a collective rival that will be able to react and attempt to boycott and delegitimize the organization, with considerable possibilities of success. When attacked, corruption bites back, so to speak. The study of the Argentinean ACA makes it possible to observe how these organizations operate in contexts that continually force them to seek legitimacy to survive, as a first condition for obtaining external support that allows them to be able to act and obtain results over time.

This case, then, will make it possible to observe a first strategy which has been attempted in Latin America to control the intricate social logic of corruption. We can say that this is the orthodox, traditional strategy: an anticorruption agency, inspired by the successful cases of Hong Kong and Singapore. Given the pernicious social logic of corruption, it is necessary to besiege the political system, creating an organization which, autonomously and therefore parallel to the formal logics of checks and balances and constitutional functions of the powers of the state, will monitor and punish wrongful acts. The contradiction is obvious: an organization that is created and sustained by the very powers and organizations that have to be watched and punished.

The Conceptual Logic of ACAs

ACAs are part of the substantive tools that have been experimented with under the traditional paradigm termed the "anticorruption industry" in this book. In other words, it is based on a normative logic: corruption as a social cancer, a curb on economic development, since it undermines the effectiveness of organizations, weakens the legitimacy of governments, reduces the welfare of societies, inhibits the economic development of countries and makes cooperation in social relations more expensive (Alcaide, 2005; Anechiarico, 2010; Rose-Ackerman, 2001; ASF, 2012). Under this logic, it is necessary to invest new resources and ideas in reducing corruption through multifunctional mechanisms, which ultimately and relatively quickly make credible threats of punishment to those who act corruptly.

The problem with this normative view of corruption is that, although it suggests a quick, forceful diagnosis, it leaves solving extremely intricate dilemmas to practice because of the way various practices can be classified as corrupt acts. As we have seen, acts that are usually classified as corrupt are often diverse and heterogeneous, so that a vision of punishments, credible threats and the vision of waging a "war" on disease is only useful as an initial metaphor. In practice, it comes up against a wealth of deeply rooted social practices, politically embedded in parties and governments. Numerous empirical studies have shown the complexity of the problem: that it is difficult to pigeonhole corruption as a single act or normative concept and that the social legitimacy of these acts tends to be supported by very different social justifications. This makes explaining, modeling and predicting this phenomenon of corruption a slippery, risky affair (Chugh, 2013; Jancsics, 2013; Jávor & Jancsics, 2013).

For the "anticorruption industry", however, this complexity can be addressed through a simple logic. International institutions such as the OECD, Transparency International and the World Bank have strongly promoted a debate and an agenda of policy recommendations to prevent, investigate, punish and reduce corruption under a concrete paradigm: as long as the punishment of corruption is not credible, impunity will remain. If the costs of being corrupt are less than the possible benefits, any actor (assumed in this paradigm), if they are rational, will maintain a propensity for acts of corruption (European Union, 2011; OECD, 2008; UN-ODCCP, 2002; Huther & Shah, 2000; Stapenhurst & Kpundeh, 1999). While corruption may have deep social and political roots, these solutions based on the rational decision of people view corruption as a problem that can be solved by attacking the rational logic of costs and benefits of individuals.

These proposals, which focus on the decisions of individuals, define corruption by ignoring the importance of the interactions that occur between people, companies, governments, and parties. These interactions construct resilient networks of practices, justifications, and forms of organization. Attacking the incentives of people will have a limited effect because the critical question is: What changes in interactions do these changes of incentives produce? Not only this but perhaps more importantly: What reactions in the interactions in the networks bring about the change in incentives directed at individuals? Expecting social interactions and networks to simply remain passive, not to react, and even to counter-react, is basically naive.

Failure to consider these contextual issues and to anticipate the crises and reactions that affect the networks of interactions that support corrupt practices is probably a major limitation of this individualistic perspective.

The simplicity of the individualistic paradigm has the advantage of providing easy answers to implement under a simple, direct causal logic. Consequently, the mechanisms prescribed to deal with the problem of corruption tend to be of two types: on the one hand, control and, on the other, punishment. In this respect, the most common recommendations are to increase penalties (costs) according to the rule of minimum quantity and sufficient ideality. The first rule states that crimes occur because they provide an advantage (benefit), so that if the idea of a greater disadvantage is linked to crime (cost), the idea of being corrupt would be undesirable. The second rule consists of the undeniable efficacy and correspondence of punitive incentives for any criminal act. In other words, increasing costs and the high likelihood of detecting corrupt behaviors are the most effective and, in time, efficient alternatives for reducing the problem according to the rational–instrumental perspective proposed in standard international recommendations.

At the same time, the corruption model proposed by Klitgaard (1988) provides the basis for the development of controls in the rational–instrumental approach. Klitgaard said that corruption is more likely to occur when there is a high degree of monopoly power with discretion and without transparency. Thus, the alternatives for addressing the phenomenon have been to strengthen democratic participation, limit the discretionary use of authority through rules and regulations, and increase transparency in decision-making processes. The disadvantage is that countries with a widespread problem of corruption, and which have implemented these control mechanisms, continue to suffer the costs of the problem together with increasing costs of public administration (OECD, 2008; Serra, 2010).[1]

Generally speaking, the more widespread it is, the more difficult corruption is to explain and address. Corruption usually occurs recurrently in processes of iterative improvement, with forms of cooperation among the members of the organization(s). The complexity of systemic corruption is characterized precisely by the fact that:

- the actors create methods—processes, languages, discourses, and customs—of iterative management to interact and avoid detection and punishment (Arellano, 2012/2018; Brunsson & Olsen, 2007);
- the actors create hierarchies and parallel networks of information and power flows inside and outside formal organizations (Jávor & Jancsics, 2013);
- the need to maintain secret operations leads to the specialized definition of functions among network actors, and to a distribution of benefits according to the participation and responsibilities assumed;
- the specialization among actors enables operations to be carried out in the spaces of normative ambiguity; or openly against statutory rules and laws; or, covertly, as "administrative errors" (Jávor & Jancsics, 2013);
- the stability achieved, the solidity and dividends of the grid, make it possible to admit in connivance with actors responsible for activating the alarms and formally established administrative control mechanisms (Raab & Milward, 2003); and
- the extent of the phenomenon facilitates its normalization (trivialization) in society, to the point where corruption is considered omnipresent and an essential barrier to cross to acquire a benefit or gain access to certain spaces. This aspect has a strong historical, cultural component requiring a detailed analysis to understand the endemic problem.

Anticorruption Agencies: Conditions and Context

The establishment of ACA is a strategy regularly adopted to address the problem of corruption in contexts where it is widespread: it is a desperate strategy that attempts to work in parallel with formal institutions that have failed and been taken over by corruption (Charron, 2008; De Speville, 2008). These formal institutions are supported by laws, and constitutions and continue to have, at least on paper, their important functions of checks, balances, control of public expenditure, bidding processes, audits, and fiscal controls. But they will do so in this respect, overseen by a meta-political organization. They are meta-organizations in the sense that an ACA is not a traditional counterweight, but one specializing in the issue of corruption, yet with sufficient powers in that specific area, to investigate, accuse, and prosecute people from formal state institutions. In these situations, establishing an ACA begins with the same individualistic assumptions described earlier: it involves realigning incentives, improving information systems, and establishing mechanisms that modify the behavior of individuals based on controls and punishments. But it does so from *sui generis*, emergency organization, which usually experiences enormous problems in being justified in a politically and legally congruent manner. Because, how can one justify having a parallel organization, with broad powers of investigation and sometimes persecution, against the state agencies themselves, in either the executive, legislative, or judicial branches? Who is there to report to if one finds that state institutions have been taken over? Worse still, what limits them or how is their political sustainability assured if it depends in many respects on the resources, support, and cooperation of the organizations that are assumed to be captured and are therefore unreliable?

The practical solution is neither obvious nor simple. Various formulas have been experimented with, all contingent on the particular case in its particular political and social context. Some generic issues can be observed: ACAs are distinguished from other public organizations because, first, they have an area of independence (command and budget autonomy) that enables the fulfillment of their mission; second, they have special powers and competencies to investigate and prosecute cases; third, there is a strong inclination to establish transparency and accountability mechanisms (horizontal and vertical); and, fourth, they have clear procedures for sharing and collaborating with other control agencies and judicial powers (Pilapitiya, 2008; Heilbrunn, 2004; Sousa, 2009; Meagher, 2005).

These recommended variables for an ACA seek to establish as clearly as possible the minimum design elements that have been experimented with in various cases. The paradox of these organizations is their constant: the search to build effective organizations instrumentally within a context of the systemic capture by corruption of formal state institutions. The first challenge is to construct its origin and conformation, as a strange, external, parallel organization. The second is to quickly establish its instruments in such a way that it will be able to produce results soon. The third is to link it to the state organizations themselves: without their data, cooperation, and legitimization, however minimal, it would be difficult for an ACA to undertake its activities with even a modicum of success. And, lastly, there needs to be the creation of conditions for its long-term sustainability: corruption will bite back, resist, and attempt to sabotage the ACAs, which as organizations are often extremely vulnerable, for all these reasons. If corruption is systemic, there is no doubt that the actors involved in the network of interactions and practices that support corruption will seek to boycott the agency or find new legal or ambiguous mechanisms to protect themselves or delay judicial proceedings against them.

There are certain international cases that have become paradigms of the possible success of these agencies: Singapore, Hong Kong and, recently, Indonesia. Various characteristics of these cases, however, make them difficult to repeat or reproduce:

1. The power and faculties exercised by the ACA are so extensive and invasive that they foster a climate of fear, fragility, and uncertainty for the potentially corrupt subject. The agency poses a serious threat to the benefits that could be acquired by the individual. The dynamics generated are a kind of panoptic in which a significant part of private life can be monitored: review of financial accounts, phone tapping, confiscation of goods, witness protection laws, black lists, covert operations, actions with potential damage to individual reputation (Princeton University, 2013; MacMillan, 2011; Mao, Wong & Peng, 2013).
2. The mechanisms for the detection, control and punishment of corrupt practices are so severe that the traditional concepts of a liberal democracy of presumption of innocence are reduced.
3. In these countries, political support usually becomes vertical: Their power lies, at least initially, in a political will at the highest level, with a willingness to apply the law directly, with few counterweights and obstacles to establishing traditional due process.

These kinds of circumstances are difficult to reconcile with liberal democratic systems of government, which recognize human rights and the importance of due process. They are also difficult to reproduce in a society that would require an almost personal will from the highest sphere of government to sustain itself. Senior public authorities in a standard democracy usually change from time to time (De Graaf, 2007). In such circumstances, in order to be functional, an ACA must know how to negotiate and survive in a context of changing political actors, who may feel threatened and counterattack a strange agency working in parallel. Corruption networks can be sufficiently organized to achieve attacks from within the system against these agencies. This boycott does not necessarily have to come from corrupt actors, but from actors who, without being so, may fear being used as scapegoats. In effect, many public policies are complex; many hands are involved. A government official responsible for a particular policy does not necessarily control each and every one of the steps, so he or she may be accused of corruption without having been the main person responsible for a certain process. The creation of an ACA means a risk, in its real dynamics, both for corrupt actors and for those that are not but act within the complexity of a contemporary state.

130 Latin American Anticorruption Strategies

An ACA is therefore a living organizational creature, which requires great intelligence, negotiation skills, and the conviction to be able to even begin acting. Understanding how these organizations resolve these dilemmas in practice seems important. It is expected to be a tortuous history, of resistance, errors, and boycotts of offensives. This is precisely what we will see in the oldest, most resilient ACA in Latin America: the Anticorruption Office of Argentina (OAA), which in practice has had to adapt and define the means of dealing with a scenario of systemic corruption.

The Argentinean Anticorruption Office as a "Strategy"

This case is not analyzed from a formal, procedural design perspective, but by understanding the OAA as a strategy for combating corruption framed in a particular political context, with historicity. In order to guide the discussion, one of the five definitions of "strategy" suggested by Mintzberg (1987) has been adopted: strategy as "position", in other words, as "the means of locating an organization in an environment, a mediating force—or pairing—between the organization and its internal and external context".

An analysis of this type requires understanding the OAA, not as the result of a rational, linear decision process, as if there were a single direct line between the decision to create it and its implementation. Instead, it means understanding it as an effort involving many actors with different interests, at different times. The result is that nowadays, the OAA is due to the interaction between disorganization and the variables of all these political processes and multiple decisions by different actors. In accordance with the most widely accepted practices and methods for the study of organizational strategies (Mintzberg & Waters, 1985), this section presents a longitudinal analysis of the OAA and the main phases of its evolution, with the aim of tracking its strategy over time and seeing how it has changed since its inception.[2]

Phase 1: From Public Scandals to the Creation of the OAA

Argentina in the 1990s represented an aggressive effort to implement neoliberal economic policies—since the election of Carlos Menem as president—through a systematic reduction of the state, deregulation, and privatization of public assets. These policies were defended by the government using a discourse focused on the structural nature of Argentine corruption. In other words, the state had to be profoundly reformed to control the corrupt practices produced by the excessive regulation of economic activity and an oversizing of the provision of public services by the state (Pereyra, 2006).

Paradoxically, it was the national government itself that promoted the reform policies to modify and neutralize the administrative control systems that existed previously in the country, thereby creating inconsequential, accessory mechanisms in terms of the fight against corruption, such as the National Public Ethics Office and the Code of Ethics of Public Administration, and limiting the independence of the Judicial Branch. Thus, the enormous transfer of resources implied by the privatizations took

The Anticorruption Agency of Argentina 131

place in a context prone to the multiplication of political and administrative corruption practices. Corruption scandals soon became common—especially cases of the violation of civil service duties, embezzlement, and bribery—while public opinion consolidated its perception of a period of widespread corruption and impunity.[3]

Opposition parties took advantage of the opportunities offered by this context of social disillusionment with the rampant corruption observed. Many of the electoral campaigns used this topic as a strategy, ultimately proposing that a new form of politics could be created that did not depend on dishonesty. Thus, a party coalition (La Alianza) led Fernando De la Rúa to win the presidential elections in 1999, and largely focus his government program on a promise to correct the legacies of the Menem administration: the social costs of privatization reforms, the stagnation of economic activity, repeated abuses of power and corrupt practices (Torre, 2003). Regarding the latter, just four days after taking office, Law 25.233 was passed. This law created the OAA as a body under the Ministry of Justice and Human Rights, with the purpose of preparing and coordinating anticorruption programs in the national public sector, applying the principles of the Inter-American Convention against Corruption (CICC).

Since its inception, the institutional design of the OAA has reflected the basic structure of the CICC, which establishes investigative and preventive policies in order to break the logic of reactive work that had characterized traditional control agencies, such as the Prosecutor's Office of Administrative Investigations and the General Audit of the Nation (De Michele, 2001, see Table 3.1). One of the most original aspects of the OAA's investigations—in comparison with these control bodies—is that it has worked on the basis of the criteria of institutional, economic and social significance to prioritize the most relevant or emblematic cases or those in which there is a social expectation of more severe punishment.[4]

Thus, following international guidelines (in force during the 1990s), the activities of the OAA were designed to restore the bond of trust between society and the state. After a decade of Menem's administration, it was necessary to send signals that it was moving steadily to meet the greatest social demands: achieving greater justice, transparency, equality in the eyes of the law and putting an end to the impunity of politicians and officials (Oficina Anticorrupción, 2001). With its technical, professional, and multidisciplinary approach, the OAA was portrayed as the most effective strategy for achieving these objectives and dealing with the complexity of corruption as a social problem (De Michele, 2001).

TABLE 3.1 Design and principal functions of the OAA

The OAA is divided into functionally independent but complementary areas.
1. The *Department of Investigations*, responsible for denunciations of corruption in the National Public Administration and related agencies.
2. The *Department of Transparency Policies* has the duty to design policies to increase transparency and prevent corrupt practices. It also administers the system of declarations of financial information of government officials.

Source: Compiled by the author.

132 Latin American Anticorruption Strategies

Phase 2: From the Initial Enthusiasm to the First Problems (1999–2001)

The OAA swiftly became the favorite place to investigate and denounce the most emblematic cases of corruption during the Menem administration. In just two years, the OAA opened up 1,784 investigations, 28% of which (489) ended in complaints to the Ministry of Justice (the OAA was a complainant in 31 of them).

Parallel to the performance of anticorruption functions, the early years of the OAA were marked by the need to undertake two complementary tasks. On the one hand, to defend its legitimacy and faculty to file complaints with the justice system, in order to deal with the denunciations received. And on the other, to overcome the police/legal view of corruption and understand the phenomenon from a more comprehensive structural perspective, with the aim of complementing the investigation with far-reaching preventive measures.

To illustrate the first aspect, it is useful to mention some symptomatic data: in 12 of the 27 cases the OAA filed as a plaintiff in 2000, several courts denied it this legally attributed power, whereas in other cases, OAA staff were not allowed to view or photocopy records to evaluate the relevance of the participation of the OAA in the process. The OAA was therefore forced to issue numerous new legal processes, appeals, and complaints to carry out its work, which implied a significant waste of resources for the OAA and for the administration of justice in general. Likewise, the OAA began to face other obstacles in the judiciary to discharge its functions, many of which still affect its performance: the lack of signals that show impartiality in the application of justice; swiftness of sanctions; rejection of the collaboration of the OAA in the judicial processes; and a static or obsolete attitude toward the modalities of the fight against corruption within the rules of the Rule of Law (Oficina Anticorrupción, 2001).

Regarding the second task, a comprehensive view of corruption, after a year of work, the OAA managed to map and diagnose the types of corruption in the public sector to determine the structural conditions that facilitated corrupt practices, to discover constants—both in the means in which events were performed and in the criminal juridical framework attributed to them—and to identify the characteristics, facts, and organizational conditions that encouraged their prevalence.[5] On the basis of this study, the OAA identified eight predominant types of corruption mainly attributed to the dismantling and lack of effective controls, excessive discretionality on the part of officials, administrative chaos, and a lack of transparency and accountability mechanisms.[6]

The findings of this diagnosis showed that, beyond the legally established punitive aspects, fighting corruption could be more effective if measures were taken to expand access to information, improve the quality of the decision-making process in the administrative sphere, establish public audiences in criminal cases, reduce the discretionality of public services in the process of purchases and hiring and implement participatory rule-making processors with actors from civil society and the private sector (De Michele, 2001). The OAA focused precisely on these aspects in 2000–2001 in order to propose policies and projects with a broader scope. These

The Anticorruption Agency of Argentina **133**

included a new system of sworn financial disclosures by public officials; bills concerning access to information and publicity for lobbying; agreements with the Head of the Cabinet of Ministers to achieve greater coordination among National Public Administration agencies (APN); strengthening the institutional capacities of the OAA; and draft decrees for public hearings and the participatory drawing up of standards. However, these efforts, which were innovative for the region, were interrupted by the profound social, economic, and political crisis of December 2001, which plunged the OAA's representation, legitimacy, and credibility—and the entire APN—into a trough.

Phase 3: Crisis, Transition and Opportunity (2002–2003)

After the 2001 crisis and the election of a transition government (2002–2003), it was essential to implement urgent political and economic changes that left the visibility of the transformation processes initiated by the OAA on the back burner. Although some major points of the crisis have been attributed to problems of corruption, such as the weakening of the notion of "the public sphere", the erosion of the state's control capabilities, market distortion, and the deterioration of the goods and services provided to the most disadvantaged sectors, it gave the OAA the opportunity to establish itself as an axis of concrete actions to reverse citizens' distrust of the state and its institutions (Oficina Anticorrupción, 2002).

The diagnosis made within the OAA was that the success of the Office depended on the quantity and quality of the signals it managed to send, in terms of compliance with the norms that protect public assets and demand integrity from officials. However, if the files were stuck at the investigation stage and acts of corruption only rarely reached the stage of oral trial—where citizens obtained reliable knowledge of the facts and the justice system showed signs of effectiveness (i.e. criminal sanctions)—social trust in the state could not be restored (Oficina Anticorrupción, 2002). Consequently, in its investigative function, one of the priorities the OAA set was the strengthening of its role as a plaintiff so that lawsuits would reach the oral prosecution stage more quickly and the cycle of scandal and impunity could be interrupted. Thereafter, the promotion of sanctions was understood by the OAA as an activity as important as preventive and investigative functions.

During this stage, the OAA focused on (re)building the bonds of cooperation and coordination with various social actors and local and international organizations. The post-crisis context showed that the result of the fight against corruption and the recovery of public trust in the state not only depended on an organism or a court, but on an interaction between the administrative, legislative, and judicial sectors, the media, and civil society. The activities were designed to: strengthen the relationship with permanent committees of Congress whose function is to control specific areas of the state; achieve cooperation agreements with local governments to implement the requirements of the CICC; raise Argentina's profile in the international context; and improve coordination with international organizations that promote the fight against corruption to develop effective policies.

134 Latin American Anticorruption Strategies

Regarding the involvement of civil society—within the framework of the Procedure for Standard Setting—the OAA promoted the participation of academics, NGOs, businesspeople, journalists, legislators, and public officials to develop the Access to Information Bill. However, despite having achieved a text that had enjoyed significant consensus among legislators from all sectors of the political spectrum, the project was not included on the agenda of extraordinary sessions. Another problem the Argentinean anticorruption fight had to overcome was becoming increasingly evident: the lack of a widespread, sustained political consensus on the need for a long-term transparency policy.

Phase 4: Repositioning and Strengthening (2003–2009)

Néstor Carlos Kirchner's election as president, in 2003, as head of the *Frente por la Victoria*, ushered in a period of political and economic stability which had a favorable impact on the development of the OAA. The decree on "Improving the Quality of Democracy and its Institutions", signed in December 2003, resumed several bills drafted by the OAA—which had previously been "dormant" in the legislative and executive areas—granting the Office a key role in the regimes of Access to Public Information and Interest Management (lobbying); and the Procedures for the Participatory Standard Setting and Public Hearings.

Likewise, the growth in the volume of work highlighted the need to update the organization, especially in the research field, to solve one of the systematic problems the OAA had faced since its inception: the excessive average length of investigations, which seriously affected the political legitimacy of the OAA in the eyes of public opinion. The main external causes of this delay are attributable to the complexity of the cases; to criteria applied by judges to demand evidence and resolve the procedural situation of the accused; the length of time required for experts' assessments; the appeals filed by the defendants; and the obvious selectivity of the penal system (Oficina Anticorrupción, 2004). To these external factors should be added internal problems of the OAA—fragmentation and dispersion in the area of investigations—which delayed the processing of a significant number of files (Oficina Anticorrupción, 2005). As a result of these considerations, in 2005, the reorganization of the area of investigations was promoted through the creation of the Admission and Derivation Unit, which is responsible for receiving complaints; classifying them in terms of importance and severity, and referring them to the corresponding jurisdiction (provinces or municipalities), their dismissal, or the opening of a case file. This reorganization enabled the other Investigation Units to follow up on complaints and investigations with a sufficient evidential framework.[7]

The year 2005 saw the start of the "Institutional Strengthening of the Anticorruption Office" (FIOA) project, designed to reinforce preventive policies. This project was developed in two stages (2005–2007 and 2008–2009). The first led to the development of an identification map of problematic nodes in government procurement processes; distance training for NPC officials; and education in values and ethics aimed at secondary school students and teachers. During the second

The Anticorruption Agency of Argentina 135

stage, aspects of the previous phase were improved and institutional diffusion incorporated into transparency issues. The objective was to develop a strategic plan of dissemination and institutional communication of the OAA as a result of the need to give greater visibility to its products and achievements.

The FIOA Project had a twofold purpose. On the one hand, to comply with the CICC regarding the provision referring to the dissemination, education and training of public officials in ethics in the exercise of public administration and the need to extend these tasks to society in general. On the other hand, there was an urgent need to reverse the low profile of the OAA if it was to positively affect the perception and trust of citizens. Nowadays, the majority of Argentinean society is unaware of the existence of the OAA. As one of the informants interviewed declared:

> ...despite the public exposure the OAA had in the beginning in 1999 and 2000, in recent years it has adopted an extremely low profile... if one conducted an opinion poll in Argentina at the national level, the percentage of citizens who know that there is a national anticorruption office would be very low, because the OAA does not intervene in substantive discussions... If one thinks about the incidence or effectiveness of anticorruption policies speaking exclusively of anticorruption organizations such as the OAA or the Prosecutor's Office, I do not believe that there is much public perception regarding the importance of these organizations [sic].

Phase 5: Continuity (2010 to 2013)

In order to address the need to improve the visibility, communication, and dissemination of the OAA, during this phase, the FIOA Project was reformulated to include new components and improve existing ones: 1) development of a system of information and documentation of the OAA, to more efficiently administer information, documentation and archives; 2) values education through training workers and the adaptation of resources for their distribution in digital format; 3) e-learning for government officials; 4) cooperation and technical assistance with sub-national governments to promote the implementation of anticorruption conventions; and 5) cooperation and technical assistance with the private sector to build a platform of dialogue on anticorruption policies.

In a complementary manner, after identifying the operational bottlenecks in evaluating and controlling the sworn disclosures of the officials, the Plan for Strengthening the Sworn Disclosure System was launched. The objectives were to optimize and stiffen the regulations and controls on patrimonial evolution and the activities of public officials; train the areas responsible for its management in the NPC; design and apply new compliance control mechanisms; and present the OAA as a plaintiff in the cases of non-compliance. However, despite these significant advances in strengthening anticorruption work, the OAA still faces major challenges. Internally, for example, the Sworn Disclosures Control and Follow-up

136 Latin American Anticorruption Strategies

Unit has a staff of no more than 14 people, who must carry out their work in a universe of 36,000 employees obliged to present the development of their assets. This Unit must undertake the mandatory control of 3,500 officials and have random control over the rest. The limitations suggested by the small staff are by no means small if one recalls that the sworn disclosure of assets is one of the main inputs for an investigation into illicit enrichment. The lack of presentation of statements and control over the evolution of the officials' assets is precisely what hinders the criminal prosecution of that crime, which is generally the one that society usually links to the idea of "corruption" and for which an exemplary sentence is expected.

In the external field, the delay in the start of oral and public debate hearings in the cases in which the OAA intervenes has been a problem without a clear solution. This can partly be explained by the appeals of the accused who, exercising their right of defense in court, have succeeded in postponing the acts in which their procedural situation should be defined. This trend significantly increased in the year 2012.

Another factor of delay is that, in the event of arriving at the instance of oral and public debate, it is important to point out that—given the amount of lawsuits, the number of accused involved, the complexity of the defense maneuvers and the amount of documentation to be processed—the participation of the OAA implies the almost exclusive dedication of the staff involved in each of the cases over the course of several weeks or months. This situation no doubt considerably affects the resources available to the agency to fulfill its missions. This aspect has yet to be reviewed.

Then, at the strategy level, the Argentinean case favors the understanding of the challenges faced by a ACA—beyond technical aspects of design—both within the framework of the possibilities and limitations imposed from its context and because of the dynamics of the organization itself. This brief description of the five phases the OAA has undergone since its inception shows how an agency of this type is continually affected by the political situation and the organizational limits discovered along the way. The characteristics of corruption as a complex, dynamic problem, for which there are no clear-cut solutions—since there are no precise definitions of their causes—suggest that the use of traditional mechanisms (controls and punishments) to influence the behavior of citizens is insufficient. Moreover, implementing innovative and dynamic measures to motivate and commit individuals and organizations to actively cooperate suggests interesting changes in social behaviors that could encourage the reduction of corruption to manageable levels.

Lessons from the OOA

The analysis of the Argentinean case suggests the following lessons and challenges to understanding the challenges of an ACA in a situation of systemic corruption:

The Anticorruption Agency of Argentina **137**

1. The OAA was established on the basis of the idea that corruption should be treated from a comprehensive and systemic perspective, as a political–administrative problem in the broad sense and not only as a strictly legal problem. However, this view, which sought the silent transformation of ethical, evaluative, and cultural aspects, has been subsumed and relegated by the legal/criminal approach (i.e. the promotion of the sanction and the role of the OAA as a complainant have acquired central importance over the years). In the initial phases of the OAA, at a time when far-reaching public policies were designed, corruption was once again thought of as individual acts and, therefore, the legal aspect predominated. One of the explanations of this fact is that there was a certain gap between the systemic view of the phenomenon and the common-sense view, which was more closely linked to the scandals which drove the creation of the OAA at the end of the 1990s. What has once again shifted measures to fight corruption toward a more legal approach is the logic and dynamics of scandals, since this creates a demand and an expectation of almost immediate punishment that is opposed to the more diffuse view of the long-term transformation of institutions, values, and culture. This is where this gap occurs, where the systemic view is unable to respond to shorter-term social expectations.

2. Conversely, the predominance of the criminal perspective also reflects the way the Judicial Branch works. Justice can do no more than operate on a case-by-case basis, identify corrupt acts, evaluate them, and judge according to the law. Due to the principle of the division of powers, criminal justice cannot issue a verdict saying that it is necessary to transform the internal procedures of a particular entity so that there are no opportunities for acts of corruption. The idea of anticipation does not exist in the logic of a judge. In other words, if there is no act, there is no crime, no attempt and, therefore, no case to investigate. Accordingly, it is possible to suggest that the predominantly legal approach to corruption is not due to the confused approach of the OAA which has failed to understand every aspect of the phenomenon, but rather to the fact that it must meet the shorter-term demand for punishment that will grant it social legitimacy and the need to adjust to the way criminal justice operates. The Mexican anticorruption body should therefore try, in principle, to reflect on corruption from a systemic approach and to act in the short term with a view to the future. Systemic corruption is normalized corruption: practices become institutionalized and normalized, so they can be considered illegal or improper in abstract terms. In other words, they may be improper in an abstract sense, but the practices mean that evaluations of what is wrong are carried out on a case-by-case basis, with the participation of many people who can justify and rationalize these practices as "normal".

3. As for the design, the fact that the ACA depends directly on the Executive Branch has at least two important implications. On the one hand, without being a decentralized and autarkic organism, the OAA never had, nor does it have, the capacity to intervene with respect to the functioning of the

138 Latin American Anticorruption Strategies

administration in the present—the incumbent government and officials. On the other hand, as has been seen over the years, the OAA has been tied to the political ups and downs and crises that have affected the government of the day, undermining its bases of legitimacy and public confidence. The Argentinean OAA has not reached the traditional extreme of the ACAs of running parallel to institutional political power, at least not completely. The issue of the autonomy of a ACA is a critical issue, whether it is small or large.

4. The OAA undertook programs to strengthen preventive measures and dissemination and institutional communication until 2005 and 2010, respectively. ACAs need to be legitimized and it is clear that the reduction of corruption can be achieved in the long term. This has created a logic that can be contradictory: giving the agency far-reaching powers. It is contradictory because operating problems and the large amount of cases to be dealt with usually surpass the actual capacities of an ACA, as can be seen in this case of the OAA. However, it is logical that in a scenario of this operational complexity, an ACA has the possibility of participating in the public debate and of being an important element of awareness and social education. Although this adds more work and risks to the action of an ACA, the Argentinean case appears to show that it can be very important in the long term: to convey to society the importance of its participation in reducing corruption, which turns out to be not only a phenomenon of illegal acts committed by unethical people, to ensure that this capacity for education and awareness is explicit from the beginning, which would allow society to legitimize an ACA without excessive expectations. In the Argentinean case, there was no such discussion at the time of enacting the law that created the OAA nor was it clearly established what its responsibility, scope and meaning should be: it was to be a control agency with the capacity to intervene ex officio in the operation of the NPC, or an agent of change that would affect public opinion, concerned with the perception of corruption outside the purely administrative sphere. In fact, the OAA was halfway between the two; it was not the office that led major denunciations in the justice system and public opinion, nor did it create public policy oriented to transforming the forms of administration or the criteria for recruiting civil servants.

Likewise, corruption as a campaign agenda does not create problems, in fact, quite the opposite. However, when one wishes to put the anticorruption fight on the government agenda, the challenge is much greater because it implies recognizing the limits of this struggle. These limits can undermine the bases of legitimacy on which the ACA was created. In other words, promoting a frank, open discussion of the scope and meaning of this type of agencies is a double-edged sword: both promising more than what it is really going to achieve, as well as recognizing a limited impact on the problem of corruption—at least in the short term—can undermine the foundations of social trust and even question the need for the existence of this kind of agency.

It can be argued that a ACA is not simply an organizational tool dedicated mainly to punishing and controlling through reports and information flows. In fact, an ACA is a social creature which, over time, will require legitimacy and a strategy. Like any other government organization that deals with a complex problem, it must plan its objectives sensibly and achieve them incrementally, in stages. Construction of this roadmap is neither linear nor direct. It implies recognizing the ACA not as a silver bullet, but as an open subsystem, an organization that depends on communication and interaction with the outside (Meagher, 2005). In particular, in the case of corruption, the promotion of a dynamic social perspective in governmental action begins to seem necessary in view of the dominance of a normative, and sometimes arbitrary, rationalistic approach, which has proven to be fairly ineffective to date.

Notes

1 The ACA of Kosovo, the Commission for the Prevention of Corruption in Slovenia and the ACA of Sierra Leone are cases where corruption has not undergone major changes. Moreover, disciplinary procedures are hampered by overlapping responsibilities, while horizontal accountability limits the independence of agencies to investigate cases (Doig, Watt, & Williams, 2007; Dionisie & Checchi, 2008).
2 For reasons of space and argumentative clarity, not all the activities of the OAA are presented, only those that we consider relevant to understanding how the strategy has changed over time.
3 Between 1990 and 1999, Pereyra (2012) counted 122 corruption scandals published in the three main national newspapers (*Clarín, La Nación*, and *Pagina*).
4 The economic criterion allows an a priori estimation of the amount that, explicitly or implicitly, is reported as irregularly managed. It is a quantitative evaluation. This criterion is applied as a priority and allows the first discrimination of the complaints presented: it excludes those who do not exceed a certain amount. All the complaints that have been excluded by this first parameter must still be examined with the other criteria, which involve judgments and qualitative evaluations (Oficina Anticorrupción, 2000).
5 This diagnosis was the result of the "Exploratory Study on Transparency in Argentine Public Administration: 1998–1999".
6 Modalities of corruption identified in the NPC: 1) irregularities in the competition of bidders for the contracting of services; 2) favoritism in the selection of effectors/beneficiaries/licensees/suppliers; 3) payment of surcharges; 4) sub-services/products; 5) diversion of funds in outsourcing (intermediation); 6) irregular delivery of state assets; 7) return order; 8) favoritism in state control of privatized service concessions.
7 The effect was that the OAA assumed the role of complainant in seven cases in 2004; in 2005 the figure rose to 11.

Bibliography

Alcaide, L. (2005). Corrupción: obstáculo al crecimiento y a la competitividad. *Economía Exterior*, 31, 125–132.
Anechiarico, F. (2010). La corrupción y el control de la corrupción como impedimentos para la competitividad. *Gestión y Política Pública*, XIX(2), 239–261.
Arellano, D. (2012/2018). *¿Podemos reducir la corrupción en México?* Mexico City, Mexico: CIDE.

140 Latin American Anticorruption Strategies

Auditoría Superior de la Federación (ASF) (2012). *Cámara de diputados. Compilación técnica. Corrupción, ética y fiscalización.* Mexico City, Mexico: ASF.

Brunsson, N., & Olsen, J. P. (2007). *La reforma de las organizaciones.* Mexico City, Mexico: CIDE.

Charron, N. (2008). *Mapping and measuring the impact of anti-corruption agencies: A new dataset for 18 countries.* Paper presented at the New Public Management and the Quality of Government conference, Sweden, November 12.

Chugh, D. (2013). The motivations behind and conditioning of corruption in India. In *Psychology of corruption.* Lady Shri Ram College for Women. Retrieved from http://ssrn.com/abstract=2117247.

De Graaf, G. (2007). Causes of corruption: Towards a contextual theory of corruption. *Public Administration Quarterly,* 31(1–2), 38–86.

De Michele, R. (2001). The role of Anti-Corruption Office in Argentina. *The Journal of Country Inquiry, Country Report,* Autumn-Winter, 17–20.

De Speville, B. (2008). *Failing anti-corruption agencies – causes and cures.* Paper presented at the workshop Empowering anti-Corruption Agencies: Defying Institutional Failure and Strengthening Preventive and Repressive Capacities, Lisbon, May 14–16.

Dionisie, D., & Checchi, F. (2008). *Corruption and anti-corruption agencies in Eastern Europe and the CIS: A practitioners' experience.* Unpublished document. Retrieved from www.ancora ge-net.org/content/documents/dionisie-checchi-corruption_in_ee.pdf.

Doig, A., Watt, D., & Williams, R. (2017). Why do developing country anti-corruption commissions fail to deal with corruption? Understanding the three dilemmas of organisational development, performance expectation, and donor and government cycles. *Public Administration & Development,* 27(3), 251–259.

European Union (2011). *Supporting anti-corruption reforming partner countries: Concepts, tools and areas for action.* Brussels, Belgium: Publications Office of the European Union.

Fjeldstad, O. H., & Isaksen, J. (2008). *Anti-corruption reforms: Challenges, effects and limits of World Bank support. Background paper to public sector reform: What works and why? An IEG evaluation of World Bank support.* Working document. Washington, DC: Independent Evaluation Group, World Bank.

Heilbrunn, J. (2004). *Anti-corruption commissions: Panacea or real medicine to fight corruption?* Washington, DC: World Bank Institute.

Hodgson, G., & Jiang, S. (2008). La economía de la corrupción y la corrupción de la economía: Una perspectiva institucionalista. *Revista de Economía Institucional,* 10(18), 55–80.

Huther, J., & Shah, A. (2000). *Anti-corruption policies and programs: A framework for evaluation.* Policy research working papers. Washington, DC: The World Bank.

Jancsics, D. (2013). Petty corruption in Central and Eastern Europe: The client's perspective. *Crime, Law and Social Change,* 60, 319–341.

Jávor, I., & Jancsics, D. (2013). The role of power in organizational corruption: An empirical study. *Administration & Society,* XX(201), 1–32.

Klitgaard, R. (1988). *Controlling corruption.* Berkeley; Los Angeles: University of California Press.

MacMillan, J. (2011). Reformasi and public corruption: Why Indonesia's anti-corruption agency strategy should be reformed to effectively combat public corruption. *Emory International Law Review,* 25(1), 587–630.

Mao, Y., Wong, C. S., & Peng, K. Z. (2013). Breaking institutionalized corruption: Is the experience of the Hong Kong Independent Commission Against Corruption generalizable? *Asia Pacific Journal of Management,* 30, 1115–1124.

Meagher, P. (2005). Anti-corruption agencies: Rhetoric versus reality. *The Journal of Policy Reform*, 8(1), 69–103.

Mintzberg, H. (1987). The strategy concept I: Five Ps for strategy. *California Management Review*, 30, 11–24.

Mintzberg, H., & Waters, J. A. (1985). Of strategies, deliberate and emergent. *Strategic Management Journal*, 6, 257–272.

OECD. (2008). *Corruption: A glossary of international standards in criminal law*. [s.l.e].

Oficina Anticorrupción (2000, 2001, 2002, 2004, 2005). *Informe anual de la oficina anticorrupción*. Argentina. Retrieved from www.argentina.gob.ar/anticorrupcion/inform es-de-gestion.

Otáhal, T., & Wawrosz, P. (2013). *Corruption and competition: Toward economic theory of corruption*. Proceeding of the 17th International Conference of Current Trends in Public Sector Research, Masaryk University, Brno, Czech Republic.

Pereyra, S. (2006). La lucha contra la corrupción y las políticas de transparencia: Un programa global, un problema local. In A. Grimson & S. Pereyra (Eds.), *Conflictos globales, voces locales* (pp. 89–134). Buenos Aires, Argentina: Prometeo.

Perayra, S. (2012). La política de los escándalos de corrupción desde los años 90. *Desarrollo Económico*, 52(206), 255–284.

Pilapitiya, T. (2008). *Creating the institutional support for successful Anti-Corruption campaigns*. Paper presented at the 13th IACC Conference. Athens, Greece, Casals & Associates, November 2, 2008.

Princeton University (2013). Interview with Bertrand de Speville. Interviewer Gabriel Kuris. In *Innovation for successful societies*. United Kingdom. Series Anti-corruption, Interview no. H2. Retrieved from https://successfulsocieties.princeton.edu/interviews/bertrand-de-sp eville.

Raab, J., & Milward, H. B. (2003). Dark networks as problems. *Journal of Public Administration Research and Theory*, 13(4), 413–439.

Rose-Ackerman, S. (2001). *La corrupción y los gobiernos: Causas, consecuencias y reforma*. Mexico City, Mexico: Siglo XXI.

Serra, D. (2010). *Combining top-down and bottom-up accountability: Evidence from bribery experiment*. Florida State University. September 14. Retrieved from http://ssrn.com/abstract= 1534107.

Sousa, L. (2009). Anti-corruption agencies: Between empowerment and irrelevance. *EUI working papers RSCAS*, August. European University Institute, Robert Schuman Centre for Advanced Studies.

Stapenhurst, R., & Kpundeh, S. J. (1999). *Curbing corruption: Toward a model for building national integrity*. Washington, DC: World Bank.

Torre, J. C. (2003). Los huérfanos de la política de partidos: Sobre la naturaleza y los alcances de la crisis de representación partidaria. *Desarrollo Económico*, 42(168), 647–676.

UN-ODCCP (2002). *Global Programme Against Corruption: Anti-corruption tool kit*. Vol. 1. Vienna, Austria: UN-UNDOC.

4

THE MEXICAN NATIONAL ANTICORRUPTION SYSTEM

White Elephant or World-Class Innovation?

Introduction

Mexico is a country where corruption is widespread, systemic, and organized. It could even be said to be historical; in other words, the dynamics of corruption have built up over the centuries (Nef, 2001; Villarroel, 1785/1994). The Mexican political system, now with democratic elections after over 70 years of single–party domination, continues to be supported by rampant clientelism on the part of all the political parties, a public administration in which there is no real civil service, a system that is federalized in form yet which in practice is highly centralized and with almost absolute power by the governors who behave almost as feudal lords.

Corruption has therefore accompanied this country from its earliest days as a colony and then as an independent country. It is a country which today has a very open economy, the eleventh largest in the world, with a population of over 120 million people (without considering the millions of Mexicans who have emigrated to the United States). The combination of these elements of size and importance, and the fact that it is one of the most corrupt countries in the world, are important elements to consider in understanding its current situation in this matter.

In order to measure the phenomenon of corruption in Mexico, it is worth mentioning (with all the limitations already discussed in Chapter 1 of the book) the Corruption Perception Index of Transparency International (TI), which has always classified Mexico as a country with high corruption levels. In 2001, the country ranked 51st out of 91 countries evaluated with a rating of 3.7 (on a scale of 0 to 10, where 10 means absence of corruption and 0 total existence of corruption). In 2015, it scored 35 out of 100 (at the level of Armenia or the Philippines), ranking 95th out of 167 countries evaluated (Transparency International, 2015). These indices clearly point to the fact that Mexico is a country in which the perception of corruption is stably high. For its part, the Global Corruption Barometer indicates

The Mexican National Anticorruption System **143**

that Mexico went from a weighted average perception of corruption in its institutions of 4.5 in 2004 to 4.6 in 2013 (where 1 means "not at all corrupt" and 5 "very corrupt"). The police, civil servants, the judicial system, and political parties are the institutions that fared worse of the 12 options analyzed.

Data are also available from the National Survey of Government Quality and Impact 2013 (ENCIG, in Spanish) published by the National Institute of Statistics and Geography (INEGI, in Spanish), an organization with operational and technical autonomy, and the authority to undertake the national census. This survey showed that, according to people surveyed throughout the country, corruption is an extremely serious problem, surpassed only by "insecurity and crime" and unemployment. The ENCIG also records the prevalence of corruption; in other words, the frequency with which the population which had contact with a public servant had an "experience of corruption": at the federal level, a prevalence of 12,080 cases was recorded for every 100,000 inhabitants. In terms of corruption per level of government, there is a much higher rate at the state than at the federal and municipal levels. With regard to the corruption incidence rate—number of acts of corruption, of which the respondent may have experienced one or more—the survey estimates that nationwide, there were 24,724 acts of corruption per 100,000 inhabitants. In more detail, the survey indicates that the two procedures with the highest percentage of corruption experiences out of a total of 21 analyzed are: "Contact with public security authorities" (50.6%) and "property-related permits" (24.8%). Regarding the prevalence of acts of corruption that affect firms, in another survey, the INEGI found that 82.2% of the country's economic units find frequent acts of corruption (ENCIG, 2017).

While these data should be considered with caution, given the difficulty of using data to measure and study a phenomenon which, by its very nature, is illegal and often based on collusion between different parties, the evidence is very clear: Corruption is a normalized phenomenon in this country. Other studies have shown its prevalence in critical spaces such as the police (Arteaga & Lopez, 1998), the judicial branch (Ríos, 2018), and in the relations between government and companies (Arellano-Gault, 2018). It is in the political system, but also at the social level in widespread practices such as *palancas*, analyzed in Chapter 2. Corruption and the practices of exchanging favors and influences may be very tightly integrated. In the Mexican case, it is: the practices and the ways of relating and exchanging favors are the basis of corruption in Mexico. In Mexico, people "have" *palancas, palancas* are lent, *palancas* are "created and fed", every day, in many social and economic spheres.

Palancas give prestige and those who know how to "invest" in them are socially appreciated. *Palancas* are a deeply entrenched social mechanism in the country: they are the way people increase the likelihood of obtaining what they want or even what they should be able to obtain through legitimate organizational channels, but which for various reasons is difficult to do so. When the authorities are untrustworthy and unstable, having *palancas* is a necessity and even a symbol of intelligence and skill. *Palancas* are so widespread that they not only operate between citizens and government, but between citizens and private companies, between private individuals, and even within the government bureaucracy as an essential management mechanism necessary for the organization to function (Arellano-Gault, 2018).

If the authorities are unreliable, they are not considered impartial, and *palancas* may be the only way to achieve what is sought. If *palancas* are institutionalized, then everyone seeks *palancas* to achieve what they want: it is not only considered necessary but a rational, logical act. Accordingly, a person with *palancas* has prestige. And he/she manages to increase it not only by what he/she achieves with *palancas* but with what he/she obtains by "lending" his/her *palancas*. A person who does not achieve what he/she wanted from obviously unreliable authorities, will therefore feel frustrated not only with those authorities but with himself/herself (and probably will even be criticized by his/her family) for not having the ability or intelligence to obtain the right *palancas* to satisfy the needs of his/her family. The following conceptual map shows the *palanca* as a mechanism with a social impact.

It may be that, throughout this journey, the search for *palancas* did not involve engaging in strictly corrupt acts. But it is very likely that, at bottom, *palancas* perpetuate corruption in a country such as Mexico. It provides a known and rational social

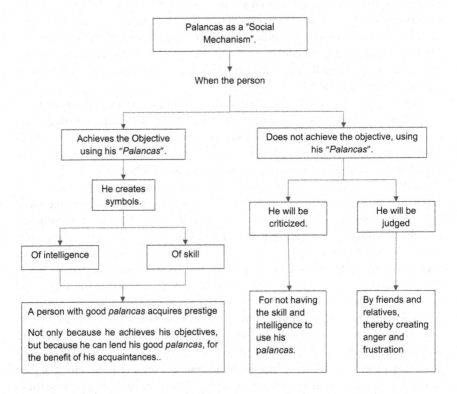

SCHEME 4.1 *Palancas* as a social mechanism
Source: Compiled by the author with data from Nuijten (2003).

The Mexican National Anticorruption System **145**

path, a language, and a social conception. It even provides hope for those who do not have power or many resources, yet who, can through the right *"palancas"* do and achieve something (Nuijten, 2003). The social skeleton that supports the *palanca* is dense and extremely rich in languages and practical codes. It is undoubtedly a clue to understanding the social fabric of corruption normalized in this country.

In Mexico, the authorities (both public and private) are perceived as far from the ideal type of impartiality (as in many societies affected by high levels of corruption; Mungiu-Pippidi, 2015), allowing people to find, in acts that can be classified or that can lead to acts of corruption, a successful way to negotiate, to find a way around formal rules and thus obtain what they need. Corruption in Mexico is a successful form of social relations, but also a social trap: everyone would be better off without it (corruption is extremely costly economically and socially), but it seems that there is no social actor with the capacity or knowledge necessary to break this kind of social agreement that condemns society to organize through this set of practices that end up being dubious and causing behaviors that cannot be measured.

Explaining the social dynamics of corruption in Mexico is an important step toward understanding how to act to control it successfully (Kaiser, 2014). This is why the reflection that has been emphasized in this book explicitly chooses not to take an "institutional" perspective on corruption as a basis, even though it can be productive. Institutions, rules, and norms, whether formal or informal, are important. They are, as some rather simplistically argue, "the rules of the game". However, the reflection that has developed up to now starts from a different place: not from a normative vision, or from an important but very limited discussion of what the rules of the game should be. Instead, it has sought to understand how the practices and forms of action of everyday life are constituted as strong networks of exchange and interaction between people, thus giving such a strong meaning and legitimacy to these practices that they become widespread. In other words, everyday practices explicitly seek to "get round" formal rules. And this bending of the rules constitutes a legitimate practice, socially speaking. Corruption, then, in a country like Mexico, may be a disruptive and illegal phenomenon, but at the same time, paradoxically, it is sustained by social exchange practices seen as substantive by people on a day-to-day basis. They are also seen as perennial, that is, as immutable over time: as true in the colony as in the era of single-party rule as in the current electoral democratic phase.

Mexico therefore experiences a powerful paradox: socially speaking, improper acts (and sometimes clearly corrupt acts) can be seen (unconsciously or at least informally or secretly) as legitimate and necessary because they are effective mechanisms for surviving in a context where the authorities cannot reasonably be expected to be impartial. It is a complicated game: the authorities are formally impartial, but everyone knows that, in practice, such a thing is a facade. On the surface, the game is based on the logic of apparently impartial authorities, although in everyday relationships, things are clearly different. The social game that produces this logic is rich and interesting. It is a social context that forces people and organizations to be extremely innovative to cope with the dense set of practices, traditions, symbols, and rules they must "know how to play" in the game of relations with *palancas* and acquaintances. The game produced by non-impartial authorities is actually a very vivid game. First of all, people have to learn to play the game and learn how to use different strategies for each situation. There is a need to create and reproduce various social mechanisms, artifacts, and symbols that allow people to deal with authorities that are said to be de jure formal and impartial, but in practice, de facto, are obscure, accept and seek informal agreements, and are influenced by various practices involving the exchange of favors. This social game is, logically, very stable although it is informal thanks to the fact that, over the centuries, it has been able to create dense structures of relations of reciprocity between the various groups and social strata.

In Mexico, *palancas* speak of the social construct of power that is obtained thanks to "someone who knows someone", which create a network of reciprocities of different levels and sizes. These personal relationships make it possible to overcome the injustices created by unreliable authorities. In this respect, the use of *palancas* can be seen by people as fair or at least indispensable. But it is also a mechanism that makes it possible to skirt the rules and obtain privileges (Zalpa, Tapia, & Reyes, 2014). Scheme 4.2 shows the way the use of *palancas* generated a network of reciprocities, creating a social construct.

This contradiction is probably experienced or justified by people in this country not without some difficulty. It can be defended as a mechanism of justice at a certain moment (people get what they need despite the rigidity of bureaucratic rules, for example) and at the same time be seen as perpetuating the injustice and bias of those who have authority (when it is observed that the richest or most influential people are able to have more and obtain more benefits, for example).

The same concept jokingly used to talk about these mechanisms is in itself a code, a way of normalizing what should be an exception but in fact is everyday behavior (however contradictory this may sound). *Palanca* (finding support to move any obstacle) in Mexico, and *Jeitinho* (a "shortcut", the skill and cunning to find a solution to something that seems impossible) in Brazil, are two words that speak of intelligence, ability, and cunning. They are two codes used to explain everyday forms of interaction and give them an ambiguous meaning that speaks of the combination of an act that is not entirely illegal, not entirely hidden, but not entirely legitimate or transparent either. It also requires extremely specific forms of action. There are those who are more skilled, charismatic, and astute, and

SCHEME 4.2 Sequence of the use of *palancas* in Mexico
Source: Compiled by the author with data from Zalpa, Tapia, & Reyes (2014).

therefore, able to make better use of these mechanisms. So having *palancas* or doing *jeitinho* therefore has some merit. But the code is also able to communicate that these are acts and practices that run parallel to formal rules.

Palancas in Mexico are present as a practice in all social strata and in the most diverse contexts. People find out about them very early on, at home and in their neighborhood. They learn to use and seek them from a very early stage. They are seen as an important skill that must be nurtured and learned, including: the more *palancas* you get, the smarter and more cunning you are. If *palancas* produce negative short- and long-term effects, it is difficult for many people in these countries to observe or accept this. If there were injustices which, due to the *palancas*, affected the rights of people without *palancas* or if *palancas* serve to reproduce a political system that is legitimized through these informal practices, it is not easy for the people involved to observe this directly. The vicious circle is clear: faced with a partial authority, the use of a *palanca* can achieve a good result for the person capable of using it. The problem is that the long-term effect is to reproduce the logic of social relations based on informal privileges and exchanges, rather than socially accepted general and impartial rules and principles. The game of *palancas* is reciprocal, producing networks that may be very extensive and to a certain extent organized. Networks of *palancas* can become so solidly organized that they become closed or semi-closed circles of privileges that are difficult for anyone to access, since they have particular entry rules. For many in these societies, *palancas* can be seen as a mechanism of "justice" by allowing "anyone" a mechanism to solve the most intricate social problems. In practice, they can become quasi-mafias of networks of friends and acquaintances that support and help maintain their privileges for members of the circle or network alone. It can therefore be said that the game of *palancas* produces the reason for its reproduction. It is a rational game played by people in a generalized way, but globally it becomes an unfair game, which reproduces the logic of the authorities and privileged groups to continue excluding the vast majority of people from exchanges and social solutions. The pathological, but by no means less stable and "functional" link, in a certain respect, between *palancas* and corruption is obvious (Nuijten, 2004). The mental map in Scheme 4.3 explains the quasi-mafias of *palancas*.

Corruption therefore forms part of a set of reciprocal strategies. It is a glue that links or entangles governments, people, civil society organizations, and companies in a specific social agreement that makes corruption a strategic political instument to survive, reciprocate, and build stable relationships (as anthropological studies of corruption have long shown; Haller & Shore, 2005; Olivier de Sardan, 1999; Torsello & Venard, 2016).

The Mexican case is extremely severe: it is a political system and an administrative regime which has corruption as a modus operandi, culture, and way of working. One might think that it is systemic corruption, which many (not without some cynicism or at least desperation) regard as functional. There is logically a high degree of resistance to change due to vested interests, among those accustomed to this way of relating and this way of obtaining income. Various aspects of corruption in Mexico can be considered a true form of *expertise* valued in various political and economic circles.

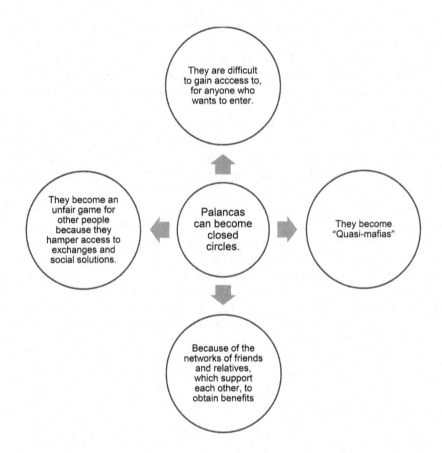

SCHEME 4.3 *Palancas* as quasi-mafias
Source: Compiled by the author with data from Nuijten (2004).

Trying to reduce corruption in such a country requires a long-term effort with a long-term view. There is no silver bullet: there is an awareness in this country that it will be necessary to experiment with many instruments, to exert constant pressure to force the political and administrative system, companies, and society in general, to abandon these practices that lead to corruption becoming functional. For many people in Mexico, it is obviously up to society to promote a generalized conception that corruption is an undesirable element that cannot be justified through everyday practices such as *palancas* or clientelism.

Making changes in this regard will require patience and long-term commitment to change things. At the time of writing this book, the country was struggling to implement the most recent experiment to deal with the problem of corruption in the country: the National Anticorruption System (SNA).

This ambitious legal and institutional transformation is a desperate measure to combat the levels of corruption reached in the 2012–2018 federal administration. And it is an experiment, an innovation, and, obviously, a risky attempt. In Mexico, a more ambitious and risky option was chosen than creating an anticorruption agency. The reasons have to do with the high likelihood that a corrupt political system that creates an anticorruption agency will end up manipulating and sabotaging it. As discussed in the introduction to Section II of this book, the experiences of the slightly more than 50 existing anticorruption agencies (Doig, Watt, & Williams, 2007) speak of the major obstacles they face in achieving their objectives (De Speville, 1997; Rotberg, 2017, p. 110). There are several reasons for this, but as has been said before, it is usually due to the resistance and even the attack that political forces launch on these organizations as soon as they begin to act. Most of these agencies have their budgets trimmed, are attacked legally or in the press, lose autonomy, and are actually trapped by the very system of corruption they attempt to fight. Famous exceptions in the literature which are actually very scarce obviously include those of Hong Kong and Singapore. In this same category of exception, we can find another anticorruption organization that has been successful, which we will study in Chapter 6: the CICIG in Guatemala. Nevertheless, at the time of writing, CICIG is being fiercely attacked by the Guatemalan political system in order to expel it from the country.

In large part, because of these difficulties in ensuring that there is a successful anticorruption agency in conditions of systemic corruption, as we discussed in Chapter 3 with the case of the Argentinean agency, Mexico refused to consider creating this type of agency as an option. For some, this option of a specialized anticorruption agency was quickly scrapped. However, the reasons given for this are logical: the chances of political groups launching an operation of resistance and capture against this agency were so high that it was thought not to be a realistic option.

While it is true that anticorruption agencies face a major challenge that increases the chances of failure, it is also true that the most successful cases show that, beyond the original or legal design, it also depends on the strategies, capabilities, and organizational strengths these agencies are capable of using. The cases where they have worked, always with enormous challenges, are an interesting lesson in the efforts, strategies, and circumstances linked to understanding the probabilities of success of this type of instruments. The case of CICIG in Guatemala (which we will analyze in Chapter 6) speaks of a successful organization precisely because it concentrated on having focused organizational capacity for criminal investigation (Zamudio, 2018). The case of Argentina already studied in Chapter 3 refers to the same: it takes time and perseverance to create the organizational and political capacities needed to build viable, focused, and specialized mechanisms to control the various acts of corruption which, in a country with systemic corruption, are persistent and widespread. And this time and perseverance is needed to establish solid capacities, as a minimum floor, for obtaining solid, valid results in dealing incrementally with the most urgent cases. In other words, there is a long way to go and it is imperative to create an organization that builds its capacities step by step, by gradually supporting the transformation of the judicial system, investigation, and combating fraud in its most diverse expressions. The strategy of these agencies, although problematic, has an advantage: they require an incremental strategy, that learns, advances, and is able to modify and reinvent itself since it is not an all-or-nothing bet.

This is precisely the problem of the Mexican SNA: after quickly ruling out the option of learning through a specialized agency, an integral system was proposed, which connects all the national pieces in a broad network that is expected to address all the problems of corruption in the country in an integral, complete, and coordinated way. This is an exciting, daring, and innovative idea. For this reason, there are no similar references to predict whether or not it will work. In other words, today we have some information about why anticorruption agencies do not work. And some knowledge about what conditions can make it work. But the Mexican innovation of the SNA implies that it is not easy to know whether it will work or how to fix it if it begins to fail. One thing is clear: the SNA will be resisted and attacked, and sabotaged by the systemic logic of the corruption of the Mexican political system. The question is whether the SNA will be able to survive these attacks and yield reasonable, prompt results.

It is worth asking: What does it mean and how can one measure that the SNA is working? This is not a trivial question and unfortunately the answers are ambiguous. A system, as a basic conceptual logic, does not generate results based on what its parts or elements achieve in isolation: the results of a system are the combined product of the interaction of the parts with each other and with a dynamic, uncertain context. Therefore, from a systemic point of view, the synergy created by the interaction between the parties and between the system and the context is key. And that synergy is created through everyday actions, and the integration, cooperation, and coordination of its elements. But also, fundamentally, it is created through its adaptation to contextual changes. No system can completely control all these relationships and effects, by definition. The interaction acquires a life of its own, so to speak, and it is in that logic that it is possible to improve interaction and expect this adaptation to be successful in adapting to its context. The SNA will obtain results insofar as the interaction between its different parts (a broad array of organizations and institutions) manages to create that myriad of actions which will eventually have the ability to break the equilibrium of the corruption system and encourage a new equilibrium, in which corruption can be reduced and controlled. The causal logic of a system, in the way the SNA is proposed, makes it difficult to establish concrete goals and specific situations to understand whether it is in fact working. Reducing certain types of corruption, or ensuring that different parts of the political system coordinate to produce new processes or create new anticorruption instruments, are not in themselves indicators that the system is working.

The experience of anticorruption agencies provides a clear lesson: they elicit immediate resistance and are objects of prompt, expeditious attacks (Charron, 2008; De Speville, 2008, 2010; Heilbrunn, 2004). The SNA will undoubtedly suffer the same fate. The key, as with anticorruption agencies, will be to understand how it will be able to withstand that attack and the sabotage it will soon suffer (and worse than in the case of an anticorruption agency because the SNA is in fact a cluster of organizations and agencies that can be boycotted from different angles and by different interests). If one part of the system fails, the entire system will be challenged.

In any case, the SNA is an innovation. Its results and effects remain to be seen. If the SNA works, Mexico will have taught the world a lesson in how to root out corruption through a complex, variegated, and expensive mechanism. If it does not work, it will become an international case study that will provide lessons on what not to do. Let us now analyze the logic of this Mexican innovation.

The Logic of the SNA

The Mexican National Anticorruption System (SNA) is a mechanism that seeks to unite "institutional efforts supported by transparency and accountability, and strengthen the confidence of citizens in institutions in a framework of promoting legality and good practices" (SFP, 2016). The SNA works with the intervention of various governmental organizations and a participation committee comprising distinguished members of civil society. The relationship is between a Coordinating Committee (responsible for establishing coordination mechanisms among members of the SNA) chaired by the Citizen Participation Committee (CPC). Six public organizations also interact: the Secretariat of Public Administration (SFP), the Superior Audit Office of the Federation (ASF), the National Institute of Transparency, Access to Information and Data Protection (INAI), the Council of the Federal Judiciary (CJF), an anticorruption prosecutor of the General Prosecutor's Office (FGR), and the President of the Federal Court of Administrative Justice (TFJA). Construction of this institutional framework began in 2012, when launching an anticorruption office or prosecutor specializing in the issue occupied a more important place on the public agenda. At the time of writing this book, the implementation of all the pieces is not yet complete, although the system as such has been operating since 2017. Scheme 4.4 outlines a timeline of the history of the SNA.

The Anticorruption Reform Proposals (2012–2016)

The government of Mexican President Enrique Peña Nieto (2012–2018) had proposed, since his transition to the presidency of the country, establishing a National Anticorruption Commission whose objective would be to achieve an honest, effective government. The proposal stated that this agency would have autonomy and that its director would be proposed by the president and confirmed by the Senate. As discussed at the beginning of this chapter, this proposal immediately generated a great deal of suspicion due to the permanent contradiction of an anticorruption agency that in many ways relies on the political system itself, which is affected by the high levels of corruption that led to its creation in the first place. In November 2012, the president submitted a bill for the creation of this Commission to Congress. However, the proposal was not well received by the political

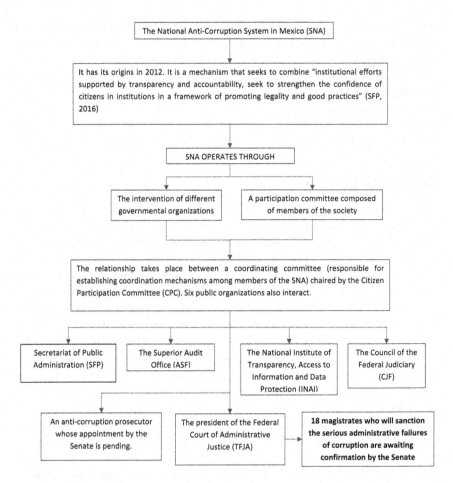

SCHEME 4.4 Mexico National Anticorruption System, 2016
Source: Compiled by the author using data from SFP (2016).

class nor by public opinion in general, because its institutional design lacked coordination mechanisms between the entities involved and real autonomy with respect to the executive. The bill was not discussed in Congress until nearly two years later. This institutional scheme was seriously criticized as a mechanism of transparency and good governance by various civil society organizations.

In this proposal to create a traditional anticorruption agency, the homogenization of the classification of crimes and penalties linked to violations of administrative and criminal responsibilities derived from the fight against corruption was contemplated. The National Anticorruption Commission would have the power to prevent, investigate, and punish acts of corruption by public servants, but also by the firms involved. The Commission would also be accompanied by the coordination of work in the sanction of courts specializing in the issue to process the lawsuits filed for acts of corruption. The work of the Commission would be accompanied by the efforts of a Supreme Audit Institution and a National Council for Public Ethics: a huge council with members of the federal government in matters of transparency, the Senate, the Chamber of Deputies, the Superior Audit of the Federation, a member from every state in the country and of the Commission itself. This reform proposal also included the creation of local commissions to combat corruption for all states.

In November 2012, a second bill was submitted to Congress. The Party of the Democratic Revolution (a left-leaning opposition party) also submitted a reform bill to the Senate to fight corruption. Unlike the proposal of the party in power, this reform project proposed the creation of a National Agency for the Fight against Corruption with the option of handling cases, whether federal or state, in criminal matters that could be shared with the Public Prosecutor's Office. This Agency would be run by seven prosecutors proposed by citizens, but appointed by the Senate. The main institutional interrelationships would happen with the Public Prosecutor's Office and the Superior Audit of the Federation (the oversight body in the legislative branch), but also with a proposed Citizens' Council to monitor the agency's performance at the three levels of government. This proposal was accompanied by mechanisms to compensate for the damage caused by acts of corruption by public servants, where the reintegrated resources would be used primarily to support young people, invest in science and technology, and strengthen the country's secondary and higher education.

In January 2013, a third reform proposal was promoted in Congress. Now the right-leaning party, the National Action Party (PAN, a party with conservative tendencies), also submitted a bill to the Senate for the creation of a National Anticorruption and Control Institute (INAC) with a more centralizing notion of functions and powers. Broadly speaking, the INAC could oversee, monitor, control, inspect, evaluate, or sanction any official at the three levels of government, autonomous bodies, institutions, or persons related to public resources. It also proposed a Specialized Prosecutor's Office for the criminal action of acts of corruption, directed by a Senior Prosecutor.

In April 2013, the PAN itself submitted a reform bill to create a National Anticorruption System. This new reform initiative proposed to divide criminal action lawsuits between the Public Prosecutor's Office and a General Prosecutor's Office to Combat Corruption, create a General Law to Combat Corruption to define responsibilities, procedures, origins, crimes, and sanctions derived from acts of corruption and sought to draw up a Register of Public Servants, together with their assets. This proposal envisaged the action of three organizations, generally related to the investigation and sanction of cases: the Federal Inspection Entity and the General Prosecutor's Office to Combat Corruption (and 32 local counterparts). The National Commission to Combat Corruption was proposed to sanction individuals and public servants involved with public resources. Operationally speaking, every state would have a replica of the Attorney General's Office and the Commission. In order to coordinate the system, the National Corruption Combat Council was proposed, with representatives from the three branches and the presiding commissioners of the Federal Commission to Combat Corruption, the State Commissions, and the Federal District. This Council would work hand in hand with the Advisory Body comprising five citizen councilors (academics and members of civil society organizations), who would be elected by the Senate. Table 4.1 shows the four reform proposals, and the origin and design of each one.

None of these four proposals was approved by the Senate. Each initiative made the institutional framework and the creation of new public organizations seeking to combat corruption more complex.

However, these reform proposals were accompanied by two important decrees that formed the basis for both the executive and legislative branches to continue designing options. The first, which occurred in February 2014, established the transformation of the Attorney General's Office, which has basically been the organization dependent on the executive branch to deal with all related legal and judicial issues, in the Attorney General's Office (FGR). It gave it constitutional autonomy, legal personality, and its own assets. This transformation envisaged that one of the two specialized prosecutors, answerable to that Prosecutor's Office, would be in charge of combating corruption. At the time of writing this chapter, a Prosecutor General has not been appointed since neither the executive nor the Senate have managed to reach an agreement after all these years. This is a symptom of how worried the political class is about the consequences of launching this anticorruption process. The second decree, enacted in March 2014, created the Public Prosecutor's Office specializing in crimes related to acts of corruption, as part of the structure of the Attorney General's Office. This Specialized Prosecutor's Office would handle, within its own structure, the work of the Special Unit for the Investigation of Crimes Committed by Public Servants and against the Administration of Justice that was already in place.

Thus, the lobbying of the reform in the fight against corruption lasted just over a year, going through several design options and a great deal of discussion between the political parties and various organizations of society. This discussion led to the final proposal, an innovation that will be discussed later.

Anticorruption Reform

On April 16, 2015, the bill for the constitutional amendment, expansion, and constitutional repeal of anticorruption matters was approved in the Senate. This was followed, on May 27, 2015, by the approval of the decree for the constitutional amendment of anticorruption matters, after the discussion and approval of the Chamber of Deputies. In particular, the reforms of constitutional articles focused on seven fundamental issues:

1. The creation of the National Anticorruption System (Art. 113 of the Constitution).
2. The recognition of the faculty of Congress to issue laws that establish the bases of the National Anticorruption System.

TABLE 4.1 Mexico: The anticorruption reform proposals, 2012–2016

The anticorruption reform proposals (2012–2016)	Origin	Objective	Observations
Federal government (2012–2018)	The government of Mexican President Enrique Peña Nieto 2012–2018.	The proposal indicated that this agency would have autonomy. Its director would be proposed by the president and confirmed by the Senate.	Its institutional design lacked coordination mechanisms between the entities involved and real autonomy with respect to the executive branch. The bill was not discussed in Congress until nearly two years later.
Democratic Revolution Party	Left-leaning opposition. 2012.	Creation of a National Agency for the Fight against Corruption with the option of handling cases, whether federal or state, in criminal issues that could be shared with the Public Prosecutor's Office.	The reintegrated resources would be used primarily to support young people, invest in science and technology, and strengthen the country's secondary and higher education.
National Anticorruption and Control Institute (INAC)	In January 2013, National Action Party (PAN).	It could oversee, monitor, control, inspect, evaluate, or sanction any official at the levels of government, autonomous bodies, institutions, or persons related to public resources.	It proposed a Specialized Prosecutor's Office for criminal proceedings for acts of corruption, directed by a Senior Prosecutor.
National Anticorruption System	In April 2013, PAN.	It proposed to divide criminal action proceedings between the Public Prosecutor's Office and a General Prosecutor's Office to Combat Corruption, to create a General Law to Combat Corruption.	Typify responsibilities, procedures, origins, crimes, and sanctions derived from acts of corruption.

Source: Compiled by the author.

3. It established the responsibilities of public servants and individuals who engage in acts of corruption.
4. It concentrated the capacity for investigation and substantiation of administrative offenses in the Internal Organs of Control of the dependencies (Art. 28 of the Constitution) and authorized the Courts of Administrative Justice to resolve cases classified as corruption (Art. 109 of the Constitution).
5. It granted the Superior Audit of the Federation the function of overseeing federal resources in the three orders of government (Art. 79 of the Constitution).
6. Creation of the Special Administrative Justice Tribunal to impose sanctions for serious administrative offenses (Art. 73 of the Constitution).
7. Obligation to submit affidavits (Art. 108) and adjustment of penalties for corruption offenses (Art. 109 of the Constitution).

The debate took place on a national scale, in each of the states and in the midst of a process of change of representatives in the Chamber of Deputies. Accordingly, it was not until July 2016 that the secondary laws of the National Anticorruption System were published. Thus, the creation of the National Anticorruption System was accompanied by a series of secondary laws, four of which were newly passed laws and three of which were amendments. Table 4.2 explains the Anticorruption Reform (SNA) and its seven secondary laws.

Moreover, the dimensions and functioning of the SNA were designed as a complex institutional framework that depends on the performance of three orders of government: federal, state, and municipal. In the state governments, the publication of the constitutional reform marked the start of a process of legal harmonization in the 32 State Congresses, to determine and provide normative support for the implementation of 32 Local Anticorruption Systems (SLAC).

It is worth noting that the SNA emphasizes an administrative logic of corruption, in other words, assuming that the main or at least the most urgent task is to reduce the corruption that is a consequence of the bureaucratic dynamics of public administrations. Accordingly, the SNA seeks to ensure that the coordination and mutual monitoring among all its multiple component parts will make it possible to create more rational and effective action, based on the cooperation and surveillance among the various organisms involved. And it makes certain citizen actors, in other words, academics and representatives of civil society organizations, responsible for coordination and oversight. Table 4.3 explains the basic pillars of the implementation of the fight against corruption.

The next section explains how the system as a whole was implemented, which has been accompanied by bureaucratic and political stagnation in recent years.

Implementation and Stagnation (2016–2018)

One of the first tasks after the approval of the constitutional reforms that led to the SNA was to set the system as a whole in train. There were three fundamental tasks that

TABLE 4.2 Mexico Anticorruption Reform. Secondary laws: 2015

On April 16, 2015, the bill for the constitutional amendment, expansion, and constitutional repeal of anticorruption matters was approved in the Senate.

The anticorruption package was accompanied by seven secondary laws:

General National Anticorruption System Law	This law established the coordination mechanism between the Federation, the states, municipalities, and the Mexico City boroughs for the operation of the SNA, with four basic institutions: • Coordinating Committee • Executive Secretariat • Citizen Participation Committee • Governing Committee of the National Control System
General Law on Administrative Responsibilities	Faculties of the orders of government to determine the responsibilities, obligations, and sanctions of public servants for the acts or omissions which they commit. Obligation of public servants to submit their statements: assets, tax, and interests Declaration of assets and interests of "any natural or legal person who receives and spends public funds or contracts under any modality with public organizations in the Federation",
Organic Law of the Federal Court of Administrative Justice	Law created to establish the Federal Court of Administrative Justice (TFJA), establish its integration, organization, powers, and operation. The law empowers the TFJA to find out about the administrative responsibilities of public servants and individuals linked to serious misconduct.
Law of Fiscalization and Accountability of the Federation	This law reinforces the role of the Superior Audit of the Federation because it establishes criteria so that it can audit the federal participations granted to entities and the public debt of states.
Organic Law of the Attorney General's Office	Reformed law to establish the functions and powers of the Specialized Prosecutor's Office in matters of crimes related to acts of corruption. There are three main aspects of this law: 1. The Prosecutor's Office has the power to request information that is useful or necessary for its investigations without it being denied. 2. It can propose the appointments of public prosecutors specializing in corruption. 3. Establish relationships and collaboration mechanisms to investigate corruption offenses with other authorities.
Federal Penal Code	It typifies and stiffens penalties for public servants who engage in acts of corruption, with up to 18 years in prison, and for private persons for establishing relationships that influence public servants to do or arrange business with up to 6 years in prison.
Organic Law of Federal Public Administration	This law appoints the SFP as the authority responsible for the internal control of the Federal Public Administration and orders it to maintain close collaboration with the National Anticorruption System and the National System of Control.

Source: Compiled by the author.

158 Latin American Anticorruption Strategies

TABLE 4.3 Basic pillars of the SNA

The SNA covers three basic pillars for implementing the fight against corruption		
Denunciation mechanisms	Investigation	Sanction

Source: Compiled by the author.

had to be carried out to begin operating the system: 1) to launch the public organizations created as a result of the reforms: Committee on Citizen Participation, Executive Secretariat, Governing Committee of the National Supervision System; 2) appoint judges and officials concerned with the operation of the Special Tribunals, the General Prosecutor's Office, and the Specialized Office on Corruption; and 3) the harmonization of the 32 state constitutions to provide legal support for the operation of their corresponding Local Anticorruption Systems.

On July 19, 2016, the seven SNA laws came into force. The first organ of the SNA to be formed was a Selection Commission; it had 90 days to achieve this (October 19, 2016)—and would be responsible for appointing five members of the Citizen Participation Committee of the SNA. This Commission was integrated within the deadline by nine members in an honorary capacity, five from institutions of higher education and research and four members of civil society organizations dedicated to matters of control, accountability, and the fight against corruption.

The next body that was created was the Committee of Citizen Participation, which involved an exhaustive process of reviewing the files of citizen candidates interested in participating in the call for submissions launched by the Selection Commission. A first round of interviews was carried out with 17 candidates, five of which were elected in an open, public process for citizens on January 30, 2017. However, this process did not escape being questioned by various media and political organizations, for having selected a group of academics and members of civil society who are not very pluralistic and have been part of a relatively formal network for several years.

The third organization which was supposed to begin operating was the Coordinating Committee. This Committee was supposed to include seven members: a representative of the Committee of Citizen Participation, the Head of the Superior Audit Office of the Federation, the Head of the Specialized Prosecutor's Office to Combat Corruption, the Head of the Ministry of Public Administration, the Representative of the Council of the Federal Judiciary, the President of the Federal Institute of Access to Information and Protection of Personal Data, and the President of the Federal Court of Administrative Justice. This Committee had 60 calendar days after the integration of CPC to be established and hold an initial session of the Coordinating Committee. At the time of writing this chapter at the end of 2018, this committee had not yet been fully integrated; the appointment by the Senate of the Special Prosecutor for the Fight against Corruption is still pending.

In order to implement the decisions arising from the Coordinating Committee, the CPC must issue the appointment of a Technical Secretary. This appointment took place on May 31, 2017, and he will occupy this position for five years.

The Steering Committee of the National Supervision System (CRSNF) is another body that was to have been established. The CRSNF is composed of the directors of the Superior Audit Office of the Federation, the Secretariat of Public Administration, and seven members of the local supervisory bodies and the secretariats responsible for internal control in the states. This Committee was supposed to operate as soon as the National Inspection System began to function. On June 7, 2018, they held their first meeting of the year in which they submitted their first annual activity report.

The Federal Court of Administrative Justice, responsible for punishing serious offenses, must have three magistrates from the Superior Court (with a 15-year term of office) and five Regional Chambers with three magistrates each. They are constituted by short lists the president proposes for approval by the Senate. Although these magistrates were to be appointed before July 19, 2017, it was not until April 2018 that the president proposed 18 magistrates. The point is that they were not ratified by the Senate due to various criticisms from the media and the citizen committee itself, regarding the lack of guarantees of a transparent, merit-based process. The CPC promoted an injunction trial to review the suitability of the magistrates and guarantee transparency in the process. On August 2, 2018, a judge ordered the president and the Senate to publish the criteria on the basis of which the merits of each person would be measured for them to be eligible as a magistrate.

The Office of the Special Prosecutor for crimes related to corruption, despite being one of the keys that opened the door to the reform of the SNA, has not yet had a Special Prosecutor nominated. This prosecutor must be appointed by two-thirds of the members of the Senate, although the executive may object to his/her appointment.

Moreover, both the Secretariat of Civil Service and the Superior Audit of the Federation had to ratify or appoint new directors of the control and inspection areas. These appointments did not elicit any conflict.

Finally, the constitutional reform set a deadline of July 18, 2017 for anticorruption matters in state constitutions to be brought into line with the Constitution of the country and to begin implementing the SLAC. By this time, the states had only achieved minimum progress. The Mexican Institute of Competitiveness (an NGO), Transparency Mexicana, and the Regional Confederation of the Mexican Republic (a Mexican entrepreneurs' organization) documented the progress that had been made up until then in the states in the areas mentioned above, highlighting the enormous disparity in progress in various states in the country. Thus, ten states had managed to achieve a constitutional reform that was equated with the functions and characteristics of federal reform. With less success in the harmonization of their law, only three states had managed to reform their constitutions, but their reform failed to achieve complete harmonization. These reforms lacked basic elements such as the establishment of a Coordinating Committee or the granting of powers to the Supreme Audit Office of the State, the General Comptroller's Office, and the Internal Control Bodies, to determine,

160 Latin American Anticorruption Strategies

investigate, and substantiate serious and non-serious administrative offenses; as well as sanction non-serious ones; or lacked the definition of the regime of the Attorney General of the State, to achieve genuine autonomy from the state executive. Of the 19 remaining states, three had poor reforms with a risk of unconstitutionality. The rest (16 states) failed to harmonize their local constitution within the agreed period. Despite this, these organizations sought reform initiatives that were under discussion or in the process of being approved. Only one state reform initiative complied with the harmonization; five failed to comply with a harmonization, but had most of the elements and another reform initiative was deficient (its modification failed to include the minimum elements of harmonization). By the time the deadline had expired, nine states had failed to begin their anticorruption reform process. After the SNA had been operating for a year, only 15 of the 32 states had managed to bring the objectives of the general law into line with local legislation, while the rest had done so partially. Moreover, no oversight system had been set up in 20 states. One state had not succeeded in having its local Congress issue its anticorruption law in 2018.

The Substantive Challenges of the SNA in a Country such as Mexico

The Mexican SNA is obviously an innovation. Risky, complex, and expensive, it has proved difficult to get off the ground. No country in the world has attempted to build a national anticorruption system as ambitious as this. Perhaps the closest is the recent effort in Brazil, which will be mentioned in the next chapter, with the National Strategy to Combat Corruption and Money Laundering. As one can see, it is a system because it attempts to connect all parties, in a coordinated fashion, to all instances of the federal government, through versions in each of the 32 local or state governments. It is odd that in Mexico there is so much trust in the instruments of a systemic logic. The SNA is simply the latest version of the systemic metaphor that implements a huge number of public policies in the country: these include the integral family system, the national transparency system, the national audit system, the national control system, the national fiscal coordination system, and an almost endless list of systems. Mexico appears to be a country with a firm belief in the systemic approach. The idea behind a systemic logic varies, but in general it is clear: the whole is more than the sum of the parts, each part has a function and it is in the relations of interdependence and coordination of the parts that the final effect of the system is achieved. And all effects depend largely on the relationship with "the context". The idea behind the SNA is that, by integrating all the federal and state actors, with their clearly defined functions, and with a very precise logic of separate and overlapping functions (prevention, detection, investigation, prosecution, and sanction), the widespread and organized corruption in the country will be controlled and reduced.

However, the SNA can also be seen as a complex version of an anticorruption agency. And if this is the case, it will experience the same contradictions as those agencies: technical and operating problems due to the wide array of acts that comprise corruption (as discussed in Chapter 1 regarding the limitations of an umbrella concept of corruption that ends up being everything and nothing at the same time) and resistance and counter-attacks from the political system itself that will threaten its structural and historical logics of corruption. These logics are already stable and supported by an intricate network of interests and modus operandi. Nothing actually makes the SNA immune from the same attacks as an anticorruption agency. An anticorruption agency is a parallel path to the political system: an organization that runs parallel to the traditional logic of checks and balances of the political system. It is a kind of intruder, a strange, different, exogenous power, which is responsible for monitoring and punishing the members of the state powers (legislative, executive, and judicial) since they are unable to perform their function of counterweights and overlapping surveillance, effectively monitoring each other. In this respect, the SNA apparently is different from an exogenously imposed anticorruption agency, since the political powers have a critical role within the system and are part of it. It is assumed then that more than a parallel path to the political system, it is a reorganization or rather a reorganization of the way the powers coordinate and monitor each other. However, this last point is important: the SNA is a bet on the procedural and orderly construction of the way the powers mutually monitor and control each other through a basic hope: that they can be organizationally, legally, and administratively coordinated in a practical or effective way to reduce corruption. In other words, it is assumed that political agents are part of a system of corruption that can be gradually dismantled if each party is monitored and coordinated in a certain way that will reduce the scope for corruption and, at best, overcome the inertias and interests that support corruption as a stable system in the country. The SNA has the enemy, so to speak, within its own structure. What suggests that they will effectively coordinate and thereby destroy the inertia and logic of corruption? The Mexican SNA can also be said to have an exogenous logic: the organization is not exogenous as in the case of an anticorruption agency. What is exogenous is the legal and organizational mechanism that is supposed to instruct the actors and organizations on how to coordinate, monitor, and control each other. Who leads that effort? Supposedly the citizen committee that heads it: a group of citizens who become public servants because they receive a salary, but who remain (it is not clear how or why) impartial guards of the other agents who are members of various state apparatuses. They are also citizens, who have to play their cards politically first to be elected and then be able to retain their positions. It is ultimately a political game, which, at least in its first implementation, that is, in the election of the first representatives, was developed and directed by a group of identifiable people with their own political interests.

In the end, the SNA has critical ingredients that are also exogenous and it depends on the proper functioning and legitimacy, pressure, and surveillance capacity of that exogenous, citizen body, but one that is rapidly politicized. In the long run, this subtlety can make the difference. Scheme 4.5 outlines the political powers as part of the SNA.

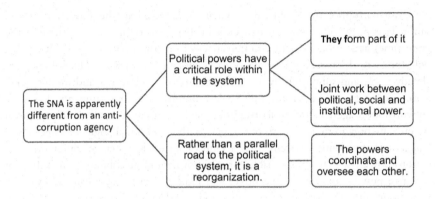

SCHEME 4.5 Mexico SNA features
Source: Compiled by the author.

It is likely then that the only thing that distinguishes the SNA from a traditional anticorruption agency is the idea that it can intervene in the powers of a state to control the systemic corruption that characterizes them through another system that forces them to coordinate and to be monitored in a particular procedural manner. This is accompanied by the very systemic hope that this coordination will become virtuous because it has become interdependent. In other words, each part of the system depends on the other, which will force them to coordinate. The critical step is that this interdependence must be built, in practice, over time, and through actions. And, like a traditional anticorruption agency, it requires substantial resources and support from the political actors it is supposed to monitor and control, and punish if necessary. If several of the political actors, in the national or local arena, try to encourage the process from the inside, influence decisions, or affect resources in a "guerrilla warfare" logic, so to speak, it is unlikely that the systemic hope that the scheme will function will be able to be sustained for a long time.

The challenges of the Mexican innovation of the SNA are enormous. Perhaps the most important thing the SNA has achieved is precisely to be born: it required an enormous number of debates, laws, regulations, creation of organizations, and selection of people. Corruption has obviously been placed on the public agenda as a serious problem. That may be key in time. Some people in Mexico assume that the other critical step has been the role of civil society organizations that are part of the system and remain its fundamental promoters. This could undoubtedly be by far the most important difference. Not because civil society organizations are really neutral or represent the general interest or have not intervened at times with political agendas that are neither clear nor transparent. Many organizations of this type that have participated in the SNA are financed by entrepreneurs or international organizations, for example. In other words, they have diverse interests and may defend the political agendas of interest groups. This is normal in any democratic society: organizations in society are also organizations with interests. The point is for them to become transparent, which did not always happen in the construction of the SNA.

In any case, what this Mexican innovation achieves will be seen in time (Morris, 2018, p. 132). The structural forces of corruption in a country like Mexico will probably be affected when different social dynamics (such as *palancas*) and policies (such as patronage and clientelism) become socially undesirable. Rothstein's skepticism (2011) regarding the ability to build institutions and overlapping organizations as a solution to a dilemma of collective action and political dynamics such as corruption, will be corroborated, or otherwise when the failure or success of the Mexican SNA is observed.

Final Reflections on the Mexican Case: Political Corruption as the Mother of Administrative Corruption

Corruption in Mexico, as we have discussed in this chapter, is systemic. In other words, it is intimately embedded in political, social, cultural, and administrative life. In this respect, the political aspect is critical, because it is one of the bases of administrative corruption (in other words, it is expressed through civil servants and public administration). Administrative corruption (the kind which SNA laws are primarily designed to reduce) is the symptom of a bigger problem: in this case, the political practices that support the political regime itself (the apolitical nature of traditional anticorruption solutions could be part of the problem, as Mungiu-Pippidi, 2006 notes).

Two elements must be considered: clientelism and the booty system. The first refers to the intimate interaction between the political class and society: political action as a distribution of perks and privileges, both within the political class itself and as a mechanism for liaising with the voting society. Clientelistic practices are so solid that for much of the Mexican population, this is the "natural" way of interacting with the political class. In this respect, democratic logics and institutions are only a screen for a concrete system that is behind the curtain and the true mechanism of political interaction: one based on clientelism. This logic creates multiple, perverse effects: the vote is a spare part, democracy is a screen, accountability an empty phrase. Clientelist logic reproduces extremely powerful, ingrained practices such as the *palanca*, which have been discussed here.

The SNA, if it hopes to obtain success, will have to generate strategic impacts in this social clientelistic logic. Otherwise, by basically attacking administrative corruption, it will probably be attacking a symptom rather than a critical cause.

As for the booty system, a complex phenomenon, it can be summarized in one point: the political system exists because it controls the administrative apparatus as a subordinate, manipulable piece. Losing control of the administrative apparatus, even minimally, is unthinkable at this time for the political class of the country. It is through the administrative apparatus that the government has control of the budget, a highly discretionary control. Without a bureaucracy which has its hands tied and is totally subordinated to the logic of the political class, this control would be significantly reduced.

164 Latin American Anticorruption Strategies

A true civil service requires greater political agreement: where the different groups observe and agree to mutually "have their hands tied" in order to build a professional, stable administrative apparatus, not linked to the political rules and normal vicissitudes produced by elections and power switching. This political agreement is a fundamental condition for the viability of a professional civil service. It is clear that this moment of agreement and political clarity has not reached the country (Pardo, 2016). But without a civil service, administrative corruption will remain a natural product of the political structure of the regime. This is an endless battle the SNA will hardly be able to solve in the short term and without which its results will scarcely be recognized.

Systemic corruption like the one that Mexico experiences speaks of an intricate network of actions, practices, and organized routines that sustain it. Bribes, frauds, collusions, and conflicts of interest are not only discrete events that can be treated individually as specific cases. It is possible to expect the opposite: every case of bribe, fraud, collusion, or diversion of funds is potentially part of a chain of other acts, many of them effectively and efficiently organized. In these circumstances, detecting these acts, investigating them professionally, documenting them appropriately, and prosecuting and accusing them effectively, entails a major organizational challenge. It requires people who are highly skilled in various sophisticated research and documentation techniques. It requires time, financial and human resources, intelligence, and experience. All this is scarce at this time in Mexico.

Creating the organizational capacities for the SNA to work is a critical step. Several examples immediately emerge. It is essential to create the capacities for true internal control which does not persecute corruption as an end, yet which professionally and systematically creates the conditions for risk reduction in governmental organizations and their decisions and processes (Arellano, Hernández, & Lepore, 2015). It is also crucial to train people and give them the organizational conditions to carry out solid anti-fraud, anticorruption research. And to integrate the capacities of forensic auditing, investigation, and criminal analysis as critical substantive elements of the system. All must be done to assemble the cases, which are not isolated but involve criminal chains and collusion which establish the dynamics of fraud, bribe, and diversion of funds. And, of course, the judicial part can process these with speed and professionalism, in order to reduce the impunity in this type of case that has reigned in the country.

These organizational capacities are critical. They will not appear spontaneously; they must be built. Moreover, these capabilities are required in different parts of the system, in different organizations with their own specificities. This will be a great challenge: the logic of the SNA is for each element to play its part so that the interaction creates the expected result—to reduce corruption effectively and promptly. But each part needs to play its role very well for the interaction to work. And at this time, it is not clear how each party will create these minimum indispensable organizational conditions. One could say that there is already experience in different organizations for each of the challenges raised here. Perhaps. Although perhaps it would be more sensible to begin with the possibility that this does not

The Mexican National Anticorruption System **165**

happen: that the experience in the country on internal control, anti-fraud investigation, analysis and criminal investigation, prosecution of cases, and prosecution before the courts is extremely limited and insufficient. That is to say, that there is virtually a need to start from scratch to create these critical organizational capacities.

Corruption in Mexico is part of the glue created by the current political system. The question is how to change the political and social logic that sustains corruption in a country like this. Since it is a social practice and the modus operandi of the system, "de-normalizing" corruption will require a great deal of time, patience, and legal, organizational, and political experimentation.

The case analyzed in this chapter offers interesting elements to be discussed in the context of societies with systemic corruption, as is the case in many Latin American countries. Rather than creating an anticorruption agency, a daring, innovative approach has been chosen in Mexico: a complete system, on a national scale. Since it is an innovation, one does not have many elements to understand *ex ante* what will make it succeed or not. But three major challenges remain. The first is the variegated, expensive, and complex scheme in which it is based. Its first problem is to begin to act, creating in practice the logics of coordination and cooperation between all parties, which is ultimately, the crux of this system. The rules, regulations, and institutional design do not suffice to ensure that the system achieves its final effect, as expected. As any student of the systems theory knows, the results and effects of a system in its context cannot be entirely planned or foreseen. They are seen only in the interaction between the parties and their capacity to adapt, affect, and modify an ever-changing and contingent context. The second challenge is that it will have to face the fierce resistance of the political system to modify the chains of interests and interrelationships that have made this political system stable or at least exist. Clientelism, patronage, and the exchange of influences and privileges constitute the glue in this political system. Changing it implies more than will or self-control or coordinations. The third challenge is also important: the SNA was born without any clarity about how to build the technical, organizational, and management skills that will be critical to its success. How, in particular, the technical and organizational capacities for investigation, prosecution, legal treatment, and prosecution will be created has been placed on the back burner. Creating these capabilities will be essential.

The SNA, apart from the fierce attack it will suffer (as has happened to all the anticorruption agencies in the world), suffers from a logical problem of its design: the dispersion of responsibilities. Its very design as a metaphor for a system that requires the virtuous coordination of its elements to produce results is an extremely high-risk factor given the political conditions of the country. Just as it is important for each part of SNA to have solid technical capabilities, it is fundamental for it to have technical capacities for inter-organizational coordination as a whole. This is not going to happen spontaneously or by decree. The game of guilt will be inevitable (Hood, 2010).

On the basis of the assumptions constructed throughout this book, corruption is not an accident or an anomaly, although this sounds paradoxical. It is the "normal"

166 Latin American Anticorruption Strategies

modus operandi of the political system. *The challenge is to denormalize corruption.* To make it undesirable and at the same time politically ineffective. One of the critical steps is to reopen the debate on clientelism as a political pattern. Elections and the party system are a reality in the country. But not the reorganization of the relationship between parties and society. Financing parties and campaigns is part of the clientelistic circle that reproduces very questionable instruments as political practices, yet which, under this logic, are extremely effective: pork barrel, *moche* in Mexico, the clientelistic distribution of goods or services, and the patrimonial use of resources. Political corruption is the base and origin of administrative corruption. Without addressing the role of clientelism as the basis of the party system and then the relationship between elected governors and society (a deeply cynical relationship of course), the fight against corruption will continue to be confused between acts of constant theft by public servants and the essence of the political relationship that is explicit in the clientelist logic of governments.

Lastly, it is worth mentioning a critical element that profoundly defines this case, unlike other Latin American countries: the lack of a real civil service. The organizational base of public administration is called the booty system: the governmental apparatus constitutes booty for the groups that come to power. The discretionary use of government resources (human, financial, and material) is therefore the rational political logic in a booty system. The political class has refused to build a true civil service: one that "ties their hands" so that they will not be able to intervene excessively in the government apparatus as if it were their right. Promoting and creating the political conditions to make a professional civil service viable and acceptable is a critical step toward denormalizing corruption (Pérez & Flores, 2011). If you create it, you will not see the results immediately and it will not be easy to create it (in addition to the logical problems all civil service generates, which are many). The objective is to enter into a political negotiation to understand and make a real professional civil service indispensable as a long-term structural step to break the modus operandi of political corruption generated by administrative corruption.

Initiating the dismantling of clientelism and the booty system seem to be substantive conditions for making it possible to speak about a certain possibility of reducing and controlling corruption in countries like Mexico. Addressing them using specialized mechanisms could be an important solution but not necessarily the only basis for success in these situations.

Bibliography

Arellano, D., Hernández, J., & Lepore, W. (2015). Corrupción sistémica: Límites y desafíos de las agencias anticorrupción. El caso de la Oficina Anticorrupción de Argentina. *Reforma y Democracia*, 61, 75–106.

Arellano-Gault, D. (2018). Government corruption: An exogenous factor in companies' victimization? *Public Integrity.* doi:10.1080/10999922.2018.1433425.

Arteaga, N., & Lopez, A. (1998). *Policía y corrupción: El caso de un municipio en México.* Mexico City, Mexico: Plaza y Valdes.

Charron, N. (2008). *Mapping and measuring the impact of anti-corruption agencies: A new dataset for 18 countries*. Paper presented at New Public Management and the Quality of Government conference, Sweden, November 12.

De Speville, B. (1997). *Hong Kong: Policy initiatives against corruption*. Paris, France: OECD.

De Speville, B. (2008). *Failing anti-corruption agencies – causes and cures*. Presented at the Empowering Anti-Corruption Agencies: Defying Institutional Failure and Strengthening Preventive and Repressive Capacities workshop, Lisbon, May 14–16, 2008.

De Speville, B. (2010). Anticorruption commissions: The 'Hong Kong model' revisited. *Asia-Pacific Review*, 17(1), 47–71. doi:10.1080/13439006.2010.482757.

Doig, A., Watt, D., & Williams, R. (2007). Why do developing country anti-corruption commissions fail to deal with corruption? Understanding the three dilemmas of organizational development, performance expectation, and donor and government cycles. *Public Administration and Development*, 27, 251–259.

ENCIG. (2017). *Encuesta nacional de calidad e impacto gubernamental*. Mexico City, Mexico: INEGI.

Haller, D., & Shore, C. (2005). *Corruption: Anthropological perspectives*. London: Pluto Press.

Heilbrunn, J. (2004). *Anti-corruption commissions: Panacea or real medicine to fight corruption?* Washington, DC: World Bank Institute.

Hood, C. (2010). *The blame game: Spin, bureaucracy, and self-preservation in government*. Princeton, NJ: Princeton University Press.

Kaiser, M. (2014). *El combate a la corrupción: La gran tarea pendiente de México*. Mexico City, Mexico: M.A. Porrua.

Morris, S. (2018). Corruption in Mexico: Continuity amid change. In B. Warf (Ed.), *Handbook on the geographies of corruption* (pp. 132–150). Cheltenham, England: Edward Elgar.

Mungiu-Pippidi, A. (2006). Corruption: Diagnosis and treatment. *Journal of Democracy*, 17(3): 86–99.

Mungiu-Pippidi, A. (2015). *The quest for good governance*. Cambridge, England: Cambridge University Press.

Nef, J. (2001). Government corruption in Latin America. In G. Caiden, O. P. Dwivedi, & J. Jabbra (Eds), *Where corruption lives* (pp. 159–173). Bloomfield, NJ: Kumarian.

Nuijten, M. (2003). *Power, community and the state: The political anthropology of organization in Mexico*. Sidmouth, England: Pluto Press.

Nuijten, M. (2004). Between fear and fantasy: Governmentality and the working of power in Mexico. *Critique of Anthropology*, 24(2), 209–230.

Olivier de Sardan, J. (1999). A moral economy of corruption in Africa? *The Journal of Modern African Studies*, 37(1), 25–52.

Pardo, M. C. (2016). *Una introducción a la administración pública*. Mexico City, Mexico: El Colegio de Mexico.

Pérez, F., & Flores, E. (Eds.). (2011). *La prevención de la corrupción y el servicio profesional de carrera*. Mexico City, Mexico: Senado de la República.

Ríos, J. (2018). *El déficit democrático: Nepotismo y redes familiares en el Poder Judicial de la Federación*. Mexico City, Mexico: Mexicanos Contra la Corrupción.

Rotberg, R. (2017). *The corruption cure*. Princeton, NJ: Princeton University Press.

Rothstein, B. (2011). *The quality of government: Corruption, social trust, and inequality in international perspective*. Chicago, IL: Chicago University Press.

Secretaría de la Función Pública (SFP). (2016). Sistema Nacional Anticorrupción. Retrieved from www.gob.mx/sfp/acciones-y-programas/sistema-nacional-anticorrupcion-64289.

Torsello, D., & Venard, V. (2016). The anthropology of corruption. *Journal of Management Inquiry*, 25(1), 34–54.

168 Latin American Anticorruption Strategies

Transparency International. (2015). *Impact report*. Retrieved from www.transparency.org/whatwedo/publication/2015_impact_report.

Transparency International. (2015, 2016, 2017). Corruption perception index 2015, 2016, 2017. Retrieved from www.transparency.org/news/feature/corruption_perceptions_index_2017#table.

Villarroel, H. (1785/1994). *Enfermedades políticas que padece la capital de esta Nueva España*. Mexico City, Mexico: CONACULTA.

Zalpa, G., Tapia, E., & Reyes, J. (2014). El que a buen árbol se arrima… Intercambio de favores y corrupción. *Cultura y Representaciones Sociales*, 9(17), 149–176.

Zamudio, G. L. (2018). *The International Commission Against Impunity in Guatemala (CICIG): A self-directed organization*. Mexico City, Mexico: Universidad Iberoamericana.

Official Documents

Código Penal Federal (CPF). *Diario Oficial de la Federación el 14 de agosto de 1931*. Mexico City, Mexico. Retrieved from http://cgservicios.df.gob.mx/prontuario/vigente/r200719.pdf.

Comisión de Selección del SNA. (2017) *¿Quiénes somos?*Mexico City, Mexico. Retrieved from http://comisionsna.mx/.

Comité de Participación Ciudadana. (2018). *Avances sobre sistemas locales anticorrupción*. Mexico. Retrieved from https://cpc.org.mx/2018/02/23/avances-sobre-sistemas-locales-anticorrupcion/.

Comité de Participación Ciudadana. (2018). *Nota sobre la sentencia de Amparo que ordena nombramiento de los magistrados anticorrupción*. Retrieved from https://cpc.org.mx/2018/08/02/nota-sobre-la-sentencia-de-amparo-que-ordena-nombramiento-de-los-magistrados-anticorrupcion/.

Constitución Política de los Estados Unidos Mexicanos (CPEUM). *Diario Oficial de la Federación el 5 de febrero de 1917*. Retrieved from www.diputados.gob.mx/LeyesBiblio/htm/1.htm.

Instituto Mexicano de la Competitividad. (2016). *La ruta de la implementación del Sistema Nacional Anticorrupción*. Retrieved from https://imco.org.mx/wp-content/uploads/2016/09/2016-SNA-Documento_Completo.pdf.

Ley de Fiscalización y Rendición de Cuentas de la Federación (LFRCF). *Diario Oficial de la Federación el 18 de julio de 2016*. Retrieved from www.diputados.gob.mx/LeyesBiblio/pdf/LFRCF.pdf.

Ley General de Responsabilidades Administrativas (LGRA). *Diario Oficial de la Federación el 18 de julio de 2016*. Retrieved from www.diputados.gob.mx/LeyesBiblio/pdf/LGRA_120419.pdf.

Ley General de Transparencia y Acceso a la Información Pública (LGTAIP). *Diario Oficial de la Federación el 4 de mayo de 2015*. Retrieved from www.diputados.gob.mx/LeyesBiblio/pdf/LGTAIP.pdf.

Ley General del Sistema Nacional Anticorrupción (LGSNA). *Diario Oficial de la Federación el 18 de julio de 2016*. Retrieved from www.diputados.gob.mx/LeyesBiblio/pdf/LGSNA.pdf.

Ley Orgánica de la Administración Pública Federal (LOAPF). *Diario Oficial de la Federación el 29 de diciembre de 1976*. Retrieved from www.diputados.gob.mx/LeyesBiblio/ref/loapf/LOAPF_ref61_30nov18.pdf.

Ley Orgánica de la Procuraduría General de la República (LOPGR). *Diario Oficial de la Federación el 29 de mayo de 2009*. Retrieved from www.oas.org/juridico/spanish/mesicic3_mex_anexo23.pdf.

Ley Orgánica del Tribunal Federal de Justicia Administrativa (LOTFJA). *Diario Oficial de la Federación el 18 de julio de 2016*. Retrieved from www.diputados.gob.mx/LeyesBiblio/pdf/LOTFJA.pdf.

Secretaría de la Función Pública. (2018). *Encabezan SFP y ASF primera reunión 2018 del Comité Rector del Sistema Nacional de Fiscalización*. Retrieved from www.gob.mx/sfp/articulos/encabezan-sfp-y-asf-primera-reunion-2018-del-comite-rector-del-sistema-nacional-de-fiscalizacion-160506.

Secretaría de la Función Pública. (2016). *Sistema Nacional Anticorrupción*. Retrieved from www.gob.mx/sfp/acciones-y-programas/sistema-nacional-anticorrupcion-64289.

Senado de la República. (2013). *Dictamen...en materia de combate a la corrupción*. Retrieved from http://rendiciondecuentas.org.mx/wp-content/uploads/2013/12/Dictamen-Anticorrupcion.pdf.

5

BRAZIL

The Success and Crisis of a Decentralized Mechanism for Controlling Corruption

Introduction

The cases of Argentina and Mexico show two countries that have taken what one could call desperate measures: creating *ex profeso* mechanisms, but above all, somehow acting in parallel to the traditional institutions of a democracy, one of whose functions is supposedly to control corruption. Anticorruption agencies (ACAs) and the strange Mexican SNA are ultimately mechanisms designed to combat corruption in a specialized way and from spaces specially designed to do what current formal political institutions are unable or unwilling to do. It is a desperate act because it means accepting, at some level, that the traditional instances of checks and balances of a democracy are unreliable, do not work, and require a parallel entity which monitors, controls, and even punishes them when they fail.

It is obviously an extraordinary path. Interestingly, since they are extraordinary routes, one might think that they should also be regarded as temporary: they would only exist until traditional institutions played their role properly and these extraordinary mechanisms were no longer necessary. But it seems that this reflection of the temporary nature of this type of effort has not been made explicit either in Mexico or Argentina: instead, they regard themselves as organizations and permanent schemes, which is a paradox. If corruption has become systemic and has affected the "normal" process of the powers of a country, one of the goals should be to create the conditions to return to that "normal" dynamic where a solid and autonomous judicial power, a vigilant and balanced legislative power, and an executive power that is controlled and monitored would constitute a sufficient basis for preventing major excesses and therefore controlling corruption in all its forms, from diverse spheres, norms, and organizations.

If systemic corruption exists, it is almost certain that judicial power does not function as such, and that it has poor or limited autonomy. Legislative power

Controlling Corruption in Brazil 171

probably does not serve as a counterweight to executive decisions and is incapable of controlling itself in the light of competition between parties and groups. And without counterweights, the executive has very little ability to self-regulate, monitor, and punish the corrupt acts of elected and appointed officials and politicians. In keeping with this idea, the creation of an anticorruption agency or an anticorruption system that runs parallel to the organizational and political process would seem extraordinary constructions, which run parallel to the political power that is institutionally incapable of monitoring and controlling itself. It would even be worth thinking that these organizational schemes (anticorruption agencies and systems) should be created with an expiry date. In other words, with a term that defines the commitment to creating the conditions for its disappearance given that progress has been made in a return to a logical state of affairs: it is the autonomy of the judiciary, checks and balances, which work in such a way that corruption can be controlled without the need for special organizations and which run parallel to the formal political process.

As has been discussed throughout this book, corruption is an umbrella concept for a multiplicity of different phenomena. All these phenomena have specific, particular social and political aspects. To think that corruption as a concept describes a unique and homogenous phenomenon, which can be "attacked" using a standard recipe for both Argentina and Mexico, may in fact be naive. Moreover, since corruption in Latin America, as discussed in Chapter 2, is a phenomenon deeply rooted in past social and political practices and traditions with great social stability, the difficulty of locating, diagnosing, and controlling it can only multiply.

We could say then that the extraordinary strategy of creating organizations that run parallel to the political and judicial process is opposed to a more logical strategy, although under certain conditions, one that is more difficult to achieve: strengthening the normal conditions of a process of checks and balances, of overlapping functions and authorities, which then enables its various parties to function in such a way that, when a problem of corruption is located, each part of that system can do what it is supposed to do, within its own logic and capabilities. The logic of control and surveillance in various democratic governments is actually found in several different spaces. The detection, investigation, and punishment of improper acts is usually the responsibility of various overlapping organizations, with other functions apart from persecuting wrongful acts. It is even possible to find that, within a single power, there are different organizations that participate in a rather disperse network of functions and responsibilities distributed among different organizations. Thus, one could say that the "normal" or logical way is that, within the multiple functions of different organizations, particular and specialized spaces are contained in the rather heterogeneous and multiple process that produces the effect of keeping undue acts under control. It could even be said that what is common in many countries is that corruption is treated as an event, as a possibility created within a very broad, intricate process of government and business activities. From this perspective, it is somewhat paradoxical to create organizations and institutions specifically dedicated to controlling corruption as the only function. This

172 Latin American Anticorruption Strategies

implies, for example, intervening as an external actor in a common process of public contracting or service payments, assuming from the start that what is going to be found is corruption. At the end of the day, this is what standardized corruption is about: it is expected to be found everywhere and at all times. The point in any case is that creating an anticorruption agenda or an elephantine anticorruption system can only be strange, extraordinary, and disruptive solutions in a traditional logic of checks and balances between powers and political institutions typical of a democratic logic. We will see later with the case of Guatemala and the CICIG that this organization realizes it is extraordinary because it understands that one of its critical roles is to return to the "normal" institutionalism of a democracy: that is, one where the judicial, legislative, and executive bodies do their work in a specialized manner, with verifiable organizational capacities, and where, as part of their functions, they control corrupt acts in their different modalities.

For this reason, the case of Brazil is both interesting and important. Brazil is a country that has advanced enormously with regard to having effective anticorruption strategies. And it has done so, not by betting on an organization or a centralized system, but on the virtues of the logic of different spaces in different powers which, without needing to coordinate perfectly, and with each one doing its part, have been able to change the spectrum of the control of corruption in the country. In other words, the Brazilian case shows the importance of a decentralized logic, where detection, investigation, and punishment are carried out in various organizations, with different and specialized organizational capacities. And they manage to function in this way, coordinating when necessary.

Brazil is a country that has suffered from systemic corruption like practically all the countries in Latin America (with the possible exception of Costa Rica, Uruguay, and Chile). *Jeitinho* as a social phenomenon, studied in Chapter 2, has been and continues to be an established and solid practice for people to deal with the force of particularism in interactions between citizens and authorities. At the same time, in recent years, an encouraging dynamic has been observed: Brazilian institutions, from their different functions and capacities, have taken an important turn and achieved success in breaking the systemic dynamics of corruption in the country.

The rather decentralized and multiple logic of Brazil's anticorruption scheme will now be analyzed, and its action will be studied in the famous Operation Car Wash case. This case is undoubtedly extremely complex and shows that every anticorruption fight ends up being entangled with politics, for better or for worse. The central point of this chapter is to see how a more institutionalized logic of overlaps between different powers and institutional frameworks is capable of being effective, not without consequences and political impacts, in countries that face the social and political logics of systemic corruption.

The Brazilian Institutional Anticorruption Framework

The Brazilian anticorruption scheme is a complex structure that has been rapidly transformed since the beginning of the 21st century. Its tendency is relatively clear:

a set of legislative changes and transformations of organizations which, in different spheres and according to different logics, will be involved in addressing acts of corruption.

Brazil is a country with an extremely significant population, territory, and economic power in Latin America and, in fact, worldwide. Its potential has been diminished by a series of political traditions characteristic of Latin American countries after centuries of colonialism: patrimonialist regimes with pronounced political instability over time. The contemporary history of Brazil ranges from coups d'état and military regimes to constant economic instability. But together with this complex process, Brazil has slowly made progress in structuring a relatively coherent legal and institutional framework that has been gradually consolidated. For example, its civil service is an example to follow in nearly all the countries in the subcontinent that lack such a political institution.

In this context, the transformation of the Brazilian institutional structure to fight corruption has been constant and a fundamental and pivotal issue for the country for at least the past three decades. In particular, the constant scandals that have highlighted the links between businesspeople and politicians in various organized crime and money laundering schemes have been important. Small-scale corruption, so to speak, has been widely tolerated in Brazil, but the collective awareness that uncontrolled levels of corruption have been reached has taken root in this country for some years now. The logic of *jeitinho*, and of the networks of relatives and acquaintances, have created an extremely intricate and powerful social sub-layer which, based on these practices, has built a network of interests that permeate politics and companies. Large-scale corruption is normalized, so to speak, by what becomes a practice dependent on the association of several people who link the formal economy with well-organized corruption networks, and are therefore able to avoid laws and the authorities (Rose-Ackerman & Palifka, 2016).

Faced with a phenomenon of corruption that has been systematically intertwined with, or even congruent with, formal politics and economics, the attempt to stop corruption would have to solve a constant paradox in Latin American countries: the same people who are supposed to attack corruption, that is, state institutions, are intimately and cohesively embedded in an extremely effective, organized informal level of interests, exchanges, favors, reciprocities, and interdependencies. Accordingly, Brazil has decided to focus on strengthening a structure of organizations to combat corruption; organizations with different functions and capacities for action and management, from the three branches: executive, legislative, and judicial. The institutional structure envisaged by the Constitution contains various mechanisms of control and monitoring, whose main objective is precisely to prevent and detect corruption and punish potential agents engaged in that practice (Freitas & Joppert, 2016).

The next step is therefore to briefly analyze this Brazilian institutional framework, describing the regulations that underpin the anticorruption scheme and, as a result, disclose the actors involved and their functions.

Normativity

The laws shaping the Brazilian anticorruption scheme are many and diverse. Here only the most important ones will be mentioned in order to determine how in the Brazilian case, a decentralized structure and multiple agents and organizations in charge have been shaped. The first norm associated with the prevention of corruption is the 1988 Constitution itself. In article 37, it stipulates the principles that should govern the public administration, which are: legality, impersonality, administrative morality, and publicity (Carreiro, 2010; CPRFB, 2018).

In addition to this, the Constitution grants the Legislative Branch broad powers to control resources. In this respect, article 79 states the following:

> The accounting, financial, budgetary, operational and patrimonial control of the Union and of the states in direct and indirect administration, regarding the legality, legitimacy, economy, application of the subsidies and waiving of income, will be exercised by the National Congress, through external control, and the internal control system of each Branch.
>
> *(CPRFB, 2018)*

The second related norm is the Penal Code. Although the penal norms concerning the fight against corruption can be found in different points of the order, most of them are in Title XI (Crimes against Public Administration). This section dates back to the 1940s (Freitas & Joppert, 2016).

This law defines the acts regarded as crimes. In this respect, in Chapter I, the types associated with corruption practiced by a public official are 1) the appropriation of public goods and resources, called embezzlement; 2) tips; and 3) bribery, called passive corruption. Chapter II, which deals with the crimes committed by the individual, includes bribery, only initiated by the individual, called active corruption. Chapter III focuses more on the operation of the judiciary in which there is a special classification of bribery, called exploitation of prestige (Carreiro, 2010, p. 123).

Chapters I, II, and III have been in the Penal Code since its inception in 1940, and reflect the concerns of the time. Some crimes related to corrupt practices had already been provided for in the Penal Code of 1890. Only in the 1940 Code was active corruption typified; in other words, before 1940, the corruptor was not punished, only the person who allowed himself/herself to be corrupted (Carreiro, 2010, p. 125).

The Penal Code has undergone modifications. At least two main changes can be said to deal with corruption. The first of these was effected by Law No. 9.127 / 1995, which introduced the criminal offense of influence peddling. In fact, this type replaced the criminal type known as exploitation of prestige. The second amendment was promoted by Law No. 10,467 / 2002, which included a chapter on crimes committed by individuals against the foreign administration in the Criminal Code.

The third norm established is the Code of Conduct of the Federal High Administration, applicable to ministers, secretaries of state, and chiefs. This standard is part of the stage of preventing corruption. Its main objective is to clarify situations where there are conflicts of interest, as its preamble acknowledges. "The public sector has become increasingly dependent on the recruitment of native professionals from the private sector, exacerbating the possibility of conflict of interest and the need for greater control over the private activities of the public administrator" (Carreiro, 2010, p. 138).

In Brazil, the fight against money laundering became more relevant following the signing of the Vienna Convention in 1988. In order to enhance international cooperation in the matter, Law 9.613 / 98,521 was approved, which defines the crime of money laundering and establishes preventive and repressive measures to combat it. In this respect, this legal device created the Department to Combat Illicit and Financial Changes in the Central Bank and the Financial Activities Control Council (COAF), linked to the Ministry of Finance. The COAF is regarded as a Financial Intelligence Unit (Carreiro, 2010, p. 159).

The COAF establishes as "politically exposed persons" all public agents, their representatives, family members, and close collaborators who hold or have held positions, jobs, or relevant public functions in the past five years in Brazil or abroad, and who have engaged in acts of corruption (Carreiro, 2010).

In these conditions, over the years, Brazil has amalgamated a fourth norm, one of the most important regarding the fight against corruption, namely the Law of Administrative Probity to regulate the behavior of Brazilian public officials. However, this document has been watered down by the constitutional interpretation of the Supreme Court (Ferreira, 2014; García, 2006). Administrative probity, which would only be properly regulated by Law No. 8.429 / 92, was already mentioned in the Federal Constitution as a cause of various punishments, such as the suspension of political rights and the loss of public office (Ferreira, 2014). This law will be discussed in detail later.

The fifth norm is the main legislation on public servants, still in force in the country, which is Law No. 8.112, enacted in 1990, and establishing the principle of impersonality in administrative practice. Civil service has proved to be one of the main ways of consolidating a systematic process of fighting corruption. This legislation provides for competitions as the main form of admission to public service, although in fact there has been a fairly consolidated civil service in the country since the 1930s. This legislation also provides for the disciplinary regime applicable to public officials, including duties and prohibitions. These include making use of public office for one's own advantage or that of a third party (Article 117, IX) and receiving a tip or commission for something which it is their duty to grant (Article 117, XII). This legislation shows that the public servant has extensive civil, criminal, and administrative responsibility in the event of the irregular performance of his/her job (Articles 121 and 127) (Freitas & Joppert, 2016).

The sixth norm involves Law 12,813, adopted in 2012, with the aim of regulating situations concerning a conflict of interest in the exercise of positions in the

176 Latin American Anticorruption Strategies

Federal Executive Power and impediments subsequent to holding these positions. The law is applied to high public officials (ministers, presidents, and directors of municipalities and public companies, among others) and agents with access to privileged information (Freitas & Joppert, 2016, p. 63).

The seventh norm, particularly important in the matter, is the Anticorruption Law, which emerged with the aim of filling the existing gap in the legal system, which implies the possibility of establishing the responsibility of legal persons for engaging in unlawful acts against the public administration. The text establishes civil and administrative liability for acts of corruption committed by individuals and corporations. Fundamentally, it is a law of strict liability and some experts say that it has placed Brazil in a good position to combat corruption on a global level. (Valencia, 2015)

The weak points of the Anticorruption Law emerge when one thinks about who and how many people have the capacity to enforce it. "At the federal level there is only one competent authority: the Office of the Comptroller General of the Union, but at the state and municipal level, everything remains in the hands of the same authorities that engage in corrupt practices" (Valencia, 2015). This is, as noted, one of the main challenges facing Latin American countries: it is the agents themselves within the state who must apply the law and the norms, who are intimately involved in the networks of economic and political interests that sustain and organize acts that can be considered as corrupt. However, legal progress has made a significant contribution to distributing the different roles and responsibilities in organizations with particular functions and specific capabilities.

It is important to mention that the 2015 reforms emphatically sought to establish mechanisms to provide the judiciary with greater transparency and the Public Prosecutor with autonomy. Prosecutors propose, among other things: a) penalizing illicit enrichment by public agents and increasing the length of sentences to sanction crimes of corruption and b) reducing the number of appeals in the context of the penal process (Nascentes, 2018).

The following section describes the organizations or agencies that perform functions concerning the fight against corruption, whose performance is also based on various legislation.

Actors Involved

These institutions are usually either inserted into one of the three powers of the Union or are independent, and perform different functions. The institutions involved in the issue are:

1. The Court of Accounts of the Union (TCU)
2. The Federal Police (PF)
3. The Public Prosecutor's Office (MP)
4. The Office of the Comptroller General of the Union (CGU)
5. Civil Society

Controlling Corruption in Brazil **177**

6.   The Public Ethics Commission (CEP)
7.   The National Strategy to Combat Corruption and Money Laundering (ENCCLA)

The Court of Accounts of the Union (TCU)

The TCU is an advisory body of the National Congress, and therefore within the sphere of the Legislative Branch. Its powers lie in the Federal Constitution and can be classified as: 1) supervisory; 2) jurisdictional; 3) advisory; 4) informative; 5) sanctioning; 6) corrective; and 7) auditing (Consentino, 2014).

This institution, headquartered in the Federal District, has a staff of its own and acts at the national level. It is an autonomous body, and is not subordinate to the Legislative Branch, although it assists it. It is composed of nine ministers: 1) one-third of the ministers are appointed by the president on the basis of a triple list following approval by the Federal Senate; 2) and two-thirds are freely nominated by the National Congress (Carreiro, 2010).

The diversified composition of the TCU tends to attribute an eminently technical action to assist the National Congress in the a posteriori external control of the Union (Carreiro, 2010). The main function of the TCU is to undertake so-called "public financial control", which consists of the "set of measures of an auditing nature, exercised on the movement of money and valuable goods of an economic nature, managed by public administrators, within the administration" (Carreiro, 2010, p. 48).

In the 1988 Constitution, the prerogatives of the TCU were substantially expanded. The TCU was authorized to assist the National Congress in the accounting, financial, budgetary, operational and patrimonial control of the Union and the states of direct and indirect administration, regarding the legality, legitimacy, economy, application of the subsidies and waiving of income (CPRFB, 2010).

In general, the courts of accounts are responsible for playing the role of external control of public accounts (Freitas & Joppert, 2016).

The Court, in the exercise of the financial and budgetary audit and with a view to the judgment of these responsible accounts or entities due to their illegality or irregularity, adopts measures to cure or prevent recidivism. Politicians often complain about the control measures adopted by the TCU, which, for example, they accused of stopping works and services suspected of exceeding their faculties and the suspension of transfers to federal states that do not contribute accounts (Carreiro, 2010).

In relation to one of the main tasks of the TCU, that is, the examination of the accounts of the President's Office, it should be noted that the main obstacle to the effective performance of this function is the National Congress itself. The TCU is responsible for drafting the opinions on accounts, rating them as regular, regular with reservations, or irregular. But it is the National Congress which has the prerogative to vote on those opinions, approving them or otherwise. The process

178 Latin American Anticorruption Strategies

of approving the accounts has become a field of political dispute, acquiring merely formal aspects in many cases and instruments of pressure in others (Freitas & Joppert, 2016).

The Federal Police

Within the sphere of the Executive Branch, the Federal Police play a key role in the fight against corruption, mainly as a result of coordinating with other public entities, particularly the Federal Public Ministry, the CGU, and the Secretariat of Federal Income (Freitas & Joppert, 2016).

The Federal Police has its powers provided for in the Federal Constitution (Article 144), such as "determining infrastructures against the political and social order or to the detriment of the goods, services and interests of the Union or its autarchic entities and public companies, as well as other offenses the practice of which has interstate or international repercussions" (Freitas & Joppert, 2016).

It is important to mention that the Federal Police is answerable to the Ministry of Justice (Dec. No. 6.061 / 2007), and is not formally granted autonomy. One of the problems pointed out by the OAS (2012, p. 25) refers precisely to the non-existence of an organic law for the Federal Police, establishing the parameters for its functioning, a structure of positions and careers, and more details about the qualifications and requirements for fulfilling management positions, including that of Director General.

The Federal Police is an institution whose functions lead to constant contact with offenders. Studies have shown that there is a correlation between police corruption and contact with criminals. The Brazilian police themselves recognize the existence of high corruption rates. Moreover, it does not enjoy the same constitutional guarantees as members of the judiciary or the Public Prosecutor's Office. Thus, police delegates and investigators are more subject to political interference by the occupants of the Executive (Carreiro, 2010).

The police face additional difficulties in dealing with sophisticated white-collar crime, especially at present, when assets derived from illicit enrichment are no longer given to family members, but legalized in sophisticated family money laundering schemes available to offenders (Carreiro, 2010; Gonzaga, 2008).

Despite these limitations, the Federal Police has played a key role in undertaking criminal investigations, the use of advanced technologies for detection and persecution, as well as professionally capturing and prosecuting powerful actors involved in acts of corruption.

The Public Prosecutor's Office

When corruption is typified as a crime, the Public Prosecutor's Office is exclusively responsible for public criminal proceedings. According to the 1988 Constitution, the Public Prosecutor's Office has broad powers to "promote civil investigation and public civil action for the protection of public and social assets, the environment, and other diffuse, collective interests" (Carreiro, 2010, p. 153).

The crucial role of the Public Prosecutor's Office in the fight against corruption in Brazil was due to a process one could call evolutionary. Despite the fact that the Federal Constitution establishes its role in the "defense of the legal order, the democratic regime and social and individual interests" and establishes the protection of public assets as its function (article 129, III), it was not always its effective function (Freitas & Joppert, 2016). The path adopted has been one of strengthening. The Ministério Público (MP) has been assigned the role of ensuring compliance with the principles relating to public finances and respect for national assets, and has sought to guarantee its competence for the effective implementation of both civil investigation and the proceedings for dealing with the various cases of corruption (Freitas & Joppert, 2016). The Public Prosecutor's Office therefore has the ability to promote, through its own authority, and within a reasonable time period, criminal investigations, provided they respect the rights of and guarantee assistance for suspects and any person under investigation by the state (Freitas & Joppert, 2016).

As part of the expansion of its functions, the attribution of corresponding rights and guarantees was considered necessary, both in the individual sphere of MP members (rights of vitality and immobility, among others) and in the institutional sphere (functional and administrative autonomy) (Freitas & Joppert, 2016).

The expansion of the capacities of the MP have not gone unnoticed due to their possible negative effects. In other words, there have been reports of the abusive use of requests for temporary and preventive detention, endorsed by the Public Prosecutor's Office and approved by the judiciary. This has been indicated as a "technique" for punishing the defendants in investigations *ex ante*, without having to regulate the development of due process of law. There is a real fear that the evidence is insufficient or illegitimate to support a criminal conviction in various corruption cases (Carreiro, 2010). The performance of the Public Prosecutor's Office has therefore been strengthened, but there is concern that it will begin to act on its own political logic or by skipping and bending the rules to facilitate its work (Carreiro, 2010).

However, in general terms, the strengthening of the Public Prosecutor's Office has been seen as a positive step. It is a step that has sought to isolate it from political pressure so that it can more easily perform its constitutional tasks (Carreiro, 2010). This would make it possible to achieve the separation of the Public Prosecutor's Office from the judicial representation of the Treasury and from the defense at any cost of acts committed by government entities, a task currently assumed by the Prosecutor's Office of the National Treasury and the Attorney General's Office.

The Office of the Comptroller General of the Union (CGU)

The CGU is the ministry responsible for directly assisting the president in matters related to the defense of public patrimony and increasing the transparency of management by the Federal Executive. As part of its functions, the CGU performs activities such as internal control, correction, public audit, and actions to combat corruption. The CGU also oversees the organs comprising the Internal Control System, the Correction System, and the audit units of the Federal Executive Branch (Carreiro, 2010).

Created in April 2001, the CGU began as an internal correction body for regulatory processes or shortcomings, but its activities were gradually expanded throughout the 2000s. Decree No. 4,177 / 2002 transferred to the CGU the functions of internal control and public audit of the Casa Civil (the Executive Office of the President of Brazil) and the Ombudsman of the Ministry of Justice. In addition, Law No. 10,683 / 2003 transformed the CGU into a ministry, and its director became known as the State Minister of Control and Transparency (Carreiro, 2010).

Given the size of the universe to be investigated, the main tool of action of the CGU is the audit program based on public draws. The CGU occupies a prominent position in the mechanisms in the fight against corruption, and is responsible for handling cases that configure administrative probity and all those requiring the judicial decree of unavailability of property, reimbursement to the treasury, and other measures to be taken by the Attorney General's Office (Carreiro, 2010).

The CGU assumed the role previously reserved for the General Current of the Union, instituted by Provisional Measure No. 2.143–31 / 2001. This concentration movement changed the logic of the separation of control and audit functions, respectively performed by the Federal Secretariat of Internal Control, linked to the Ministry of Finance, and the General Audit of the Union (Freitas & Joppert, 2016).

The CGU expanded its functions to include, in addition to the fight against corruption, the monitoring of public policies, the promotion of transparency, and the mobilization of civil society, by training organizations to exercise social control. It also assumed a political role, not only as a defender of the Access to Information Law, but also of public electoral financing. It also assumed an important role related to international initiatives, such as the Open Government initiative (Freitas & Joppert, 2016).

The Public Ethics Commission (CEP)

The May 26, 1999 Decree created the CEP, directly linked to the President's Office. It was designed to serve as an advisory body to the president and state ministers in public ethics issues and to elaborate and propose the institution of the Code of Conduct of the Federal Administration (Freitas & Joppert, 2016).

The regulation concerning the CEP was reformed in 2007, by Dec. No. 6.029. This decree instituted the Ethics Management System of the Federal Executive Branch, composed of the CEP and other ethics commissions, established in other areas. The ethics commissions have the authority to investigate the practice of an act in breach of the Code of Conduct of the Federal High Administration or the Code of Professional Ethics by Civil Public Servants of the Federal Executive. This investigation may be instructed *ex officio* or based on a complaint filed by any citizen, which may be anonymous. It has been observed, however, that the ethics commissions has limited powers (Freitas & Joppert, 2016).

National Strategy to Combat Corruption and Money Laundering

Despite not having a specialized agency, the Brazilian government has developed the National Strategy to Combat Corruption and Money Laundering (ENCCLA), created in 2003 by the Ministry of Justice in an attempt to centralize efforts to coordinate the systematic fight against money laundering and corruption. The ENCCLA is made up of more than 70 organs of the three branches of the Union, Public Ministries, and civil society, acting directly or indirectly, in the prevention and fight against corruption and money laundering (Ministério da Justiça, 2018).

The ENCCLA is composed of a Plenary, the Integrated Management Cabinet (GGI), Annual Working Groups, and the Executive Secretariat. The Plenary is responsible for approving proposals for the following year and evaluates the actions implemented in the current year. It usually meets in the last week of November of each year (ENCCLA, 2018a).

The GGI is composed of a group of bodies and entities that meet every three months to follow up on the implementation of specific actions. This Cabinet is divided into two groups: corruption and money laundering. The proposals of this group are discussed during the Plenary and it meets up to four times a year to accompany the actions implemented (ENCCLA, 2018a).

The Annual Working Groups, coordinated by specific bodies, according to the definition of the topic and the related institutional issues, are responsible for the implementation and follow-up of the activities to achieve certain objectives in the Plenary. Each year has a number of specific Actions defined in the Plenary (ENCCLA, 2018a).

Finally, the Executive Secretariat is responsible for the administrative functions of the Strategy. This position is exercised by the Department of Asset Recovery and International Legal Cooperation (DRCI). The DRCI is an organ of the National Secretariat of Justice and Citizenship, which in turn forms part of the Ministry of Justice and Public Security (Freitas & Joppert, 2016).

Various Federal Executive agencies participate in the ENCCLA, such as the Ministries of Justice and Finance, the Federal Revenue Secretariat, the Central Bank, and the General Law of the Union. Participants in the ENCCLA currently number 78 (Freitas & Joppert, 2016).

Through this structure, the Strategy intensifies the prevention of corruption and money laundering crimes because it combines the experience of various partners in favor of the Brazilian State, constituting a coordination center for discussions and the development of actions designed to combat this type of crime (Freitas & Joppert, 2016).

The actions carried out by the ENCCLA are annually agreed and elaborated by its members. For each one, a working group composed of institutions is created to achieve predefined products through activities. The actions of ENCCLA can have

182 Latin American Anticorruption Strategies

different objectives: the preparation of a bill to be submitted to the National Congress, the undertaking of a specific study, the development of a metric to determine the effectiveness of various measures, and establishing regulations at the infra-legal level, among others (ENCCLA, 2018a).

Some of the actions undertaken by the ENCCLA are given below: 1) the creation of the National Training Program to Combat Corruption and Money Laundering where more than 18,000 public agents were trained in every region in the country; 2) the creation of Transparency Metrics, with the application and evaluation of organs and powers in the three spheres; 3) the development of applications enabling citizens to identify patterns in the distribution of public resources; 4) the implementation of the National Cadastre of the Financial System; the standardization of the request for/response to movements in the Banking Movements Research System; 5) the creation of the Technology Laboratory against Money Laundering; 6) the creation of Commissariats Specializing in Financial Crimes within the scope of the Federal Police Department; 7) the structure of the National Group to Combat Criminal Organizations; 8) the application of computerized means in tenure and securities declarations; 9) the creation of the National Program for the Primary Prevention of Corruption; and 10) the legislative proposal that resulted in the enactment of laws such as Law 12.683/12, which updated the Money Laundering Law (ENCCLA, 2018b).

Of these actions, those that have been most important during the existence of the ENCCLA include the creation of the National Training Program to Combat Corruption and Money Laundering (PNLD), the Cadastre of Inappropriate and Suspicious Entities and the Specialized Delegations in Financial Crimes within the scope of the Federal Police (PF), and the development of the methodology used in the National Transparency Ranking, published by the Federal Public Ministry (Freitas & Joppert, 2016).

To give an example of the functioning of the ENCCLA, in 2016, the actions approved by the Plenary were organized around three axes: the prevention, detection, and punishment of both acts of corruption and money laundering (Freitas & Joppert, 2016). The most important actions undertaken were Action 1, which seeks to expand the evaluation of transparency of the National Transparency Ranking for municipal legislative powers and the Public Prosecutor's Office; Action 2, which created guidelines for the implementation and operation of internal control systems in states and municipalities; and Action 3, which drafted a bill on whistleblowing (Freitas & Joppert, 2016).

In this respect, it is important to highlight some of the limitations on the functioning of the ENCCLA. Its installation in the Department of Asset Recovery and International Legal Cooperation indicates the inexistence of an apparatus dedicated exclusively to the development of measures to combat money laundering and corruption. It lacks institutional and legal security in its operation, as well as the necessary financial and material support. As a coordination entity, the ENCCLA and its actions indirectly support the original problems of the organizations comprising it. If an organization, for example, which has a coordinating role in an action, reveals the lack of political willingness to take the necessary measures or suffer a change of command, this action could end up harming it (Freitas & Joppert, 2016).

It is worth mentioning that, in addition to the ENCCLA, there is a National Strategy to Combat Cartels (ENACC), Forums to Combat Corruption (FOCCO), and the Public Management Control Network. Among these efforts, ENCCLA is the strongest action to promote the integration of this type of control organisms. Dozens of other entities participate, at least partially, in the fight against corruption. There are therefore very few instruments of coordination between the latter, capable of lending the efforts of the public power the uniqueness and coherence to eliminate corruption. The main one is undoubtedly the ENCCLA (Freitas & Joppert, 2016).

On the basis of the aforementioned actors, it is important to state that there is no agency in Brazil exclusively dedicated to the fight against corruption. The former Comptroller General of the Union, currently the Ministry of Transparency, Control and Inspection, may be the closest approximation, although its functions are restricted to the Federal Executive Branch.

Another initiative worth mentioning is the Agenda to Fight Corruption, launched by the General Comptroller of the Union and the Ministry of Justice at the end of 2015. It brings together the initiatives implemented within the scope of the Federal Executive. It operates, to a certain extent, within the molds of the ENCCLA, but under the command and with the main initiative of the CGU. Eight objectives were established, also organized around the axes of prevention, detection, and punishment.

Given the governmental composition to combat corruption, it is important to understand the administrative structure that governs officials in order to determine whether it encourages or prevents acts of corruption. The following section describes the situation of the Brazilian public administration.

Operation Lava Jato (Car Wash)

The Brazilian anticorruption scheme, as we have seen, is one of numerous specialized structures with the participation of extremely diverse agents of different powers of the state. This has enabled Brazil to strengthen its anticorruption apparatus to detect, investigate, and sanction unethical acts by public officials and individuals. This scheme Brazil has been building for decades in order to combat corruption within its government includes an administrative structure of its own, at the request of investigators and enforcers of sanctions, and the inclusion of the three branches of government: the Executive, Congress, and the judiciary; as well as autonomous bodies and organized civil society. Coordination challenges have been a concern from the outset, but one can say that the emphasis on the technical capacities and autonomies of each part of the structure has yielded certain results in the recent past which are worth observing in slightly more detail.

184 Latin American Anticorruption Strategies

One of the anticorruption operations that has attracted the greatest attention in Brazil and internationally is Operation Car Wash, because as a result of this investigation, the authorities involved in the matter discovered acts of corruption of great significance. In addition to a large amount of money at stake, these acts involved high-ranking Brazilian public officials and prominent businessmen in that country (RPP Noticias, 2017).

In addition to this, these investigations unraveled a huge network of corruption involving senior public officials from other countries and senior managers of companies with a presence in several countries, especially those in Latin America.

This part of the chapter briefly describes what Operation Car Wash involved. An overall description is provided of the origin of these investigations, the structure of the operation, the institutions, and the actors detected through the work of the Brazilian authorities.

Origin and General Characteristics

Operation Car Wash is the largest corruption investigation in the history of Brazil (Barón, 2016). It arose as a result of an investigation of a possible case of money laundering at a gas station and a car wash. A businessman by the name of Hermés Freitas Magnus believed his small plastics company was being used by a network of politicians to launder money. The Federal Police concluded that one of the companies that sent money to Magnus was precisely a gas station (Nascentes, 2018). Until then, it was an ordinary investigation being undertaken as in any possible act of corruption of middling importance.

However, in March 2014, the money laundering investigation at this gas station led the Brazilian Federal Police to Petróleo Brasileiro S.A. (Petrobras) (Clarín, 2018), the state oil company founded in 1953. It is currently the largest state-owned company in Brazil and Latin America. It employs approximately 87,000 people and produces nearly two and a half million barrels a day (RPP Noticias, 2017).

During Operation Car Wash, those responsible for the investigation obtained information incriminating politicians who had thitherto been untouchable and entrepreneurs whose companies had a presence beyond Brazil's borders. Four years after the start of Operation Car Wash, investigations are still underway since the network of corruption has spread to the political and business elite in other countries.

This event led Brazil to increase the legislative proposals regarding corruption in the chambers. Since 2015, there has been an exponential increase in the number of accusations. This is shown in Scheme 5.1.

This is only a small example of the way in which Operation Car Wash shocked Brazil. It was an unprecedented event in which it seemed that impunity for high-ranking government officials, politicians, and businesspeople no longer existed, since the authorities responsible for detecting, investigating, and punishing acts of corruption were acting independently and autonomously. But which were the institutions that were turning the country upside down by investigating and sentencing powerful people economically and politically?

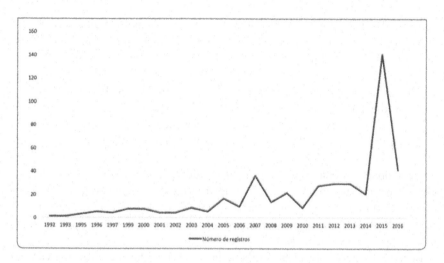

SCHEME 5.1 Brazil. Year of presentation of proposals on corruption in process in both legislative houses 1992–2016
Source: Diagnóstico institucional: Primeiros passos para um plano nacional anticorrupção (2016).

Structure and Institutions

There were three actors behind the Operation Car Wash investigation: 1) the Federal Police; 2) the Public Prosecutor's Office; and 3) the judges. All three were responsible for the detection, investigation, and punishment of the people involved in the case of money laundering in Petrobras and other private companies.

The Federal Police has been in charge of conducting the investigations. It was also responsible for the arrest of 20 people in March 2014, when everything began (Agencia EFE, 2018). Since then, it has been in charge of handling the people it arrested to present them to the Brazilian justice system.

The Public Prosecutor's Office has been in charge of investigating and dealing with the complaints filed with the judges so that they can be processed. In particular, the prosecutor at the Federal Prosecutor General's Office of Brazil, Deltan Dallagnol, has coordinated a work team that investigates and submits the denunciations to the judge for their resolution. This prosecutor has worked closely with Judge Sergio Moro, who has been in charge of prosecuting most of the politicians and businessmen thitherto regarded as untouchable, for which his work has gained notoriety in the country (Barón, 2016).

The presence of this judge has been crucial to finishing defining the structure of Operation Car Wash, because without this figure, these investigations would probably not have taken the course they did. Judge Sergio Moro became a key player in the structure, since his actions in responding to the complaints filed set a precedent in the history of Brazilian justice: he sentenced politicians and businessmen with an enormous influence on the elite of Brazil to jail.

186 Latin American Anticorruption Strategies

The judge has issued over 150 orders for preventive and temporary detention, 50 criminal actions, and has sentenced over 100 people (Barón, 2016). However, as noted by Nascentes (2018, p. 10):

> Moro had a script ready to address systemic corruption in Brazil, in the event that the correct circumstances arose, since he had studied the *Mani Pulite* operation in Italy … However, there are several dangerous elements associated with the process. To begin with, the sanctification of Moro himself.

The importance acquired by the judge is justified to a certain extent, since he was the first person able to take on the corrupt Brazilian elite. However, the "sanctification" of the judge could give him so much power that he could end up taking advantage of the Brazilian anticorruption structure as a result of the media circus that has sprung up around him.

Beyond this personal variable of the judge in charge, the fact is that the work of several organizations has been involved: that of the Federal Police, the Prosecutor's Office, and the judge. This largely explains the location and understanding of the size of the situation: the existence of a broad network of politicians and businessmen organized in a sophisticated way to link a vast number of companies, activities, and transfers of resources. They are all connected, at the end of the day, in the fraudulent increase in the sums involved in contracts for the sale of goods and services to Petrobras in exchange for obtaining other activities or concessions (Nascentes, 2018).

In the end, the success of Operation Car Wash is not due to a single person. The strengthening of the tools of the judiciary since the beginning of the 20th century has been a success due to the containment of excesses by the Executive Branch, the institutional strengthening of the Public Prosecutor's Office, the judiciary, and the police forces. It has been a process of incremental improvements (Nascentes, 2018).

Actors Involved in Money Laundering

Throughout this chapter, emphasis has been placed on the fact that Operation Car Wash has attracted so much interest internationally for two reasons: 1) because of the amount of resources that were at stake in the money laundering, estimated to have been approximately $8 billion USD from 2004 to 2012 (RPP, 2017); and 2) because of the people involved in it.

According to the sentence passed by the Court of First Instance, these acts involved: senators, deputies, governors, politicians from different parties, ministers of state, and presidents of Brazil (Cabral & Oliveira, 2017).

At the business level, names such as Marcelo Obedrecht, who was the CEO of the largest construction company in the country[1]; Leo Pinheiro, former president of the OAS construction group (Agencia EFE, 2018); and Otávio Azevedo, former president of the Andrade Gutiérrez group, have been involved to such a degree that they have been sentenced to jail and have agreed to give information to the Brazilian justice in exchange for a reduction of their sentences.

From the political point of view, the characters involved in these operations are Luiz Inácio Lula Da Silva, former president of Brazil, who at the time of writing is in prison; Eduardo Cunha, former president of Congress who was sentenced to 24 years in prison (El País, 2018); former president of Brazil, Dilma Rousseff, who was brought to trial and impeached because of the corruption cases; Nestor Cerveró, who was the director of the international area of Petrobras and sentenced to 12 years in prison (Infobae, 2015); former president Fernando Henrique Cardoso, who was involved in certain emails (Carta Capital, 2018); and the current Brazilian president, Michel Temer, currently under investigation (Clarín, 2018).

Given the size of the money laundering and corruption network that surrounds all these actors, government, and companies, both state and private, Operation Car Wash shook the Brazilian political class, with other countries coming under scrutiny. Legal problems are being investigated in Peru, Colombia, Mexico, and elsewhere in Latin America.

Organizational Analysis

The success of Operation Car Wash is no coincidence. It is the product of an institutional network that was able to coordinate effectively. The three institutions involved had well-defined functions and collaborated in compiling the investigation files. The nodal point of the structure was the judge's performance, since the leeway he had to act without fear of reprisals against him enabled his behavior to be impartial in the cases detected.

This shows that the actors, who are within the structure comprising the Public Prosecutor's Office, the police, and the judges, understood their functions and the objectives of each organization and, at the same time, helped each other create a buffer zone that would ensure that the actors would not be harmed by the political pressure exerted in an attempt to stop the investigations from continuing.

Aware of their social function within the organizational structure, the actors dealt with their spaces in a discretional way, which allowed them to conduct their investigations. They handled this discretionality in parallel with the objectives of the organizations, meaning that they were able to achieve them in cases where those involved were powerful people.

It should be noted that since these were institutions with national jurisdiction, they overlook what happens at the state and local level, meaning that corruption continues to prevail in cases at these levels, an issue that is beyond the scope of the structure.

It is important to be clear on one point. This structure is not different from the conventional structures of detection, investigation, and punishment of corruption cases in other countries. It is not like Guatemala, where an institution led by an international organization was formed to fight corruption and impunity.

It is a centralized structure to a certain extent, where there are only three organizations responsible for the corruption analysis process. This raises the question of

188 Latin American Anticorruption Strategies

what was different in this case if the structure is similar to those in other countries. The main factor is that the judge, the Public Prosecutor, and the police, as individual actors, are independent of political and economic power. This contributed to the fact that the investigations were not biased.

Due to this independence, the institutions were able to conduct impartial investigations to such an extent that they were able to penetrate the layer of impunity prevailing in Brazil's strongest social and political power circles.

Final Considerations

By February 2017, Operation Car Wash had achieved the following numbers: 1,434 procedures installed; 730 searches and arrests; 197 coercive measures; 79 instances of preventive custody; 103 temporary prison sentences; six prison sentences for flagrantly breaking the law; 131 requests for international cooperation; 71 award-winning cooperation agreements signed with individuals; 9 plea bargains and 1 behavior adjustment agreement; 57 criminal accusations against 260 different people, 25 of whom had already been sentenced for the following crimes: corruption, crimes against the international financial system, transnational drug trafficking, criminal formation and organization, money laundering, among others; and seven accusations of administrative improbity against 38 individuals and 16 companies, asking for the payment of R$12.5 billion, with the total value of the compensation received, including fines, being R$38.100 million. To date, 125 sentences have already been handed down (Freitas & Joppert, 2016).

According to the Attorney General's Office, in four years, 954 search warrants, 103 preventive arrest warrants, and 118 temporary detention orders have been issued. During the 49 stages of the investigation, 188 sentences have been handed down to 123 people, some of whom have received more than one conviction. Thus, the sentences of the accused who have been sentenced amount to 1,861 years and 20 days in prison.

In this context, the organization Transparency International (2015) states the following:

> [L]arge-scale cases of corruption, such as those of Petrobras and Odebrecht in Brazil... show how collusion between companies and politicians takes billions of dollars from national economies to benefit a few at the expense of the majority... This type of large-scale, systemic corruption results in violations of human rights, curbs sustainable development and encourages social exclusion.

Hence the importance of analyzing cases such as Operation Car Wash, since they serve as an example so that the justice systems of other countries can respond to acts of corruption and eliminate the impunity that prevails in most countries, particularly in the case of people with political or economic power.

Final Reflection on the Brazilian Case

Unlike Mexico and Argentina, Brazil has advanced a very broad and comprehensive strategy, with rules and organizations that endogenously, in other words, within the political and administrative system itself, seek to control corruption. Despite suffering from systemic corruption, Brazil has opted for a decentralized scheme of multiple organizations in various areas of the political system, acting as a network, to reduce the most serious consequences of corruption in the country. The case is striking because at the same time, the organization and depth of corruption is endemic in the highest political spheres of the country, as has been shown in recent years with cases such as Operation Car Wash and others that have erupted in media scandals. The capacity of the various Brazilian organizations, both executive, judicial, and legislative, have made it possible for these scandals not to have avoided consequences: investigations, punishments, and persecution have been the norm that has reached the highest spheres of power in Brazil. This success can be analyzed as a paradox, for at least two reasons. The first is because it has been a scheme that has begun to yield results through the rules and organizations of the political system. This has allowed it to avoid the contradiction that agencies like the OAA in Argentina and the SNA in Mexico have: attempting to act in a parallel or relatively exogenous way to control the political system which has to sustain and finance it. The second paradox is more intricate: its success has challenged the political system itself. A political system in which everything would appear to indicate that corruption is the norm is being forced to transform those practices, but at a very high speed and with a very uncertain route. In other words, success in controlling corruption has destabilized a political system that is largely managed and organized through various improper or questionable actions. Corruption can be reduced, but the route that remains pending is how corruption can be extirpated from the political system to create other practices, other ways of relating that do not involve acts and practices such as bribery, conflicts of interest, or influence peddling. It is essential to study the case of Brazil, since it could lead the way for many other countries in Latin America and other parts of the world.

Note

1 Obedrecht construction company has been involved in corruption scandals at the international level, for making illegal deals with high public officials in several Latin American countries.

Bibliography

Agencia EFE. (2018). La operación Lava Jato cumple cuatro años con 123 políticos y empresarios condenados. Brasil. Corrupción. Retrieved from www.efe.com/efe/am erica/politica/la-operacion-lava-jato-cumple-cuatro-anos-con-123-politicos-y-empresario s-condenados/20000035-3556312.

Barón, F. (2016). 7 preguntas y respuestas para entender la operación Lava Jato. CNN Español. Brasil. Retrieved from https://cnnespanol.cnn.com/2016/09/26/7-pregunta s-y-respuestas-para-entender-la-operacion-lava-jato/.

Cabral, M., & Oliveira, R. (2017). *O Príncipe: Uma biografia não autorizada de Marcelo Odebrecht.* São Paulo, Brazil: Astral Cultural.

Carreiro, L. (2010). *O combate à corrupção: A contribuição do direito econômico.* Doctoral dissertation, Universidade de São Paulo.

Carta Capital. (2018). Em e-mails, FHC pede doações a Marcelo Odebrecht: "O de sempre". Retrieved from www.cartacapital.com.br/politica/em-e-mails-fhc-pede-doa coes-a-marcelo-odebrecht-o-de-sempre.

Clarín. (2018). Qué es el Lava Jato, el caso de corrupción que estalló en Brasil y sacudió toda la región. Retrieved from www.clarin.com/mundo/lava-jato-caso-corrupcion-estallo-bra sil-sacudio-toda-region_0_HyLOyLySX.html.

Consentino, L. O. (2014). Controle Externo do TCU e suas funções accountability no debate da qualidade da democracia. In J. A. O. Moisés (Ed.), *Congresso Nacional, os partidos políticos e o sistema de integridade* (pp. 117–136). Rio de Janeiro: Konrad Adenauer Stiftung.

Constitución Política de la República Federal de Brasil de 1988 (CPRFB). (2018). Retrieved from www.wipo.int/edocs/lexdocs/laws/es/br/br117es.pdf.

El País. (2018). *24 años de prisión para Cunha, el "arquitecto" del impeachment a Dilma Rousseff.* Retrieved from www.elpais.com.uy/mundo/anos-prision-cunha-arquitecto-impeachm ent-dilma-rousseff.html.

Estrategia Nacional de Combate a la Corrupción y el Lavado de Dinero (ENCCLA). (2018a). *Quienes somos.* Retrieved from http://enccla.camara.leg.br/quem-somos.

Estrategia Nacional de Combate a la Corrupción y el Lavado de Dinero (ENCCLA). (2018b). *Principales resultados.* Retrieved from http://enccla.camara.leg.br/resultados/prin cipais-resultados.

Ferreira, F. (2014). *A prática de improbidade administrativa e as expectativas de controle decorrentes.* Associação Mineira do Ministério Público (AMMP). Retrieved from www.ammp.org.br/ inst/artigo/Artigo-96.pdf.

Freitas, M., & Joppert, C. (2016) *Diagnóstico institucional: Primeiros passos para um plano nacional anticorrupção.* FGV Direito Rio, p.162. http://bibliotecadigital.fgv.br/dspace/handle/ 10438/18167.

García, E. (2006) O combate à corrupção no Brasil: Responsabilidade ética e moral do Supremo Tribunal Federal na sua desarticulação. *Revista Brasileira de Direito Constitucional,* No. 6, Year II, 9–19.

Gonzaga, C. (2008). Os crimes de colarinho branco e as teorias da pena. DE JURE. *Revista Jurídica do Ministério Público de Minas Gerais,* 505–521. Retrieved from https://bdjur.stj.jus. br/jspui/bitstream/2011/27221/crimes_colarinho_branco_teorias.pdf.

Infobae. (2015). Condenaron a 12 años de prisión a Nestor Cerveró, ex director de Pet- robras. Retrieved from www.infobae.com/2015/08/17/1748917-condenaron-12-anos-p rision-nestor-cervero-ex-director-petrobras/.

Ministério da Justiça . (2018) Estratégia Nacional de Combate à Corrupção e à Lavagem de Dinheiro (ENCCLA). Retrieved from www.justica.gov.br/sua-protecao/lavagem-de-d inheiro/enccla.

Nascentes, L. G. (2018). *Consideraciones sobre las causas de la corrupción sistémica en Brasil: El caso de la operación Lava Jato.* Final assignment. Mexico City, Mexico: CIDE.

OAS Organization of American States. (2012). *Mechanism for follow-up on the implementation of the Inter-American Convention Against Corruption — Final Report on the Federative Republic of Brazil.* Washington, DC. Retrieved from www.oas.org/juridico/english/bra.htm.

Political Constitution of the Federative Republic of Brazil (CPRFB). (2010). Retrieved from www.acnur.org/fileadmin/Documentos/BDL/2001/0507.pdf.

Rose-Ackerman, S., & Palifka, B. J. (2016). *Corruption and government: Causes, consequences, and reform.* New York: Cambridge University Press.

RPP, Noticias. (2017). 6 claves para entender la operación "Lava-Jato". Retrieved from http s://rpp.pe/mundo/latinoamerica/que-es-la-operacion-lava-jato-6-claves-para-entender-es te-caso-noticia-943263.

Transparency International. (2015). *Impact report.* Retrieved from www.transparency.org/ whatwedo/publication/impact_report.

Valencia, L. (2015). Brasil: Virtud y defecto de la Ley Anticorrupción. LexLatin. Retrieved from http://lexlatin.com/reportaje/brasil-virtud-y-defecto-de-la-ley-anticorrupcion.

6

THE INTERNATIONAL COMMISSION AGAINST IMPUNITY IN GUATEMALA

Introduction

The International Commission against Impunity in Guatemala (CICIG) is an extremely innovative international mechanism devoted to fighting corruption in that country. It was created by the United Nations (UN) in 2006 and ratified by the Guatemalan Congress in 2007 as part of the peace agreements, particularly the Global Agreement on Human Rights, with the aim of "supporting, strengthening and helping the institutions of the State of Guatemala to investigate, prosecute and dismantle illegal bodies and clandestine security apparatuses that commit crimes and affect the fundamental human rights of citizens" (Zamudio, 2018, p. 508).

On September 7, 2007, the "International Commission against Impunity in Guatemala" (CICIG) was formally established with three central objectives:

1. Investigate the existence of Illegal Corps and Clandestine Security Apparatuses that commit crimes and affect the human rights of the citizens of Guatemala and identify the structures of these illegal groups (including their links with state officials), activities, operational modalities, and sources of financing.
2. Work with the state in the dismantling of clandestine security apparatuses and illegal corps and promote the investigation, criminal prosecution, and punishment of crimes committed by its members.
3. Make recommendations to the state of Guatemala for the adoption of public policies aimed at eradicating clandestine apparatuses and illegal security forces in order to prevent their re-emergence, including the legal and institutional reforms required for this purpose.

(Zamudio, 2018)

Illegal Security Corps and Clandestine Security Apparatuses are groups which:

a   Commit illegal acts in order to affect the full enjoyment and exercise of civil and political rights;
b   Are directly or indirectly linked to state agents or have the capacity to achieve impunity for their illicit actions.

Through this organization, the Guatemalan government attempted to address the impunity these groups had maintained, since over time they gradually became inserted into the government to control certain activities which would assure them impunity in the face of the corruption crimes committed by them (Impunity Watch, 2010).

It is unusual in that it promotes the strengthening of the local justice system within the country, working with national laws and institutions "without trying to substitute or replace its government institutions" (Zamudio, 2018, p. 510).

The CICIG can be regarded as a "hybrid" institution, which faces a major challenge in following the guidelines established by the international organization while, at the same time, respecting the Guatemalan legal framework in this area. In its 11 years of existence, the CICIG has taken on cases that have had an enormous political impact, since they have found evidence that there are politicians and influential people involved in corruption cases.

For these reasons, this chapter seeks to discuss how the CICIG is an extremely novel Latin American experiment, which has yielded major results. There are a number of reasons for these results. These include its capacity as an organization to change and adapt: from the original agenda with which it began—a highly complex, unclear agenda to reduce impunity—to another, more focused, and clearer agenda for addressing corruption. And on the basis of this, it formalized an organization with enormous technical capacities for investigation and criminal analysis. Finally, it focused on strengthening the judicial institutions of the state to eliminate impunity. However, these elements have been possible thanks to a particular condition: given that corruption is systemic in Guatemala, the strength of the CICIG lies in the fact that although it is an international organization, in principle it is solidly supported by Guatemalan state organizations. Although the fact that it is an international agency has enabled it to gain credibility to confront Guatemalan government institutions captured by the logic of corruption, its international status has become both a weakness and a vulnerability. As the CICIG has become increasingly successful, it has become a problem for the status quo of the political system and the Guatemalan state has already begun a campaign to expel the organization from the country. It justifies its actions on the grounds that the CICIG violates the sovereignty of the Guatemalan state. At the time of writing this chapter, the Guatemalan president, who is under investigation by the CICIG for corruption issues with electoral campaign funds, has said he will not request the renewal of the agreement regarding the organization from the UN.

The purpose then is to understand how these factors are part of the explanation of this innovation in the fight against corruption, by finding out how it has operated and the impact it has had. To this end, the chapter is divided into five parts:

194 Latin American Anticorruption Strategies

the first outlines the background to the creation of the CICIG to understand the context in which it originated; the second describes the regulations and organization that support the existence of this institution; the third describes the institutions involved and the role they play in the fight against corruption; the fourth lists the important people who have been involved in cases of corruption while the last one presents the final considerations.

Background

The civil war Guatemala experienced from 1962 to 1996 left a complex social composition in its wake, because the existence of armed corps opposing the state caused an unprecedented wave of violence. The 36-year conflict was the longest and deadliest in the region, with a death toll of 200,000 (OSF, 2016). The Open Society Foundation report (OSF, 2016, p. 19) says the following about this Central American country:

> ... a state incapable of controlling the violence and threats against democratic stability stemming from political corruption and organized crime. The crisis originated in the structure of Guatemalan institutions which, in turn, are the result of a lengthy, complex historical process shaped by the interests and incentives of the country's most powerful actors in the political, military and economic arena.

This condition caused an increase in the number of cases of corruption and the penetration by criminal groups of the institutional structure of the state due to its fragility (Impunity Watch, 2010). As a result of this fragility, state institutions were corrupted through links with state agents, interference in political parties, the coopting of officials, and the distortion of the processes for the selection and nomination of the authorities in key institutes of justice. If this failed to yield sufficient results for the interests of criminal groups, then they physically eliminated those considered a threat to their interests (Impunity Watch, 2010).

In this context, in 1994, Guatemala signed a human rights agreement known as the Global Agreement on Human Rights, in which the country has committed, among other things, to two important aspects: 1) acting against impunity and 2) purging and professionalizing the security forces (Impunity Watch, 2010). It should be recalled that the illegal, clandestine security groups created during the armed conflict had acquired a great deal of power in this Central American country.

On the basis of this agreement, the Commission for the Investigation of Illegal Bodies and Clandestine Security Apparatuses (Ciciacs) was formed; however, this Commission did not prosper either legally or politically (Impunity Watch, 2010). Ciciacs is the direct forerunner of the CICIG. Since it was declared unconstitutional after its creation because an international entity was granted powers which the Guatemalan legal system only permitted in the Public Prosecutor's Office, it was unable to begin operating (Impunity Watch, 2010).

Despite the signing of the 1994 agreement, since the violence and the state's weak situation continued in the country, alternative measures were sought to pacify it. Some of the formal changes involved certain security institutions such as the Civil Self-Defense Patrols (PAC), paramilitary forces that assisted the Guatemalan army. The PACs were demobilized. In addition, the Presidential General Staff, which served as a center for military intelligence and covert activities, was replaced by the Secretariat of Administrative and Security Affairs (WOLA, 2015).

In response to the sustained climate of violence, the Guatemalan government resumed negotiations with the UN and in 2006, the CICIG emerged, after the agreement to create the Ciciacs was signed on January 4, 2004 by the United Nations and Guatemala (Impunity Watch, 2010). The agreement for its creation was therefore ratified by the Congress of Guatemala and the CICIG came into force on September 4, 2007 (WOLA, 2015).

Normativity

The CICIG is based solely on the agreement mentioned in the previous section. This document, called the Agreement between the United Nations Organization and the Government of Guatemala regarding the establishment of an International Commission against Impunity in Guatemala (CICIG), stipulated the objectives, powers, functions, legal personality and capacity, organic structure, terms of cooperation with the CICIG, financing, security, and personnel protection.

As regards functions, the Commission is responsible for determining the existence of illegal security forces and clandestine apparatuses; collaborating with the state in dismantling clandestine security apparatuses and illegal security corps and promoting the investigation, criminal prosecution, and sanction of crimes committed by its members; and recommending to the state the adoption of policies to eliminate illegal organizations (CICIG, 2018c).

The Commission is an entity with absolute functional independence in the performance of its mandate, whose functions include the following:

1. Collect, evaluate, and systematize information provided by anyone.
2. Promote criminal prosecution through a criminal complaint to the corresponding authorities.
3. Provide technical advice to the competent institutions of the State in the investigation and criminal prosecution of the crimes committed.
4. Denounce public officials and employees who, in the performance of their tasks, have allegedly committed administrative offenses, to the respective administrative authorities.
5. Act as an interested third party in administrative disciplinary procedures.
6. Sign and implement cooperation agreements with the Public Prosecutor's Office, the Supreme Court of Justice, the institution of the Human Rights Ombudsman, the National Civil Police, and any other state institutions.

196 Latin American Anticorruption Strategies

7. Guarantee confidentiality for the people who participate in the functions and faculties of the Commission; request statements, documents, reports, and collaboration in general; among other functions.

In order to perform these functions, and be accepted as an international organization with investigation capabilities in a sovereign state such as Guatemala, it was necessary to build the organization with certain particularities. Although it is an international organization within Guatemala, it is not considered a UN civil service organization. The CICIG does not receive financing from the United Nations regular budget. All its funds come from voluntary donations from various countries, administered through the United Nations Development Program (UNDP). The donor group consists of Norway, Germany, Canada, Spain, the United States, Italy, Japan, the Netherlands, and Sweden, as well as the Inter-American Development Bank, the World Bank, the International Monetary Fund, the United Nations Development Program, the European Union, and the Organization of American States (Zamudio, 2018). Thus, the CICIG is a very special entity, international but with national capabilities. But it does not have the formal characteristics of an international UN organization, in order to limit the scope of its action and thus avoid the ever-present criticism of violations of the country's sovereignty. The CICIG can therefore investigate and use this investigation to support the Public Prosecutor's Office and the state attorney's office, in order for these organizations to implement the demands and prosecutions. The CICIG is a "supportive companion" of these organizations, in other words, which avoids the problem experienced by the Ciciacs, which violated Guatemalan state regulations.

The way the CICIG is organized internally is as follows: one commissioner, specialized staff, and a secretariat. The commissioner is the CICIG representative to the government of Guatemala, as well as to other states and local and international organizations. The commissioner is the only person formally belonging to the UN. Specialized personnel are then hired directly by the commissioner (in other words, they do not belong to the UN civil service), which includes technicians with experience in conducting human rights investigations, forensic experts, and information experts. The Secretariat is the responsibility of an international official, who is in charge of the general administration of the institution.

Organization

The CICIG comprises 173 people from Argentina, Canada, Chile, Colombia, Costa Rica, El Salvador, Spain, France, Honduras, Italy, Mexico, Peru, Portugal, Sweden, Uruguay, and Venezuela. The Commission also has the support of 70 agents from the Guatemalan National Police, who perform investigative and security functions and are part of a police unit that supports the Special Prosecutor's Office for CICIG (UEFAC), which is the link and direct channel of communication between the Public Prosecutor's Office and the CICIG.

The international employees hired are selected through public calls for submissions and the evaluation of their academic and professional credentials. Over half are dedicated to the investigation of criminal structures (CICIG, 2015d). Likewise, national officials are hired in accordance with the guidelines issued by the United Nations Organization, which include the selection of trained, experienced personnel with the capacity to maximize resources and efficiently perform the tasks entrusted to them (CICIG, 2015d).

The CICIG comprises three areas: the Commissioner's Office, in which a technical and executive support team participates in the work of the Commission; a Political Section, where the work of formulating recommendations for preparing public policies and legislative reforms is coordinated; and a Press Section responsible for handling the communication strategy of this Commission (CICIG, 2016).

The CICIG commissioner is appointed by the UN Secretary General. Strictly speaking, he is the only United Nations officer and is obliged to report annually on his activities through a report submitted in New York (Zamudio, 2018).

Likewise, the CICIG has a Research and Litigation Department in which the investigative activity is carried out, which, in turn, comprises investigative units and information and analysis as well as financial investigation sections that directly accompany the Public Prosecutor's Office in the investigation of cases linked to the mandate of this Commission. The CICIG has an Administrative Department, responsible for providing logistic and operational support for its substantive activities (CICIG, 2016).

The communication strategy (Press Section) makes it possible to create a link between the work of the Commission and the Guatemalan population. The CICIG communication seeks to increase knowledge and understanding of its everyday work concerning investigations (CICIG, 2016).

To inform the majority of people, the CICIG uses different tools, among which are the following: social networks; conferences and press releases; interviews with local, national, and international media (CICIG, 2016).

The language used is easy to understand for the audience in general and the response of the population in the virtual media demonstrates and expresses support and follow-up of the work of the Commission, while at the institutional level, it makes it possible to know about the concerns, doubts, and demands of the Guatemalan population, allowing direct, rapid contact between society and the CICIG (CICIG, 2016).

The communication strategy linked to the forceful actions undertaken by this institution are the reasons why the CICIG has a good reputation at a national and international level, since it has demonstrated its impartiality through certain acts and has addressed impunity and corruption, regardless of who committed the crime.

Institutions Involved

Since the CICIG is an organization independent of the Guatemalan government, it is a unique model of cooperation, since it is independent of research and at the

198 Latin American Anticorruption Strategies

same time operates under Guatemalan laws and depends on the Guatemalan justice system. Accordingly, this process of cooperation between the CICIG and the Guatemalan institutions strengthens the capacities of both (WOLA, 2015).

In this respect, the institutions with which the CICIG has close communication are, mainly: 1) the Public Prosecutor's Office; 2) the National Civil Police; and 3) other Guatemalan institutions focused on the prosecution of crimes.

The challenge of coordinating the CICIG with the institutions is enormous, because, first of all, the Commission had to find a way to work with its main partner, the Public Prosecutor's Office, an institution which had also been infiltrated by networks dedicated to influence peddling. Carlos Castresana, one of the commissioners of the CICIG, established the bases paving the way for the establishment of a link with the Public Prosecutor's Office, by forcing President Álvaro Colom to appoint a general prosecutor with whom he could work, jointly establishing an independent unit within the institution dedicated to working with the CICIG, in addition to creating the skills required for analysis, security, and phone tapping units (OSF, 2016).

The other institution with which the CICIG has an ongoing relationship is the National Civil Police, whose function is to protect public order, and detect and investigate crimes committed within Guatemalan territory (Gobierno de Guatemala, 2018).

Thus, the CICIG serves as an auxiliary of these agencies, mainly to conduct investigations in an efficient and impartial manner to sanction crimes that have been committed. It is important to mention that the Commission does not take any action other than through these institutions, since it is obliged to comply with the Guatemalan legal mandate.

Impunity Watch (2010) has identified the main weaknesses of the Guatemalan justice system as the following: the lack of effective mechanisms to monitor the performance of justice workers; failure to comply with the selection, promotion, evaluation, and dismissal criteria; the wide margin of discretion of the authorities in the Public Prosecutor's Office and the Judicial Branch; and weak disciplinary systems.

Another persistent problem contributing to impunity has been the limited protection provided by the Public Prosecutor's Office and the National Civil Police for witnesses, complainants, and justice workers during the criminal proceedings (Impunity Watch, 2010).

Although in nominal terms, the Commission is an organ created by the United Nations, it has rapidly evolved to become an extremely independent organization, managed by a commissioner who is virtually not subject to any supervision. However, this freedom to act without the evaluation and supervision of the United Nations has been extremely beneficial for the CICIG (OSF, 2016).

The first, and perhaps the most important benefit is linked to the principle of legal and political oversight of procedural discretion, a mechanism that seeks to ensure that the desire of a prosecutor does not invade the accepted limits or violate the rules governing the conduct of United Nations officers.

CICIG in Guatemala **199**

Second, the CICIG commissioner has the power to modify the structure and personnel of the CICIG, as well as to determine the political and procedural strategy of the Commission without the participation of the United Nations, to spend the $15 million USD budget of the Commission merely by satisfying internal restrictions (OSF, 2016), and to continue negotiations with Guatemala and other governments without the participation of the United Nations.

La Línea Case

One of the most emblematic cases investigated by the CICIG is the *La Línea* case, as a result of which more than 50 people were sent to trial, including former President Otto Pérez Molina and former Vice President Ingrid Roxana Baldetti Elías, for leading the customs fraud network known as "*La Línea*" in which individuals, former bosses, former employees of the Tax Administration Superintendency (SAT), and the customs offices of the country participated. The former president was specifically accused of the following crimes: illicit association, customs fraud, and passive bribery (CICIG, 2017; CICIG, 2015b).

La Línea sought to obtain bribes from the employers and users of various customs houses in the country in exchange for modifying the amount of tax importers had to pay the treasury. "One of the main issues was smuggling and in general fraud in a country that has such a great need of resources", said Iván Velásquez, leader of the UN Commission (BBC Mundo, 2015).

The investigation began in May 2014, "due to the suspicion that a group of importers were involved in smuggling, who had contact with a network of customs brokers to evade payment of the correct amount of taxes" (CICIG, 2015c). However, the investigation gradually discovered a network that provided telephone links—hence the name of the case, "*La Línea*" meaning "line"—to customs workers, businessmen, and a criminal organization that indicated the amounts of taxes and bribes importers had to pay when the customs traffic light turned red.

The criminal network needed those in charge of the inspections and agents (who review and process imports) in the customs houses to be assigned specific work schedules. The request was made by a criminal organization outside the SAT. At the same time, the organization infiltrated agents with the help of the SAT to facilitate orders for the schedules and places where agents and customs officers would be assigned to work. The CICIG investigation found that *La Línea* was used to communicate the organization strategy so that the inspectors and agents would receive orders to carry out the fraud. Customs inspectors and agents were given the task of altering the customs inspection system so that some containers were revised in such a way that smaller amounts of merchandise were declared and, therefore, the tariffs and taxes on these imports were partially or totally omitted (CICIG, 2015e). To close this circle, in exchange for modifying what the importers had to pay the treasury, they were made to pay bribes.

In this last phase, *La Línea* communicated, by means of a telephone call, the value of the tax due on each container, while indicating the amount to be charged

200 Latin American Anticorruption Strategies

in bribes ("la cola" in Guatemala), whereby businessmen paid between 30 and 40% less than the amount they were supposed to pay. Although bribe payments were not made in that place, the fraudsters built a collection system through bank deposits that were sent to the accounts of the criminal operators of the structure outside the SAT. Finally, the money reached four bank accounts of the Corpgold firm, whose representative was the driver of Francisco Javier Ortíz, one of the main leaders of the criminal structure. The money was distributed in cash at *"la oficinita"*, a place in the Guatemalan capital (Melini, 2015).

Although the total sum of the embezzlement is not known, in two weeks a member of the criminal group was able to collect 2.5 million quetzales (approximately $330,000 USD), according to the official inquiry (BBC Mundo, 2015). In the investigation, which involved 80,000 telephone taps and 5,000 email messages, the researchers found references to "The number one guy" and "the number two woman" which, according to the CICIG and the Attorney General's Office, correspond to the participation of Pérez Molina and the now ex Vice President Roxana Baldetti (BBC Mundo, 2015). On the day of the raid alone, approximately 5 million *quetzales* in cash ($60,000 USD) were taken for judicial safekeeping.

The case also implicated Omar Franco, director of the Tax Administration Superintendency, Carlos Muñoz, his predecessor, and Juan Carlos Monzón, former private secretary of the vice president and alleged leader of the criminal organization (BBC Mundo, 2015). Monzón was traveling to South Korea with the vice president when government security forces, together with the CICIG, raided offices and homes in mid-April (BBC Mundo, 2015).

As part of the network structure, other government officials who were also implicated included Sebastián Carrera, head of Human Resources of the SAT; Anthony Segura, General Secretary of the SAT union; Carla Mireya Herrera, Central Customs Administrator; Gustavo Adolfo Morales, head of the Southern Division; as well as Melvin Gudiel and Julio Robles, administrators in Puerto Quetzal.

For its part, the criminal organization, below Juan Carlos Monzón, was operated by Salvador Stuardo and at least nine people linked to the formal customs structure.

Although they did not appear in the criminal network, the former president and former vice president had very close links with the main parties involved. The former vice president was directly associated with her private secretary Carlos Monzón since he was her direct employee. Former President Otto Pérez Molina was linked to events by the appointment of SAT director, Omar Franco Chacón, in 2014, who was directly involved.

The investigation immediately began to have a significant media impact. Some economic sectors such as the Coordinating Committee of Agricultural, Commercial, Industrial and Financial Associations publicly acknowledged its satisfaction with the operations in dismantling the criminal structure in the customs offices (CICIG, 2015c). National newspapers highlighted the operation and the investigation. On April 17, 2015, the headlines of some newspapers announced "MP and

CICIG deal blow to smuggling and customs fraud structure", "Fraudsters Network Dismantled", "CICIG dismantles corruption network in SAT", "Head, former head of SAT and secretary of Baldetti directed fraud", "CICIG and MP dismantle organization led by Vice President's secretary", "Major blow to criminal structure", "Fraud network discovered and caught," "Head of SAT and Baldetti's secretary directed network", "Head, former head of SAT and secretary of Baldetti directed fraud". The articles were accompanied by images of officials being arrested and handcuffed (CICIG, 2015c). Newspaper editorials also accompanied their texts that day with an emphasis on the investigation and described the discontent and shame over the actions of those involved, especially officials.

In this sense, media and social pressure was such that both the former president and the former vice president were forced to resign from their positions, as Guatemalan society began to take to the streets to demonstrate in order to call for their resignation in the face of their exasperation with the cases of corruption and impunity in Guatemala. Although the former vice president denied her involvement in the fraud network by telling the people of Guatemala that, "Rest assured that no one at the highest level of the state is involved in this structure", at the end of April, approximately 15,000 people gathered in *Plaza de la Constitución* in Guatemala City, to demand the resignation of the president and vice president. The demonstrations spread across the entire country and by September 2015, people were clamoring for the resignation of Otto Pérez Molina: 75,000 Guatemalans in the interior of the country and another 25,000 in the capital (BBC Mundo, 2015).

After they had resigned from their positions, another stage of the CICIG investigation, related to searches of the homes of the people involved, showed that former Vice President Baldetti Elías and her husband were the beneficiaries of checks and invoices found at the home of Salvador Estuardo, one of the operators of the criminal network. On July 27, 2017, the former vice president was taken to trial, accused of leading the *La Línea* customs fraud network, together with former President Otto Pérez Molina.

For his part, the former president was linked to the *La Línea* case because several wiretappings provide evidence of the direct relationship between Pérez Molina and certain members of the structure the CICIG showed in its investigations, including Salvador Estuardo and Carlos Enrique Muñoz (former head of the SAT) (CICIG, 2015f). Moreover, the investigations in the raids turned up documents such as bribe distribution tables, changes of posts, and a memorandum addressed to former President Otto Pérez Molina.

The investigation clearly demonstrated the systemic corruption faced by Guatemala. It also revealed the possibility of highlighting a large network of connections between the government and organized crime. It also showed that systemic corruption is built over time, maintained and adapted, until it eventually becomes normalized. One of the tapped calls by Francisco Javier Ortíz (from the criminal network) recorded a conversation in which he stated that this type of operation had been operating in Guatemala for nearly two decades: "I'm a newcomer to this business, they have been working in customs fraud for over 18 years" (Melini, 2015).

202 Latin American Anticorruption Strategies

It is worth mentioning the progress made in the *La Línea* investigations showing that, in order to perform these acts of corruption in the country's customs offices, "importers created shell companies, using the names of real companies and people to obtain their tax identification numbers. This means that many of the names appearing on the lists of importers do not necessarily correspond to the actual importer" (CICIG, 2015e).This, in turn, led the Metropolitan District Attorney to investigate over 800 cases of identity theft. In some cases the same person has irregularly registered 12 firms. The investigation put an end to corrupt acts in three ways, through 1) the network established among government officials, 2) the criminals; and, 3) the part concerning those who agree to give bribes: the entrepreneurs.

La Línea marked a watershed in the CICIG, showing that it was an efficient, credible, and legitimate organization. Thereafter, everyone in Guatemala would know that no one is untouchable or, in the words of the commissioner, that "we are not condemned to live in impunity" (Zamudio, 2018, p. 532).

Thanks to *La Línea*, a new concept was created: Illicit Political-Economic Networks (RPEI). Commissioner Iván Velázquez sought to capture a much broader phenomenon, which combines actors, contexts, and legal and illegal, public and private, formal and informal dynamics (Zamudio, 2018). The difference is that it was now possible to visualize a much more complete phenomenon, which includes clientelism, cronyism, or, as the Guatemalans themselves say, an entire culture of "greed" and corruption (Zamudio, 2018).

The notion of the CICIG has not been abandoned, but under the new category, a change in the definition of the country's problems was created and far more sweeping action is possible, even within legal structures or within the everyday exercise of politics and public administration, which constituted blind spots for the CICIG (Zamudio, 2018).

Under the new operational concept, corruption was identified as a cross-cutting issue and five priority issues to be investigated were established:

1. Smuggling and customs fraud;
2. Judicial corruption;
3. Administrative corruption;
4. Illicit electoral financing;
5. Drug trafficking and money laundering.

During the period from 2007 to 2015, the CICIG investigated more than 200 cases and obtained arrest warrants for 160 acting (or retired) public officials including former presidents, interior and defense ministers, prominent members of the army and national police force, as well as criminal gang leaders (Zamudio, 2018).

The organizational change was characterized by the simplification and clearer specification of its approach and modus operandi. The five original departments were reduced to three (administration, security, and research), with the aim of "strengthening the processes of criminal investigation, making research more agile and improving the progress of context methodology" (Zamudio, 2018, p. 520).

More Investigation by the CICIG

The CICIG has published 84 cases (www.cicig.org) in which it has participated in the indictment of public servants and individuals in relation to corruption cases. CICIG investigations include several issues, such as: security cases, diversion of funds from public programs, public health, corruption in municipal governments, nepotism, the Guatemalan military industry, and cases against judges and legislators, to mention just a few.

The following cases reveal the importance of an organization such as the CICIG. Although the social and media impact was less than that of *La Línea*, it is worth clarifying that the CICIG has made a far-reaching contribution to the reduction of impunity because of the issues it is investigating and is able to make available to the Guatemalan authorities.

The Mariachi Loco Case: Public Security

In 2008, "Four members of the National Civil Police (PNC) formed a criminal organization responsible for committing robberies and organized assaults" (CICIG, 2018b). Those implicated were the former head of Police Station 11 in Guatemala, the former deputy inspector of the PNC, and two former PNC agents, accused of theft, abuse of authority, and crime simulation. Although they were sentenced to five to eight years in prison, the "CICIG appealed the ruling because the judges of the Court did not consider the aggravating circumstance that they were public officials" (CICIG, 2018b, p. 32). The four were given a 15-year inconmutable prison sentence for the crimes of which they were accused. In this case, the role of the CICIG was important in pressuring the judges of the Court to ensure that the accused were given appropriate sentences. In other words, rather than presenting evidence on those involved and bringing them before the authorities, the CICIG functioned as an organization with social interest so that the penalties imposed were appropriate.

Health Negotiators Case: Public Health

In October 2015, a network of 13 operators, employed by the Guatemalan Social Security Institute (IGSS), as well as individuals who offered medical products and services, who collaborated to favor certain drug providers in exchange for commissions (CICIG, 2015g) was dismantled. A structure with four sectors participated in this network:

1. The operators were people outside the IGSS responsible for establishing relationships with IGSS officials to benefit medical goods and service

providers, trafficking in health information, co-opting the market, and interceding with IGSS officials on behalf of providers. These operators are intermediaries for facilitating tenders, making them appear legal, and obtaining the tender for a supplier in exchange for a commission.

2. The providers paid or offered commissions to operators and beneficiaries to place their products, goods, or services. These suppliers could be individuals, companies, or associations that participated in the bids promoted by the IGSS.
3. Peripheral officers were "technical or professional IGSS officers who work in any of the patient care units" (CICIG, 2015a). Peripheral officers had the power to modify the "list of essential medicines" of the Social Security Institute, which determines which drugs are provided and prescribed by IGSS doctors.
4. The main government employees were IGSS technicians or professionals who worked in the IGSS administrative offices. These employees "intervene in the generation, development, supervision and/or decisions in the institutional acquisition processes".

(CICIG, 2015a)

The investigation stated that the operators were looking for peripheral or central officers to place medical goods or services through the promotion of medicines to be supplied by hospitals or prescribed by IGSS doctors through preferential treatment of the firms represented by the operators. The operators used to ensure or agree with the central or peripheral officers that the companies represented by the operators would be the ones who would win the bids promoted by the IGSS—the investigation even documented the fact that a group of companies, under the control of a single operator participated in the bidding processes with the same prices to force other participants out and win the bidding—in exchange for commissions which they used to call "diplomas", "chairs", or "benches", to identify them. This was verified during the documentation carried out by the CICIG during the investigation of the case by tapping phone calls.

The construction of the network and the deals revealed bidding processes arranged in exchange for commissions to IGSS officials likely to be co-opted by the commissions. The investigation also revealed the favorable treatment received by companies, medical laboratories, and private providers associated with the operators. Among those implicated in the Guatemalan government were Hugo Navas, Director of the IGSS Polyclinic; César Hernández, a doctor at the IGSS Oncology Unit; Roberto Estrada, Director of the IGSS Hospital of General Diseases; Carlos Palma, Director of the IGSS Juan José Arévalo Hospital; Marcelo Noguera, Head of the Financial Unit at the IGSS Juan José Arévalo Hospital; Carlos Salvatierra, Director of the IGSS Peripheral Unit; Gustavo Castillo, doctor at the IGSS Infectology Unit; and the General Manager of the Guatemalan Social Security Institute (IGSS), Óscar Armando García Muñoz "for buying medicines from specific providers and receiving air tickets and lodging expenses for him and his family in exchange for modifying the list of essential medicines" (CICIG, 2015a)—it is estimated that from March 2013 to May 2015 he received approximately 500,000 quetzales ($64,800 USD) and $15,000 USD.

In this investigation, the CICIG protected itself from the resolutions of the Courts that issued substitute measures to release ten of those involved during the sanctioning process. The CICIG eventually achieved the reversal of the substitute measures. Those involved were sent to trial, in addition to the former IGSS board of directors and deputy Roberto Ketsler for being linked as a partner in companies related to the process. A total of 19 people were tried for various crimes such as bribery, influence peddling, illicit association, concussion, and illicit collection of commissions.

Case of Business in the Military Industry: Army

The military industry is a government entity that is answerable to the Ministry of National Defense of Guatemala. Its purpose is to produce, acquire, market, and distribute arms, ammunition, equipment, clothing, footwear, and related military items for the Ministry of Defense and other Ministries and State Organisms.

Between 2008 and 2011, the military industry hired retired Major Rolando Enrique Hernández, as a "sales representative" for the military industry (CICIG, 2018a). However, the CICIG documented that the payments he received had several irregularities as a result of which five servicemen and seven businessmen related to the case were prosecuted.

The CICIG revealed six irregularities in the services provided by retired Major Rolando Henrique Hernández: 1) In the military industry "the figure of 'sales representative' was created (for Hernández), failing to comply with the principle of subjection to the law, duplicating unnecessary functions because there were positions that already performed the functions agreed upon for the sales representative" (CICIG, 2018a). 2) The commissions paid were agreed discretionally, without legal or technical support, and were "excessive and inoperative"—amounting to between 5% and 25%. 3) "It was not proven that the sales representative had the skills, knowledge or experience in the commercial area" (CICIG, 2018a). 4) The Major did not serve as a "representative" in several contracts. But he was paid commissions for sales he did not make. 5) He also "received payment of commissions for sales made to public institutions to which he was contractually forbidden to sell (such as the SAT, the Judiciary among others)" (CICIG, 2018a). 6) There was a discrepancy between the payments established by the contracts and the commissions charged on behalf of the major.

Moreover, the CICIG documented that the head of the military industry and the head of the Financial Department extorted money from businessmen who had a commercial relationship with this agency. The commission amounts estimated were equivalent to a cost to the treasury of 23.4 million quetzales ($3.16 million USD) with extortions of approximately 919,000 quetzales ($119,000 USD). In this case, it is striking that the Guatemalan military authorities ignored the rules for provision of information relating to protecting public resources.

Of the soldiers involved, at the time of their capture, four were retired military personnel, while the last one was commissioned as a military attaché to Brazil. They were brought to trial for the crimes of embezzlement, bribery, and conspiracy.

Cadastral Information Registry Case: A Box of Payments

As mentioned earlier, *La Línea* opened research lines that made it possible to uncover corruption networks in various sectors of the government of Guatemala, which operated even before the administration of former President Otto Pérez Molina and former Vice President Roxana Baldetti, one of them being the case of State Co-opting from which this investigation emerges.

The Registry of Cadastral Information (RIC) is an autonomous body of the government of Guatemala, with its own legal personality and assets, which seeks to give certainty and legality to land tenure in Guatemala, which is responsible for updating the cadastral data of the country. The CICIG and the Public Ministry of Guatemala documented that in that institution, payment for phantom jobs was made to people who kept a percentage of the salary, failed to comply with the object of the contract and that the remainder of the salary was paid to the person who recommended them to occupy the position, or were people who were hired by the RIC but never fulfilled the purpose of the contract; and, finally, they could be people who had been hired but carried out activities outside the contract. However, they did say they were workers of the "contact" which had invited them to work at the RIC (CICIG, 2018b).

The investigation found that there were two phases of co-opting in the RIC. The first happened when senior Guatemalan government officials such as the former vice president, the director of the RIC, Juan Alvarez Girón, Carlos Monzón (former private secretary of Roxana Baldetti and also involved in the *La Línea* case), and Omar Nájera (Monzón's contact) determined the jobs and the people who would have a job at the RIC.

The second happened when Emilia Ayuso (a close friend of Baldetti's) was appointed as interim director. Ayuso was responsible for hiring and instructing the personnel of the RIC's human, financial, and administrative resources area to fill and write reports on the phantom jobs. The CICIG estimates damage to public resources of 4.8 million quetzales ($241,000 USD). Finally, 17 people were formally accused (although another 50 hirings are still under investigation), including former Vice President Roxana Baldetti and Emilia Ayuso, as well as RIC personnel involved in hiring people to fill positions which, according to the CICIG and the MP of Guatemala, served as "tradable currency" for the payment of political favors. The crimes of which they were accused are illicit association and embezzlement.

Final Considerations

Despite the efforts made and the progress made by the Guatemalan justice system and the CICIG, it is important to note that, although the emblematic and high-impact cases of the CICIG have probably shaken the political mafias and political–criminal structures of Guatemala, the old behaviors are still present in a state apparatus incapable of occupying spaces temporarily rectified due to the activities of the CICIG and the Public Prosecutor's Office (OSF, 2016).

The CICIG is a unique case serving as an example of a way to fight corruption and impunity with the participation of the government and the UN. The Commission has currently been involved in controversy because Guatemalan President Jimmy Morales announced on August 31, 2018 that he will not renew the agreement to retain the CICIG. This would put an end to this institution which has been present for 11 years as part of the anticorruption policy (Pocasangre, 2018). Moreover, the president also decided to prohibit the entry into the country of CICIG commissioner, Iván Velázquez (CNN Español, 2018).

This has caused different impressions, since part of Guatemalan society and the international community disagrees with the elimination of this institution that has made great strides in the fight against corruption. In fact, it has been speculated that the president's decision may have been due to the fact that the CICIG recently began to investigate the alleged illicit enrichment of the campaign of the incumbent president.

The CICIG can therefore be seen as a very particular anticorruption agency (ACA). In the end, it suffers the same hardships and attacks from the political system which it is supposed to control and oversee, yet on which it also depends for its existence. As the CICIG itself has expressed in various official documents, its success has been impressive, and the support of society, critical. But if the CICIG disappeared or left the country, the logic of corruption would probably remain relatively strong and gradually return to normal. The permanent transformation of the exchange of favors, influence peddling, and use of well-known networks is not achieved quickly. Not only because corruption bites back when attacked, which is in itself disturbing and shocking. It is also because the legal, administrative, and organizational framework linking political power and corruption has crystallized and reproduces itself. Just as in Brazil, the success of its organizations in identifying and punishing corruption has produced a major political crisis in the country. In Guatemala, it is this possibility of crisis that makes various political actors willing to opt for expelling corruption from the country.

Anticorruption policies and schemes require profound reflection and a clear political strategy. Thinking that reducing corruption is exclusively a technical or legal issue, or a matter of incentives means that one is only taking some of the instruments available into account. Understanding the way the political system will be affected, together with its stability and the basic agreements that comprise it, would seem to be a critical element of the future of the instruments and strategies for controlling this group of phenomena and acts included in the concept of corruption.

Bibliography

BBC Mundo. (2015, September 3). "La Línea": El qué, el cómo y el porqué del escándalo de corrupción que tumbó al presidente de Guatemala. Retrieved from www.bbc.com/mundo/noticias/2015/05/150507_guatemala_corrupcion_escandalo_vicep residenta_baldetti_jp.

208 Latin American Anticorruption Strategies

CNN Español. (2018). Jimmy Morales vs. Iván Velásquez: ¿De qué se trata la creciente tensión política en Guatemala por cuenta de la Cicig? Retrieved from https://cnnespanol.cnn.com/2018/09/06/jimmy-morales-vs-ivan-velasquez-de-que-se-trata-la-creciente-tension-politica-en-guatemala-por-cuenta-de-la-cicig/.

Comisión Internacional contra la Impunidad en Guatemala (CICIG). (2015a). *Caso negociantes de la salud*. Retrieved from www.cicig.org/casos/caso-negociantes-de-la-salud/.

Comisión Internacional contra la Impunidad en Guatemala (CICIG). (2015b). *Capturan a ex vicepresidenta Ingrid Roxana Baldetti Elías y solicitan antejuicio contra presidente Otto Fernando Pérez Molina*. Retrieved from www.cicig.org/casos/capturan-a-ex-vicepresidenta-ingrid-roxana-baldetti-elias-y-solicitan-antejuicio-contra-presidente-otto-fernando-perez-molina/.

Comisión Internacional contra la Impunidad en Guatemala (CICIG). (2015c). *Desmantelan red de defraudación aduanera*. Retrieved from www.cicig.org/casos/desmantelan-red-de-defraudacion-aduanera/.

Comisión Internacional contra la Impunidad en Guatemala (CICIG). (2015d). *Informe de la Comisión Internacional contra la Impunidad en Guatemala con ocasión de su octavo año de labores*. Retrieved from www.cicig.org/uploads/documents/2015/COM_085_20151113_VIII.pdf.

Comisión Internacional contra la Impunidad en Guatemala (CICIG). (2015e). *Modo de operar de usuarios red "la línea"*. Retrieved from www.cicig.org/casos/modo-de-operar-de-usuarios-red-la-linea/.

Comisión Internacional contra la Impunidad en Guatemala (CICIG). (2015f). *A prisión preventiva ex presidente Otto Pérez Molina*. Retrieved from www.cicig.org/casos/a-prision-preventiva-ex-presidente-otto-perez-molina/.

Comisión Internacional contra la Impunidad en Guatemala (CICIG). (2015g). *Pronunciamiento del cacif por capturas de red criminal*. Retrieved from www.cicig.org/noticias-2015/pronunciamiento-del-cacif-por-capturas-de-red-criminal/.

Comisión Internacional contra la Impunidad en Guatemala (CICIG). (2016). *Noveno informe de labores de la Comisión Internacional contra la Impunidad en Guatemala*. Retrieved from www.cicig.org/uploads/img/2016/others/COM_087_20161124_INFORME_ANUAL_2016.pdf.

Comisión Internacional contra la Impunidad en Guatemala (CICIG). (2017). *Caso La Línea: A juicio ex presidente Otto Pérez y ex vicepresidenta Roxana Baldetti*. Retrieved from www.cicig.org/casos/caso-la-linea-a-juicio-expresidente-y-exvicepresidenta/.

Comisión Internacional contra la Impunidad en Guatemala (CICIG). (2018a). *Caso negocios en la Industria Militar*. Retrieved from www.cicig.org/casos/caso-negocios-en-la-industria-militar/.

Comisión Internacional contra la Impunidad en Guatemala (CICIG). (2018b). *Caso Registro de Información Catastral: Una caja de pagos*. Retrieved from www.cicig.org/casos/caso-negocios-en-la-industria-militar/.

Comisión Internacional contra la Impunidad en Guatemala (CICIG). (2018c). *Mandato y acuerdo*. Retrieved from www.cicig.org/cicig/mandato-y-acuerdo/.

Gobierno de Guatemala. (2018). Estructura orgánica y funciones. Retrieved from http://uip.mingob.gob.gt/1-estructura-organica-y-funciones-direccion-superior-2/.

Impunity Watch. (2010). *Cambiar la cultura de la violencia por la cultura de la vida: Los primeros dos años de la Comisión Internacional contra la Impunidad en Guatemala*. Guatemala City, Guatemala: Impunity Watch.

Melini, S. (2015). *CICIG: Cobraban soborno a cambio de evadir el pago de impuestos*. Retrieved from www.cicig.org/uploads/img/2015/others/COM_036_20150420_elpe4y5_888567.jpg.

Open Society Foundation (OSF). (2016) *Against the odds: CICIG in Guatemala*. New York: OSF.

Organización de las Naciones Unidas y el Gobierno de Guatemala (Acuerdo de creación). (2018). *Acuerdo entre la Organización de las Naciones Unidas y el gobierno de Guatemala relativo al establecimiento de una Comisión Internacional Contra la Impunidad en Guatemala (CICIG).* Guatemala City, Guatemala: CICIG.

Pocasangre, H. (2018). Jimmy Morales no renovará el mandato de la CICIG. Retrieved from https://republica.gt/2018/08/31/jimmy-morales-cicig-ivan-velasquez-mandato/.

Washington Office On Latin America (WOLA). (2015). *La Comisión Internacional contra la Impunidad en Guatemala. Un estudio de la Investigación WOLA sobre la experiencia de la CICIG.* Washington, DC: WOLA.

Zamudio, L. (2018). La Comisión Internacional contra la impunidad en Guatemala (CICIG). Una organización auto-dirigida. *Foro Internacional*, 58(3), 493–536. doi:10.24201/fi.58i3.2530.

INDEX

Page numbers in *italics* and **bold** indicate Schemes and Tables, respectively.

absolute integrity 37
Access to Information and Data Protection (INAI) 151
administrative corruption 163–164
Agenda to Fight Corruption 183
Alverez Girón, Juan 206
Andrade Gutiérrez group 186–187
Anthropology of corruption or anthropological studies of corruption?
anticorruption: campaigns 39; forms of 97; initiatives **119**; policies 18–19; reform proposals 151–154; socially constructed 7
anticorruption agencies (ACAs): affecting people and organization's behavior 123–124; combatting corruption in a specialized way 170; conceptual logic of 125–127; defined 110–111; description of 123; as desperate act 121–122; as dynamic organizations 125; establishment of 128; failure of 117–118; independence of *112*, 128; limits of 121–125; mandates *113*; obstacles for 149; overseen by meta-political organizations 128; in parallel to political systems 124, 161; recommended variables for 128–129; strategy of creating 118; systemic corruption and 121–122; *see also* CICIG (International Commission against Impunity in Guatemala)
anticorruption agency models: Corrupt Practices Investigation Bureau of Singapore 116–117; multi-purpose

agencies with power to enforce the law 113–116; National Anticorruption Directorate of Romania 117–120; types of **111**
anticorruption industry: bias created by 20–21; birth of 19; description of 18; for developing countries 20; ineffectiveness of 108–109; normative view of 125–126; repercussions of international effort 37–38; *see also* anticorruption agencies (ACAs), international anticorruption regime
anticorruption measures 110
Anticorruption Office of Argentina (OAA): capacities of 138; challenges of 136–138; defending legitimacy of 132; design of **131**, 137–138; effective measures of 132–133; establishment of 124, 137; institutional design of 131; investigation and prosecution procedures 134; Judicial Branch and 137; obstacles for 132–133; public debate hearings 136; from public scandals to creation of 130–132; repositioning and strengthening 134–135; restoring trust 131; as a strategy 130–136; strengthening preventive measures 138; strengthening role as plaintiff 133
appropriateness, social logics of 57–58
Argentina: Access to Information bill 134; Corruption Perceptions Index (CPI) 107; focused organizational capacity 149

Index **211**

authority, legitimacy of 8
autonomy, legitimacy and 124
Ayuso, Emilia 206

balanced reciprocity 63
bid rigging 204
bites 46–47
black corruption **27**, 37
blat: building social capital 70; defined 67;
  negative connotation of 70; network of
  acquaintances 67–68; as subversive
  instrument 68; use of 68–69
blatmeisters 69
blaty, gap between legal and illegal 69
booty system 163, 166
border between unethical and ethical act 6,
  35, 118
Botswana 117
Brazil: Anticorruption Law 176; Code of
  Conduct of the Federal high
  Administration 175; contemporary
  history of 173; Corruption Perceptions
  Index (CPI) 107; Federal Public Ministry
  182; Federal Secretariat of Internal
  Control 180; Financial Activities Control
  Council 175; General Current of the
  Union 180; impersonality in
  administrative practice 175; large-scale
  corruption 173; legislative proposals
  regarding legislative corruption 184, *185*;
  Ministério Público (MP) 179; Ministry of
  Justice 178; National Congress 177;
  Office of the Comptroller General of the
  Union 176; patrimonialist regimes 173;
  Penal Code 174–175; small-scale
  corruption 173; State Minister of Control
  and Transparency 180; *see also* Brazilian
  anticorruption scheme
Brazilian anticorruption scheme: Agenda to
  Fight Corruption 183; Court of Accounts
  of the Union (TCU) 177–178;
  description of 172–173; Federal Police
  178, 184, 185; laws shaping 174–176;
  National Strategy to Combat Corruption
  and Money Laundering (ENCCLA)
  181–183; Office of the Comptroller
  General of the Union 179–180;
  Operation Car Wash (*See* Operation
  Car Wash); Public Ethics Commission
  180–181; Public Prosecutor's Office
  178–179, 185
Bribe Papers Index (BPI) 43
bribery: communication of 46; defined 26,
  28; euphemisms and 46; example of
  46–47; gifts becoming 29; *guanxi* vs.

71–72; identifying 29; maintaining social
  relationships for 29; *palancas* vs. 80; of
  public servants 39; in Roman Empire 25;
  as type of corrupt act 22; *see also* fraud
bureaucratic rigidity 75–77, 81, 98

camouflage 98
cancer of corruption 17, 19
Cardoso, Fernando Henrique 187
Carrera, Sebastián 200
Castillo, Gustavo 204
Castresana, Carlos 198
Cerveró, Nestor 187
Chile, Corruption Perceptions Index
  (CPI) 107
CICIG (International Commission against
  Impunity in Guatemala) 11, 109, 149;
  ability to change and adapt 193;
  Administrative Department 197;
  background of 194–195; business in the
  military industry case 205; Cadastral
  Information Registry case 206; Ciciacs as
  forerunner of 194; commissioner
  197–199; Commissioner's Office 197;
  communication strategy 197; creation of
  192; functions of 195; health negotiators
  case 203–205; as hybrid institution 193;
  identity theft investigations 202;
  institutions involved in 197–199; La
  Línea case 199–203; Mariachi Loco case
  203; National Civil Police and 198; new
  operational concept 202–203; normative
  view of 195–196; objectives of 192;
  organization structure 196–197;
  Prosecutor's Office and 196, 198;
  Research and Litigation Department 197;
  as supportive companion 196; *see also*
  anticorruption agencies (ACAs)
Citizen Participation Committee (CPC)
  151, 158, 161
Civil Self-Defense Patrols (PAC) 195
civil service 10, 109, 131, 142, 164, 166,
  173, 175, 196
Clandestine Security Apparatuses 192–193
clientelism 8, 33, 142, 163, 165–166, 202
  see also palancas
coercion: organized crime and 55–56; as
  type of corrupt act 22
cognitive dissonance 34; 37
collective: abusing for private purposes 96;
  impact of corruption on the 36;
  separation of private and 96
collective imaginary 78
collusion, *guanxi* and 73
Colom, Álvaro 198

212 Index

Commission for the Investigation of Illegal Bodies and Clandestine Security Apparatuses (Ciciacs) 194
Committee of Citizen Participation 158
concealment: as complex operation 2–3; of corrupt acts 56–57; justifications 2–3; presentations and 56; rationalizations 3
conflicts of interest: appearance of 35–36; Brazil and 175–176; description of 23–24; establishing 55; requiring chain of events 24–25; as type of corrupt act 22
Corpgold firm 200
corrupt acts: bribery *See* bribery; coercion *See* coercion; concealment and 56–57; conflicts of interest *See* conflicts of interest; embezzlement *See* embezzlement; fraud *See* fraud; as illegitimate 24; as interaction of at least two people 53; nepotism *See* nepotism; patronage *See* patronage; as social act 22, 34; types of 22–23; undesirable 32; uses **45**
corruption: acts of *See* corrupt acts; bias created by 20–21; as campaign agenda 138; as a cancer 19–20; controlling and/or reducing 10, 17; defined 2, 18–19, **27–29**, 30; as disease **28**; forms of 1–2; for greed **28**; as heterogeneous social practices 1; investigating acts of 3; linked to social practices 107–108; logic of favors and exchanges relating to 96–101; measuring 43–44; for need **28**; as normalized phenomenon 143; as political act 37; as politically created concept 21; problems in study of 2–4; as social act 2–3, 5; social and political logic of 47; as social construction 30; as socially legitimate 6, 118; as socially negotiated concept 9, **27**, 32–33; as a social relationship 53–59; stages of 2–3; as two-way street 36; types of 25–26; as umbrella concept 21–24, 44, 171; as unethical 1; war against 19–21; World Bank and 38; *see also* galaxy of definitions of corruption, systemic corruption
Corruption, Drug Trafficking and other Serious Offenses (Singapore) 116
Corruption Law (Singapore) 116
corruption metrics 38–39, 43–44
corruption model (Klitgaard) 127
Corruption Perceptions Index (CPI) 43, 107, 142
Corrupt Practices Investigation Bureau of Singapore 116–117

Costa Rica, Corruption Perceptions Index (CPI) 107
Court of Accounts of the Union (TCU) 177–178
cronyism 35, 202 *see also pituto*
culture 23, 65–66, 67, 76, 77, 95, 109, 137, 147, 202
customs, as a social mechanism 54–55
cynicism 10

Dallagnol, Deltan 185
deceivers 53–54
decentralized logic 172, 189
De la Rúa, Fernando 131
Delphi method 84
direct exchange of favors 61–62
direct reciprocity 75
discriminatory societies 93
dynamic plasticity 64–65

Economic and Social Council of the United Nations 39
economic corruption 33
Eigen, Peter 40
embezzlement 31, 42–44, 122, 174, 200, 205–206 *see also* bribery, fraud
emotional burden 4, 5
Estrada, Roberto 204
Estuardo, Salvador 201
European Union 111
exchange of favors: acquaintances networks and 62–63; Brazilian *jeitinho* 75–78; Chilean *pituto* 78–79, 98; Chinese *guanxi* 71–74; direct 61–62, 75; future reciprocity and 73; gift-giving and 61–62; Israeli *protektzia* 74–75, 99; logic of 96–101; mechanisms involved in 66; Mexican *palancas See palancas*; plasticity of 61, 63–64; Russian *blat* 67–70; in social contexts 59–60; in social relations 67; social relationships in context of 60–61; studying mechanisms for 83–96; sympathy and charms for 77; systemic corruption and 122; Transaction Cost Economics approach 73; *see also* reciprocity
exchange relationships 61–64

Federal Court of Administrative Justice (TFJA) 151, 159
Federal Public Ministry (Brazil) 182
Federal Secretariat of Internal Control (Brazil) 180

Index 213

Financial Activities Control Council (COAF) 175
FIOA project 134–13
focus groups?
Foreign Corrupt Practices Act of 1977 (FCPA) 39–40, 42
Forums to Combat Corruption (FOCCO) 183
Franco Chacón, Omar 200
fraud: deceiver in 53–54; defined 23; description of 3–4; as type of corrupt act 22; *see also* bribery, embezzlement
Freitas Magnus, Hermés 184

galaxy of definitions of corruption 26
galaxy of definitions of corruption, legal definition 26
game theory 55
García Muñoz, Óscar Armando 204
General Current of the Union (Brazil) 180
generalized reciprocity 63
General Prosecutor's Office (FGR: Mexico) 151
gift-giving 61–62, 66, 97
gifts: as bribes 29; illegal vs. immoral 26; reciprocity and 60, 66–67
Global Agreement on Human Rights 194
Global Corruption Barometer (GCB) 43–44, 142–143
government bureaucracies: informal relationships as crucial in 87; Kafkaesque nature of 81, 82, 94, 100
gray corruption **27**, 37
guanxi: affords and advantage 98–99; as an art 73; bribery vs. 71–72; collusions and 73; creating commitments 72; defined 71; interpersonal relationships in 71
guanxixue 73
Guatemala: human rights agreement 194; National Civil Police 198; security institutions 195; state's weak situation 194–195; Tax Administration Superintendency (SAT) 199; *see also* CICIG (International Commission against Impunity in Guatemala)
Guatemalan Social Security Institute (IGSS) 203–204
Gudiel, Melvin 200
guilt 2, 4, 165

Hammurabi Code 25
Hernández, César 204
Hernández, Rolando Enrique 205
Hong Kong 129

Illegal Security Corps 192–193
Illicit Political-Economic Networks (RPEI) 202
imitations, as a social mechanism 54
impartiality principle 92–93
Impunity Watch 198
inappropriateness 57–58
Independent Commission against Corruption (ICAC): composition of *115*; independent advisors for 115; investigation and prosecution procedures **114**; laws granting functions to **114**; performance standards 115–116; priorities of 113; successes of 113
Indonesia 129
influence peddling 22
Institute of Statistics, Geography, and Information Technology (INEGI) 143
Institutional Strengthening of the Anticorruption Office (FIOA) project 134–135
Inter-American Convention against Corruption (CICC) 131
Inter-American Development Bank (IDB) 42
international anticorruption regime 18, 20
International Commission against Impunity in Guatemala (CICIG) *see* CICIG (International Commission against Impunity in Guatemala)
International Monetary Fund (IMF) 40, 41
international trade transactions 40
interpersonal dependence 62

jeitinho 75–77, 108, 172
justifications 2–3

Kafkaesque nature of bureaucracy 81, 82, 94, 100

La Línea case 199–203
large-scale corruption **27**
Law on Corruption (Singapore) 116
legitimacy: autonomy and 124; based on justification 108
Lula Da Silva, Luiz Inácio 187

mafia organization 33, 55–56
Mariachi Loco case 203
Mauss, Marcel 60
Menem, Carlos 130
Menem administration 130–131
metrics *see* corruption metrics
Mexican bureaucracy 81–82

214 Index

Mexico: Access to Information and Data Protection (INAI) 151; administrative corruption 163–164; anticorruption reform 154–156; anticorruption reform, secondary laws **157**; anticorruption reform proposals **155**; booty system 163, 166; Citizen Participation Committee (CPC) 151; corruption as social trap 145; Corruption Perceptions Index (CPI) 107, 142; Federal Court of Administrative Justice (TFJA) 151; General Prosecutor's Office (FGR: Mexico) 151; Global Corruption Baromoeter (GCB) 142–143; National Council for Public Ethics 153; National Institute of Transparency 151; Office of the Special Prosecutor 159; prevalence of corruption in 143; Secretariat of Public Administration (SFP) 151; Superior Audit Office of the Federation (ASF) 151; Supreme Audit Institution 153; transformation of Attorney General's Office 154; *see also palancas*
Ministério Público (MP) 179
minor acts of corruption **27**
Mireya Herrera, Carloa 200
money laundering 116, 175, 178, 181–183 *see also* Operation Car Wash
Monzón, Juan Carlos 200, 206
moral economy 57
Morales, Gustavo Adolfo 200
Morales, Jimmy 207
morality 29–30
moral normality 4–5
Moro, Sergio 185–186
Muñoz, Carlos Enrique 201

Nájera, Omar 206
National Anticorruption Directorate of Romania 117–120
National Anticorruption System (SNA: Mexico) 11, 109, *152*; attacks on 150–151; building interdependence 162; challenges of 160–163, 165; combatting corruption in a specialized way 170; Coordinating Committee 151, 158; creating organizational capacities for 164; description of 148–149; effectiveness of 150; as exogenous logic 161; features of *162*; functioning of 156; implementation of 156–158; pillars of **158**; secondary laws 156, **157**; Selection Commission 158; temporary nature of 170
National Commission to Combat Corruption 151

National Corruption Combat Council 153–154
National Inspection System 159
National Institute of Transparency 151
National Strategy to Combat Cartels (ENACC) 183
National Strategy to Combat Corruption and Money Laundering (ENCCLA) 181–183
National Survey of Government Quality and Impact 2013 (ENCIG) 143
National Training Program to Combat Corruption and Money Laundering (PNLD) 182
National Transparency Ranking 182
Navas, Hugo 204
negative reciprocity 63
nepotism 5–6, 35, 99 *see also pituto*
network of acquaintances 62–63, 67–68, 93, 108
Nixon, Richard 39
Noguera, Marcelo 204
non-governmental organizations: reducing corruption 4; Transparency International 37–38, 40, 43–44
normalization of corruption *see* corruption, systemic corruption
normative view of corruption 125–126
NPC 134–135, 138, 139n6

OAS construction group 186–187
Obedrecht, Marcelo 186
Obedrecht construction company 189n1
Office of the Comptroller General of the Union (Brazil) 176, 179–180
Open Society Foundation 194
Operation Car Wash: arrest statistics 188; Federal Police 185; investigation actors 185; money laundering actors 186–187; Moro, Sergio 185–186; organizational analysis 187–188; origin and characteristics of 184; success of 187; Transparency International on 188
organizational gain **28**
Organization for Economic Cooperation and Development (OECD) 40, 111
organized corruption 33, 55–56
Ortíz, Francisco Javier 200, 201
Otávio Azevedo 186–187

palancas: as adaptive mechanism 80; attributes 82; bribes vs. 80; bureaucratic rigidity and 80; bypassing anticorruption regulations 94; on case-by-case, need-by-need basis 94–95, 101;

Index 215

correcting injustices 86–87; dark side of 82–83, 91–92; defined 79–80; degrees of formalization of 94; description of 85; as double-edged sword 83–85; emotions and 99–100; etiquette rules and 88–90; fairness of 91; focus group study 84–85; as functional 100; imposition implications 89; networks 147; prestige of 144; quasi-mafias of 147, *148*; reciprocity and 81–82, 146; relationships between acquaintances 92–96; rule bending and 89–90; semiology of 83; social game with 146; as a social mechanism 108, 143; social perspective of 91–92; social relationships and 85–90; social slide 99; universal expression in Mexico 85; use of *146*, 147
Palma, Carlos 204
paradox of corruption 33
particularism 10, 94–95, 100, 172
particularistic societies 93
patronage 8, 44, 99, 165
Peña Nieto, Enrique 47, 151
Perception of Corruption Index 38–39
Pérez Molina, Otto 199, 200, 201
permeability 58
personal favors 98 *see also* bribery
personal gain **28**, 42, 175
Petróleo Brasilero S.A. 184
Pinheiro, Leo 186–187
pituto 78–79, 98, 108
Plan for Strengthening the Sworn Disclosure System 135
plasticity of exchanges 61, 63–65, *144*
police corruption 178
political act, corruption as 35, 37, 163
political actors 123, 129, 162, 207
political battle against corruption 33, 47–48
political corruption 33
positive reciprocity 63
private acts 34
private gain *see* personal gain
protektzia 74–75, 99
public confidence 113, 116
public corruption **27**
Public Ethics Commission (Brazil) 180–181
public financial control 177
Public Management Control Network 183
public office-centered acts 42
public power for private benefit, misuse of **28**
public sector, role in corruption 36
public servants: *blat* networks 69–70; bribery and 24–26, 29, 39–42; CICIG indictment of 203; damage cause by corrupt 153;

impersonality in administrative practice 175; National Anticorruption Commission and 152; National Commission to Combat Corruption and 153; *palancas* and 87, 92; social relationships with 3
public sphere 133

rationalizations 3, 57
reciprocity: chains of 75; collective imaginary and 78; defined 59; direct 75; in exchange relationships 61–62; favors 66–67; gifts and 60; *guanxi* and 72; mechanisms of 77; *palancas* and 81–82, 146; permanence of corruption and 22; as socially stabilized 37; social relationships implying 87–88; symbolic debt and 79; trust building and 46; types of 63–64; uncertainty of 59; *see also* exchange of favors
Regional Confederation of the Mexican Republic 159
Registry of Cadastral Information (RIC) 206
Robles, Julio 200
Roman Empire 25
Romanian National Anticorruption Directorate (NAD) 117–120
Rousseff, Dilma 187
routines, as a social mechanism 54–55
Roxana Baldetti Elías, Ingrid 199, 200, 201
rule bending 74–77, 80–81, 89–90, 94–95, 100, 108, 145, 179

Salvatierra, Carlos 204
secrecy 98
Secretariat of Public Administration (SFP) 151
Securities and Exchange Commission of the United States (SEC) 39
Segura, Anthony 200
shame 4, 201
Singapore 116–117, 129
smuggling 199, 201
social branding 4
social capital 62–63, 70
social clientelistic logic 163
social density: of corruption 5–6, 21, 40, 47–48; of exchanges of favors 60; of relationships between acquaintances 92–96
social exchange mechanisms 108
social interdependence 60
social mechanisms, types of 54–55

216 Index

social relationships: bribery and 29; corruption and 30–31, 34, 53–59; exchange of favors and 60–61; implying reciprocity 87–88; *palancas* and 85–90; as socially acceptable 55–56; as source of support 86
social structure and micro action 31
sociolismo 108
soft corruption 93
solidarity 74
solidarity networks 98
Soviet system 68
standardized corruption 171–172
State Minister of Control and Transparency (Brazil) 180
Steering Committee of the National Supervision System (CRSNF) 159
Stuardo, Salvador 200
Superior Audit Office of the Federation (ASF) 151
Sworn Disclosures Control and Follow-up Unit 135–136
symbolic debt 79
systemic corruption: anticorruption agencies as strategy for 121–122; complexity of 127; exchange of favors and 122; intricate network within 164; judicial power and 170; legislative power and 170–171; National Anticorruption System and 162; as normalized corruption 137
systemic logic 160

Tax Administration Superintendency (SAT) 199
Temer, Michel 187
traditions, as a social mechanism 54
Transaction Cost Economics (TCE) 73
Transparency International 37–38, 40, 43–44, 142, 188
Transparency Mexicana 159

United Nations: anticorruption measures 111; combatting bribery 40–41; Economic and Social Council 39; General Assembly 40–41; International Commission against Impunity in Guatemala 192
United Nations Development Program (UNDP) 42, 196
United States Agency for International Development (USAII) 42
Uruguay, Corruption Perceptions Index (CPI) 107

Velázquez, Iván 202

war against corruption 19–21
war on cancer 19–20
Watergate scandal 39
white corruption **27**, 37
Wolfensohn, James 40
World Bank 37–38, 40–42